When Spirits Speak

Live Spirit Ghost Box Communication

Bruce Halliday

BEYOND THE FRAY

Publishing

ISBN 13: 978-1-954528-48-2

Cover design: Disgruntled Dystopian Publications

Beyond The Fray Publishing, a division of Beyond The Fray, LLC, San Diego, CA
www.beyondthefraypublishing.com

BEYOND THE FRAY

Publishing

Contents

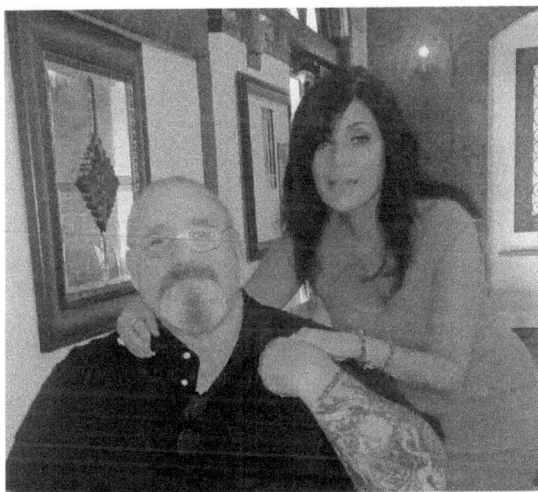

This book is dedicated to my loving wife, Melady, without whose unending patience, understanding and support over the last twenty years, this book, and career in paranormal research would not have been possible. If I had a nickel for every time I summoned Melady to listen to or give an opinion on a piece of live spirit ghost box communication, I would be a wealthy man. Since I did not get the nickels, I will be happy to settle for the wealth of having a partner in life who has stood by me and will continue to stand by me in this life and the next.

Foreword

Ron Yacovetti - ITC / DRV Researcher

In any area of interest or study, not only are dedication, attention to detail, and passion necessary to sustain the work, but chronicling it, logging it, and sharing it are equally important. In the ITC of live spirit ghost box communication, Bruce Halliday has done it all.

His work spans a sufficient number of years to show trends, efficacy of the method, and proof of concept. His voices from spirit show a connection that one would imagine only happens through repeated contact. We believe that spirits know our intentions, dedication, and perseverance to do something as extraordinary as communicating with them, especially if one considers that it has always been taught to us, from a young age, to be an act that is either evil, wrong, or downright impossible. In short, it has been discouraged; Bruce Halliday's work proves otherwise. The concept of live spirit ghost box communication, launched domestically by the late, great Frank Sumption, created an ITC offshoot path that would end up dominating the ITC world's representation in the field of "ghost hunting" as well as in all of the mainstream paranormal television shows. That influence did not get lost as many brilliant builders began an all-American ghost box revolution that continues to this day.

Moreover, while the ITC methodology of employing a sweeping radio remains suspect to many involved with scientific studies from within the world of academia, it is through the innovation and use of ghost box practitioners that it has proven to be deserving of a legitimate place in ITC history. Only with the consistency of work and chronicling of results by people like Bruce Halliday can the ghost box world earn its academic stripes and secure its foundation upon which so many pursue this research and continue to stand proud. Let this book and its content guide you through one man's enduring journey into a lifelong endeavor of live spirit ghost box communication.

DRV
Direct Radio Voice
Researcher
Ron Yacovetti

Preface

My name is Bruce Halliday. I started my journey in the
world of paranormal research over two decades ago. My
journey began as a novice paranormal investigator
running a modest team of like-minded individuals
conducting investigations of reported haunted locations
in and around New York City and southern New Jersey. I
worked exclusively in the field of traditional EVP research

for a number of years before being introduced to the device that would lead to my sole area of study and research within the paranormal field of live spirit ghost box communication. I began my research into live spirit communication with the use of a ghost box in 2006; at that time there were only a handful of individuals who actually owned a ghost box, and very few more who even knew what the device was. I am one of two original creators of live spirit ghost box communication research. I am also personally responsible for formulating the majority of theories and working protocols accepted in the field today, which are based on years of extensive solid research. I am responsible for the creation of two of the more popular ghost box "hack radios," the Radio Shack 12-470 and the Jensen SAB-55.

I have written many articles that have been published in magazines as well as on popular paranormal websites and have hosted two of my own internet radio shows dedicated to live spirit ghost box communication. I am the owner and sole administrator of the popular Facebook group "Live Spirit Ghost Box Communication Learning & Sharing" with over one thousand members, along with my YouTube channel "Halliday Paranormal." I decided to write this book to help bring the knowledge and experience I have gathered over the years in countless hours spent pursuing the truth about and validation of actual live interactive communication between the physical world and the spirit realm. I felt a growing need to try to deliver this tried-and-true knowledge to those who seek it and have few venues to attain it. My hope is that I can pass my knowledge and experience on to those who are delving into the field of live spirit ghost box communication as well as those seasoned researchers, investigators, and ghost box operators who may find it useful. I would like to state in closing that all the information set forth in this book is based on my theories and experience gained through many years of research and dedication in this extraordinary field of live spirit ghost box communication.

Chapter 1

My Paranormal Awakening

I come from a working-class Italian American family born and raised in Brooklyn, New York. I had my first paranormal experience as a child of around ten years old. I can remember it like it was yesterday. My family owned a small six-family apartment building on a street overlooking the Brooklyn-Queens Expressway. The building was a three-story walk-up with two cold-water flat apartments on each floor; all but one of the apartments were occupied by family, aunts, uncles and cousins. My grandmother lived in the right side apartment on the second floor. The house was always bustling with activity: residents coming and going, and a bunch of kids, all cousins, including myself, using the hallways as a playground. Back in those days the apartments' doors were always left open so that anyone could come and go in visitation as they pleased.

On one particular day, I happened to be alone in the hallway, amusing myself by sliding down the banister and pretending to be Batman. My grandmother was busy in the kitchen of her second-floor apartment, as usual, preparing the daily meals. After I slid down the banister to the bottom of the staircase, I would immediately turn and run back up the stairs for another slide. On one of these trips I reached the bottom, dismounted the banister, and turned to make my way back up the stairs when I saw at the top of the stairs an elderly gentleman in a vest, wearing an old fedora and smoking a small black cigar. He had a little scruffy dog in tow and was starting to make his way down the stairs. As I ran up the stairs, I passed him and remember pausing to ask if I could pet his dog, but the man and his dog had vanished. I remember thinking that I did not recognize him and thought it was odd that he got off the stairs and out of the house so quickly, but being so engrossed in my Batman adventures on the banister, I shrugged off the encounter and continued to play.

Not long after, my grandmother, having fixed lunch for me, called me to come and eat lunch. My saving of Gotham City had caused me to work up an appetite, so I raced to her apartment to devour the lunch. As I sat at the kitchen table, eating, my grandmother in her broken English Italian accent asked if I had fun playing. As I blurted out every detail of my amazing experience with the banister, I mentioned to her about the elderly man I'd seen coming down the stairs with the dog and that I did not know who he was. My grandmother was a bit concerned about a stranger in the building, but I guess she simply attributed it to a visitor to one of the apartments. She casually asked me what the man looked like, so I described him the best I could. She listened as she was busy fiddling with things around the kitchen, but as I finished my description of the elderly man and the dog, she stopped abruptly in her tracks, turned to me, and asked if the man had a mustache. I replied I think so and then asked if she knew who the man was. With a strange look on her face, my grandmother crossed herself and whispered the name Mr. Giuseppe. Although I was more interested in my lunch than in who the man was, my grandmother's expression caught my attention, and I asked if she knew him. She told me that the man was Mr. Giuseppe, and he was the gentleman my grandfather had purchased the house from, and she left it at that, which was enough explanation for me, being ten years old and much more worried about more pressing matters, like getting back to the banister and Gotham City.

Years later when I was older, I was sitting with my grandmother, and we happened to recall the encounter I'd had with the elderly gentleman that day. My grandmother confessed at that point that she had not elaborated on the incident at the time due to my young age and did not want to scare me. I asked her why I would have been scared; he was a harmless-enough-looking old guy. What she told me then did not really shock me; I just smiled and shrugged it off as an old Italian woman from the old country holding strong to her old-world superstitions. My grandmother proceeded to tell me that she had known the old man with the little dog who walked the hallway that day. He was a man named Mr. Giuseppe, and he was the man whom my grandfather had bought the house from back in the nineteen twenties. I vaguely remembered her saying that at the time; what she'd elected to leave out at the time because I was at such a fragile age was that when I had my encounter with Mr. Giuseppe, he had been dead for over twenty years. She went on to tell me that my description of the elderly man and his dog left no doubt in her mind as to his identity.

The events of that day and the subsequent confession of my grandmother as to who Mr. Giuseppe really was stayed with me somewhere in the back of my mind, an awareness of the existence of the paranormal and spirit beings that existed beyond our physical comprehension. My first introduction to the possibility of being able to communicate with spirits of human beings who have left this physical world and crossed over to an ethereal existence that we in physical form can only speculate on and what I have come to think of as an awakening came in the form of a movie. I was relaxing one evening, channel surfing as I usually did—I mean, I only had 450 channels; why should it be easy to find something to watch?—when I happened to land on a movie titled *White Noise*.

If you're reading this book, you're probably familiar with it. The movie starred Michael Keaton as a man who lost his wife and, in his search to ease his grief, came across a man who practiced a form of spirit communication known as EVP (electronic voice phenomena). The method of EVP is where it is believed that a spirit entity can manipulate and use the energy and ambient sound surrounding a running recording device to place words and phrases directly onto the recorder and have the communication discovered and heard when the recording is reviewed. At the end of this movie, there is a short documentary-style clip that explains how anyone can practice EVP with very simple equipment and rudimentary knowledge of the procedure.

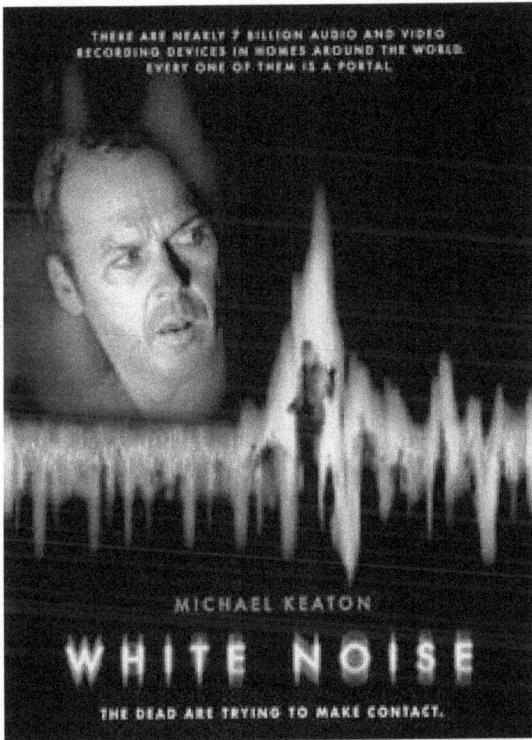

It is an understatement to say that I was intrigued. I turned off the television and went to bed. The next day with the thought of possibly being able to actually receive messages from the spirit world still fresh in my mind, I set out to prove to myself that it was just nonsense in a movie and could not be real, so I dug out my old cassette tape recorder, put in some fresh batteries and a new cassette tape, and decided to give this EVP a try. At this time I was in the habit of picking my wife, Melady, up from work every afternoon around five, so I decided to place the tape recorder in my bedroom, ask a question, and allow it to run while I went to pick up my wife so that the house would be empty and free of any noise that may pollute the recording and be mistaken by me for some sort of otherworldly occurrences, so that is exactly what I did. I started the tape recorder and asked out loud, "If there are any spirits that want to speak to me, please do so," and I promptly left the room and closed the bedroom door behind me. Let me preface the next part by saying that we never closed any doors in my home; even my child's bedroom door remained open day and night; the reason I mention this will become apparent shortly.

When I returned home, I retrieved the tape recorder from the bedroom and put it to the side, fully intending to review the recording shortly, but of course, as family life would have it, I had a million things to do around the house with family, etc. It actually took a couple of days before I remembered the tape recording and found the time to listen to what turned out to be a ninety-minute recording. I took the tape recorder and went down to my man cave, which was located in the basement of my home, sat down, and pushed play, fully expecting to hear nothing but static noise. I listened for what seemed like hours to the hiss of white noise and actually found myself being lulled into a sort of hypnotic state by it. My mind, of course, drifted to mundane thoughts of when the grass needed to be cut, and how I needed to fix that saggy ceiling tile I was unconsciously looking up at while listening to the never-ending hiss of the recording playback.

Suddenly without warning I was startled into full coherency by a voice that was what I perceived to be male but almost childlike in its tone. The voice was surprisingly loud and was delivered at a higher volume than the hiss of the white noise. I did not immediately understand what was said; it was not like hearing the sound of a normal human voice that would come from a recording. The immediate experience was kind of like if you were asleep and someone picked you up and dropped you into a pool of cold water; that's the best way I can explain it. I stopped the recorder and rewound it to listen to the voice again and again and again. After listening to that short phrase quite a few times, I decided that what I was hearing was the phrase "does he want this open." Because I had zero experience with anything paranormal and went into this experiment convinced that it was a bunch of bunk, my mind would not accept it at face value. I had to try to confirm my initial judgment that things like this were just not possible.

I decided to put on my Sherlock Holmes hat and tackle this enigma systematically step by step, either eliminating or confirming each possibility. First, I needed a second opinion on the voice in the recording, so I enlisted the aid of my wife, Melady. Let me just say that when I explained the situation to her, the first thing she did was to check the liquor cabinet to see if I had consumed every bit of alcohol in the house. When she stopped worrying that her husband had finally gone off the deep end, she tried to approach the situation and the recording with an open mind. I played the recorded voice for her a number of times, and she finally agreed with my conclusion as to what was being said and that the mysterious voice did not sound like what would be a normal person speaking into a recorder. I now had my second opinion confirming that there was something weird there; now I had to figure out what that something was or was not.

I now proceeded to try to eliminate the obvious things that could have occurred to cause a weird voice to appear on a recording being made in an empty house with the door and windows closed and nothing in the house that could render anything sounding like a voice or human speech. My first thought was that someone outside the house, a neighbor perhaps, talking could have been picked up by the recorder. Upon deliberation of this possibility, I reasoned that if this were the case, the voice would be very low and muffled and would have been simply a whisper amidst the static white noise of the recorder, so I eliminated the possibility of voice pollution from outside the house. My next thought went to ambient noise in the house, such as the air conditioning coming on, any appliances that may have been running without my knowledge, or even pipes making noise, or the periodic sound of creaking that is inherent in what I call house sounds. I went through every one of these possibilities in order and concluded that none of these occurrences could produce the voice that was heard on the recording.

After deliberating all the possibilities I could think of that would explain the voice I was hearing in this recording, I started to resign myself to the fact that the impossible was actually possible and probable in this case. The voice I was hearing on the tape recording had been placed there by an entity that was not a member of the living physical world. Now that I had basically accepted that I had indeed captured an EVP, I turned my attention to contemplating the message itself. Here is where the closed door I mentioned earlier comes into play. Like I said, there were never any closed doors in my house unless there were extraordinary circumstances, or it was the bathroom door for obvious reasons, and it would be very unusual for me to randomly close the bedroom door especially when I was about to leave the house and there would be no one home. I came to the conclusion that the message left by the entity, "does he want this open," was the entity referencing the closed door and asking if I wanted it open. Of course, this was my interpretation of the meaning of the ethereal message, and I cannot say definitively that is what the communicating entity was referring to. It was the closest I could come to adding legitimacy to the somewhat cryptic statement, which, by the way, was only the first of thousands of cryptic spirit messages that awaited me on the long journey I had just taken my first steps on.

As I look back on the years between that first paranormal experience as a child in my grandmother's house and the time I discovered EVP, I can vaguely recall a few instances that now I would deem to be possibly paranormal: the odd shadow caught out of the corner of my eye in an empty room, the faint sound of footsteps when no one was home, or the discovery of a light that was on minutes after I definitely turned it off, all shrugged off by me as being odd but never attributing these fleeting occurrences to paranormal activity, just explaining them away with the thought of just hearing things or my mind playing tricks on me. As I look back on some of these fleeting incidents now, my experience in paranormal research and investigation showcases them in an entirely different light. Following my baptism into the world of EVP and researching the paranormal, I was hooked totally. I immediately felt a hunger and passion for more. Little did I know that this one short phrase, "does he want this open," would lead me on a journey that has spanned over two decades and is still going strong.

Chapter 2

The Beginning of a Long Journey

A few weeks following my first and what I considered a successful attempt at capturing a message delivered from a spirit entity in the form of a traditional EVP in the bedroom of my home, I decided to take the plunge into the world of paranormal investigation and research; this was around the middle of 2002. This decision was made without my having an ounce of knowledge or experience. I had no equipment and, basically, no idea what equipment I would need besides the old cassette tape recorder I had used in my maiden foray into EVP. With the lack of equipment also came the lack of knowing what the hell I was doing and exactly how to get started in a field that had no solid information and no experts from whom to gather knowledge and learn from. At the time, paranormal investigation and research was not nearly as prevalent as it is today; you could literally count the number of paranormal investigating teams on your fingers. I decided that the best way to gain knowledge would be to research any and all the information I could on paranormal investigating and research. I went on the internet, such as it was back in the old days of the early 2000s, and searched for anything concerning the paranormal. I purchased every ghost-hunting magazine I could get my hands on and watched every episode of the one or two ghost-hunting television shows that aired at the time. I absorbed all the information I could gather and in a couple of months felt I was ready to embark on my journey.

I had compiled a list of all the investigating equipment that the so-called "professionals" used, including an EMF detector, temperature gun, digital voice recorder, digital camera, and video camcorder complete with tripod and noise-reducing microphones, all tucked nicely into a foam-lined aluminum carrying case; "I was ready!" Now that I had a working knowledge of the methods needed and the equipment necessary to carry out those methods, I needed a paranormal investigating team. I decided the best way for me to assemble a team was to advertise for like-minded individuals, and what better way to do this than to print up flyers and tack them to the community bulletin boards in the local supermarkets and libraries, so that's exactly what I did. After about a week, I got my first response via email; the email contained one very short question, "What is this about?" With that question, I knew putting together a team was not going to be a walk in the park. After what seemed like an eternity, I finally gathered up three people. I had the team, I had the equipment, I had the passion, the only thing I didn't have was a place to investigate.

We held our first team meeting and decided to post more flyers and reach out to friends and family, letting everyone know that we were available to investigate any location that had even a hint of believed paranormal activity. I was actually surprised at the responses and requests we received, of which about 99% were people who "heard a sound," "thought they saw something" out of the corner of their eye, generally things that ran along those lines, nothing really solid. We were very eager to get our ghost-hunting feet wet, so we decided to do a nighttime investigation at a small local cemetery. After reviewing hours of audio, video and still photos, I began to realize this was not going to be like the TV shows I watched; nevertheless I had this burning passion to keep going. I convinced myself that sooner or later a real investigation would come my way.

Some time passed, and my team and I did a few more mundane investigations that did not produce any solid evidence. The team was getting discouraged, and frankly, so was I. That's when I received a phone call from a couple who had recently moved into a home they rented and were experiencing, as they put it, "weird stuff" happening in the house. From what they described, I believed this might be our first real promising investigation. We decided to do a two-night investigation. We prepared ourselves and our equipment and headed to the home on a Friday night; we arrived and listened to the residents' story in detail, then proceeded to set up our cameras and other equipment. At 9:00 p.m. it was lights out; we let the video cameras run continuously, then proceeded to move about the house, taking still photos and doing EVP sessions. We wrapped up around 5:00 a.m. and left the home, planning to return that coming night. The second night was pretty much a repeat of the first night with no one experiencing any personal live activity during the investigation, so we wrapped everything up, thanked and reassured the residents, and told them I would contact them with a report and any findings we may have.

Time to review the data we collected and document any energy or temperature fluctuations we may have experienced. This being my first full-blown investigation, not to mention it being two full nights, with about seventeen hours of audio and visual data to review, I was not prepared for the daunting task it would be. I delegated the review of the data to each team member and kept the audio EVP data for my own review. I sat at the computer with headphones on, listening to hours of audio recording that consisted of questions being asked by team members as well as comments being blurted out by the residents and team members alike, all amidst the ambient sounds of footsteps, shuffling, the odd cough or sneeze and, of course, the background white noise ever present and more apparent in the silent moments. I believe I had about two hours of audio recording left to review when I heard a voice that was not asking a question or offering an unsolicited comment and definitely was not ambient sound. It was human speech; it was delivered in a gravelly-sounding male voice. I immediately loaded the audio into an editing program and isolated the section where I heard the voice. After raising the volume of the voice a bit, I listened to it a few times, and what I heard was relatively clear to me, a male voice saying, "Get out." I isolated this piece of audio and made a single audio file of it and saved it.

I continued my review of the remaining audio and was able to discover and isolate two other EVPs, which unfortunately were not as clear or of the same quality as the "get out" EVP. My team and I gathered to submit whatever was believed to be paranormal evidence, both audio and visual. The video had captured no evidence; the still photos caught a few orbs and a couple of light anomalies that we decided were due to dust and light refraction. Now came time for me to present the EVP evidence that was captured. When I played the EVP clips for my team members, I did not tell them what I believed the EVPs contained, I simply played them for the group and waited to hear what their interpretation of the voices was. I played the lower-quality EVPs first and received mixed descriptions of what the individual team members heard. After playing them numerous times, we came to a general consensus of what we thought was being said, nothing solid by any means; then I stated that I'd saved the best for last. I played the EVP of the male with the gravelly voice saying, "Get out," for the team, and I immediately received from each of them a unanimous confirmation that the EVP did, in fact, say, "Get out." Actually, it was so clear that it was chilling and raised the hair on more than a couple of arms in the room.

I proceeded to put together a detailed report of all the data we had collected, which I would present to the couple we'd performed the investigation for, and presented it to them, allowing them to hear the audio clips of the EVPs we'd captured. When I was finished with the evidence presented, the couple was fixated on the one EVP of the male voice. The first response from the woman resident was, "We are moving." I thanked them for the opportunity and asked that they keep me informed of any further paranormal activity they may experience. This first real investigation was my baptism into actual paranormal investigation and research.

As time went on, my team and I did numerous investigations, some good, most not so good. Overall I found myself obsessed with the gathering of audio data, namely EVP. Of course, I gave attention to the other aspects of data gathering, but my focus and passion lay with EVP and the attempt of actually establishing communication with a spirit entity. As time passed, one team member left the group and then another, and before very long I found myself the only one left. The time had arrived for me to reevaluate my priorities in paranormal research and investigation. I decided to put things into perspective. Did my passion lay in the investigating of paranormal activity in given locations, the performing of investigations, and the running of a ghost-hunting team, or was my real passion in the research, the drive to discover the who, what, why, how and if it was possible for physical human beings to interact with spirit entities that existed in another realm? I think I always knew the answer; the moment I asked myself that question, it was a no-brainer. I wanted to dedicate my time and efforts to researching the paranormal. From the very start I was drawn to spirit communication, EVP, which would become my chosen field in the paranormal: experimenting, practicing, and researching EVP. The Paranormal Investigating Team of Southern New Jersey was no more.

I proceeded to turn my man cave into an EVP research laboratory, and believe me, I use the word "laboratory" loosely. I already had the rudimentary equipment I needed, a computer, digital voice recorders, noise-canceling microphones, and a myriad of speakers and headphones. Before I go any further, let me explain the believed theory of how EVP is delivered by a spirit entity and captured by an individual conducting an EVP session. It is the accepted theory that a spirit entity can and does use the ambient energy and sound surrounding a running recording device and manipulates it to form words and phrases of human speech that are placed directly onto the recording medium, be it tape, digital voice recorder, or even the audio recorded during video capture. It is also accepted that the communicating entity needs to be in proximity to the recording device in operation in order to place the EVP; in other words, if you were performing an EVP session at one location, an entity that was present in a location a mile away theoretically would not be capable of rendering an EVP at your location and certainly would not be capable of delivering communication from the spirit realm.

I left the world of paranormal field investigation behind but kept the knowledge and experience I gained from the field investigations I had done. Today was the first day of my new career in paranormal research. I concentrated my focus on EVP and spirit communication. I started out by doing what I call controlled sessions, which are simply EVP sessions conducted in a controlled environment, which was my makeshift lab. My methods were simple at first: compile a series of questions and make sure the conditions were suitable with the least amount of noise pollution possible and the most favorable conditions I could provide to allow for optimal EVP capture. In the beginning, I started with no more than two fifteen-to-twenty-minute sessions containing on average about five questions. A twenty-minute EVP session did not just take twenty minutes and it was finished. There was the performance of the actual session and then the review and editing of the session recording, which was in and of itself a daunting task. Each second of audio needed to be carefully reviewed, and when a believed EVP was discovered, it needed to be isolated, cleaned up, and saved as an individual file.

I continued to do controlled EVP sessions in my home lab for quite a few months, but my success was, let's say, less than I would have liked. I could not figure out why the EVPs I did manage to capture came so few and far between; then one day as I sat at the kitchen table reading the newspaper, it came to me out of the blue like a stubborn splinter that was rolling around in my subconscious and finally pushed its way out. "OH YEAH," I said out loud. In order for an entity to deliver an EVP, the communicating entity would have to be in proximity to the recorder; that would mean in order for me to get more than just a passing EVP now and then, there would have to be entities consistently at my location for them to deliver their communication via EVP. So I decided to, as they say, "take the show on the road."

I researched the locations of some local cemeteries

and began to visit them one by one and perform EVP sessions. My success level began to rise; I was capturing double if not triple the number of EVPs. That's when I decided to expand my territory and do EVP sessions at locations of past accidents where there had been a fatality, you know those roadside memorials you see when driving, a bunch of flowers, a picture or a makeshift cross placed at the location where someone had passed due to an unfortunate accident. Now things really started to gather momentum; the EVPs were coming much more frequently. I decided to divide my efforts between controlled sessions at home and my road trips to locations that I suspected may have wayward entities eager to communicate.

As my research continued, I developed experience and knowledge and began to formulate my own theories on how EVP worked and whom we were receiving these otherworldly messages from. If you know anything about traditional EVP, you will know that it is very rough; the messages that are received are inherently hard to understand and require a certain amount of editing cleanup. There is a grading scale that is used for EVP quality based on the grading system used in a school test; for instance, an exceptional EVP that is clear and easy to understand by most listeners will be graded a "class A" EVP. As the quality diminishes, the grade will lower to class B, C or D. Most of the EVPs captured fall into the B to C class.

I began to try different experiments, like flooding the room where I was performing the EVP session with EMF energy by using a Van de Graaff generator or supplying various background noise like white noise, running water, and even different frequency tones to see if this would enhance an entity's ability to form and deliver EVP communication. Many of the experiments had mixed results. Sometimes they worked; other times they didn't. I could perform the same experiment numerous times with the same exact conditions, and some would produce quality EVPs, and some would not produce any EVPs at all. I performed EVP research every day for almost three years, learning from and documenting every experience, every thought, every theory.

One day as I sat at my computer, I noticed that I had received an email. The sender's name was strange to me, but I had been corresponding and connecting with so many individuals associated with the paranormal field that it came as no surprise that I would receive an email from someone I did not recognize. The email was from an individual inquiring about my paranormal investigating team and asking if I was taking on any new team members. I informed him that I was not taking on any new members for the paranormal investigating team and thanked him for his inquiry. A couple of weeks passed, and I received another email from the same individual, asking me if I had ever heard of a device called a ghost box. I had not, and I told him I'd never heard of such a device. In his replying email, he described to me basically what this device called a "ghost box" was and how it was supposed to work. After reading his explanation, I promptly informed him that I did not think any device like that would or could work, and he should not waste his time with it. He thanked me for my response, and the correspondence was ended for the moment.

In the days following my email communications about the ghost box, I found myself, no matter how I tried to dismiss the idea, thinking about it. Because I was so dedicated to my chosen method of EVP spirit communication, I had immediately dismissed the idea of something brand new and virtually untested. I decided to have an open mind and attempted to gather some information about this brand-new spirit communication device. My first step was to do an internet search on the words "ghost box." If my memory serves me correctly, there were only a couple of vague results on Google and nothing explaining the ghost box in any detail. My second step was to email the person whom I had previously corresponded with and ask if he had any more information about it, so I did exactly that. I received a response email directing me to a Yahoo group. Facebook had just been born, and no one knew what it was yet, so if you wanted to interact with other like-minded individuals via a written forum, Yahoo groups were the place to go.

The Yahoo group recommended to me was owned by a gentleman named Frank Sumption, who was the creator of the first ghost box. The group was dedicated to this new form of "live spirit communication" with the use of a ghost box; more to come on Frank later. I found the group and applied for membership; shortly after, I was accepted as a member of the group. I visited the group numerous times a day for a couple of weeks before I decided to render my first post. I gathered all the information I could on this new device and how it could allegedly allow someone to hear a communicating entity live in real time as the entity delivered the communication.

From what I could gather, Frank Sumption had at this point only produced a very small number of these ghost boxes and had only given a select two or three people the opportunity to receive one and work with it. My first post to the ghost box Yahoo group was the question "How can I get a ghost box?" The almost immediate answer to my query was "You can't." My follow-up question was "How is someone supposed to practice this new method without a ghost box?" To this question I received the answer "Manually." "OK, manually, what the heck does that mean?" I asked, to which I was told, get yourself an analog radio with a dial tuner, turn it on, and begin to sweep the radio dial back and forth from one end to the other continuously without stopping, ask your question, and listen for a response. It was further explained to me that this procedure was basically how a ghost box operated; the only difference was that a ghost box was made to sweep the radio dial automatically without the operator having to manually sweep the radio band by using the tuning knob.

As luck would have it, I had a small portable radio with a dial tuner, and of course, I was going to give this a try. The next morning when the house was empty and quiet, I retrieved my radio, put in some fresh batteries, sat at the kitchen table, and prepared to perform what would be the first of many hundreds of live spirit ghost box communication sessions. As I reached for the radio's power switch to turn it on, my mind was still filled with serious doubts and little if any expectations that this would produce communication from a spirit entity or that I would be able to hear that communication live immediately as it was delivered by that entity. My loyalty to my chosen method of traditional EVP was a strong factor; however, I was determined to go into this maiden attempt with an open mind and a glimmer of hope that somehow it could and would work. I had not established any set parameters for this, my first ever ghost box session. I decided to ask the most rudimentary questions and give it a few minutes before I ended the session and confirmed my initial doubts that this method could not possibly work.

I hit the power switch on the radio and started to turn the dial, beginning at the lowest point on the AM band and moving to the highest point and back again. I did this continuously while I asked my first question, "Are there any spirits who would like to communicate with me today?" The sound coming from the radio as I swept the dial back and forth was chaotic to say the least. It was a jumble of broken-down human speech, music, static white noise, clicks, and tones spilling out of the radio speaker seemingly all at once. Amidst this mishmash of sound, I was able to catch some words I could understand, a couple of yeses and nos, the odd full word here and there, but nothing that I discerned as an attempt at communication. I stopped sweeping the dial for a moment to think. The few intelligible words I was hearing were merely words of radio broadcasts that had escaped being chopped up by my rapid movement of the dial across the band; in my mind that was the likeliest explanation.

I decided to increase the speed of my dial sweep to as fast as was possible, so I took a breath and began again. As soon as I began the dial sweep, I heard the name Mike spoken clearly, and I realized that the word seemed to be somehow separated from the rest of the cacophony of sounds being produced. As I was concentrating on my thoughts for the moment and not the sound of the radio, I was jolted back into focus by a voice loudly and clearly saying, "Mike." I paused; did I actually hear the name Mike again within seconds of hearing it the first time? At this moment the experience that I had gathered in spirit communication kicked in, and I blurted out the question "Did you say Mike?" not truly expecting to hear a response. A low but very audible "Yes" came through. The hair on my arms and the back of my neck stood on end. Was this really happening? Was I involved in live communication with an ethereal entity?

Considering myself to be somewhat of a seasoned paranormal researcher, I gathered myself and asked the question "Is there an entity that is trying to communicate with me?" Less than five-seconds passed, and a clear understandable male voice came through the radio speaker and said, "Yes, Bruce." OK, seasoned paranormal researcher or not, I literally jumped to my feet and ran from the room. I finally stopped at the front door, realizing that I was in flight mode, and I took a series of long deep breaths. After years of listening to what I firmly believed to be spirit entity communication in my EVP research, nothing had prepared me for what just happened. I asked myself, "Did you just have a coherent live interacting communication with a spirit through a radio?" My only answer could be, yes, I did.

I went back to the radio, which was still running, sat down, and began to turn the dial again. I asked, "Did you just say yes, Bruce?" A few seconds later I heard the response "Yes," this time in a high-pitched female voice. As much as I wanted to keep the session going, I had to take some time to absorb this experience and analyze the events of the session logically in my mind. I retreated to the quiet solace of my little basement laboratory. I sat down and began to recount the manual sweep ghost box session step by step in my mind. I examined each instance of alleged spirit communication that I had heard and attempted to consider every possibility that could have caused me to hear the words of human speech that were so obvious and relevant to the questions I asked.

The one single incident of the session that sealed my decision was the response I received when I asked if the entity had said, "Yes, Bruce" in response to my asking if there was an entity attempting communication. I had taken into account that any clear responses I heard during the session could just be stray words of radio broadcast that had escaped being broken down by the sweep of the dial; what negated that possibility in this specific instance was that the spirit communication was a relevant and deliberate answer to my specific question. The cherry on top was that the entity mentioned me by name in his communication. I tried to calculate the odds of my name being able to escape being broken down into sound fragments by my rapid sweep of the dial and randomly coming through clearly at that exact moment in time to be part of a relevant and specific answer to a question I had asked only seconds before; the odds were so high against that happening that I was unable to calculate them.

After much deliberation, I could only reach one logical conclusion, live spirit communication was absolutely possible with the use of a ghost box. I was hooked! The following morning I decided to contact the individual I had been corresponding with about the ghost box, render an apology for my abrupt condemnation of the device and its method of live spirit communication, and explain the manual sweep session I had done the day before. My email was answered almost immediately. Graciously my new friend lightheartedly accepted my apology and suggested a phone call to discuss the events of my session, and I agreed. I received a call from my new paranormal colleague the following afternoon. After exchanging pleasantries and a brief bio of both our experiences in the field of paranormal investigation and research, we got down to business, the ghost box.

Following the previous discussion with my new paranormal friend, I continued to experiment with the manual sweep method I had initially performed and continued to follow the posts on Frank's Yahoo group closely. About a week had passed since my last contact with my friend. I had done a few manual sweep sessions in that time, receiving basic live spirit communication, yes and no answers and the occasional hi or hello but nothing really significant. Not that these basic one-or-two-word spirit communications were not extraordinary in themselves, it was that I was very eager to move forward and see what a custom-built ghost box would render. The sessions with the manual dial radio were sufficient; the only drawback was that because the sweep was being manipulated manually by hand, it was erratic, faster, slower, choppy, and just basically inconsistent, which I believed hindered the chances of receiving quality live spirit communication.

After finishing dinner one night and heading down to my lab, the phone rang. I answered it; it was my friend. He asked if I had time to talk; I told him of course. He proceeded to tell me that he had been working with a man called Joe Cioppi and that Mr. Cioppi had managed to create a facsimile of the Frank's Box and named it a "Joe's Box." My friend also informed me that he had been beta testing the first Joe's Box and that this prototype was not really what he had expected, and he had reported his findings to its creator. Joe Cioppi proceeded to act on the suggestions my friend had made and created the Joe's Box #2, which my friend received for the price of parts and labor. He went on to explain that he had been working with this new ghost box for a short time with limited success. My friend suggested a Skype call so that I could hear the Joe's Box in operation, and of course I agreed.

We connected over Skype that evening, and my friend proceeded to bring the Joe's Box to life, and we, of course, did an impromptu ghost box session right there over Skype. The session met with some limited success, and I managed to hear what I believed to be rudimentary spirit communication. Because this was my first exposure to a real automatically sweeping ghost box, I was excited to say the least. After the ghost box session ended, I asked my friend if it were possible for me to purchase a Joe's Box from Mr. Cioppi. He gave me Joe's contact information and suggested I contact him with my request.

The next day I contacted Joe Cioppi and arranged to purchase one of his ghost boxes. Joe told me it would take a couple of weeks to build and ship out to me, we agreed on a price, and I sent payment the next day. Two weeks had passed when I received an email from Mr. Cioppi telling me my ghost box was finished and that it would be on its way to me the next day. I thanked him and started counting the days until I would receive my very first ghost box. A few days passed that seemed like weeks, and the box had not arrived. Since Mr. Cioppi and I lived in neighboring states, I had anticipated my Joe's Box's arrival sooner. Finally, on the afternoon of the seventh day, I opened my front door to find a package sitting there; my ghost box had arrived! I rushed the package downstairs to my makeshift paranormal research lab and quickly opened it. I pulled the small walkie-talkie-looking device from the cardboard box and examined it. The device was a beige color with a silver telescoping antenna and two black knobs protruding from it. I placed it on my work desk and stared at it for a while, pausing to come to terms with the idea of now having my own custom-built automatically sweeping ghost box.

It was just after dinnertime when I called my friend on Skype to inform him that I had received my Joe's Box. He seemed almost as excited as I was. His first question was whether I had used the new ghost box yet. I told him I had not and that I wanted to have him on Skype with me for its maiden session. I turned the device on, and my Joe's Box crackled to life, spewing a blast of ghost box sweep reminiscent of what I had heard from the Joe's Box sessions done over Skype with my friend. I was not conscious of it at that moment, but flicking that power switch would not only give life to my first ghost box experience but would change not only my life as a paranormal researcher but my life overall.

I started to ask some basic questions, the first of which was "Are there any entities that wish to communicate today?" The first live spirit communication to be delivered from my Joe's Box and heard live in real time by both myself and my friend was "Here, Bruce." At that very moment, I knew that live spirit communication with a ghost box was going to revolutionize the paranormal research world, and all my efforts would be dedicated to this field. My only regret was that in my haste to formally initiate myself into the field of live spirit ghost box communication, I had forgotten to turn on my digital recorder and capture this historic session, ugh! My first ever legitimate ghost box session was now destined to live only in my memory.

I began working with my Joe's Box on a daily basis, sometimes doing multiple sessions in a day. As my work with the ghost box proceeded, so did the quantity and quality of the live spirit communication I received with it. I began to create protocols and set procedures for the performance of live spirit communication ghost box sessions; the seeds of theory as to the who, what, and how the ghost box worked and the reception of live spirit communication from the entities we were communicating with started to sprout. At this time I had begun posting audio files of the live spirit communication I had captured during my ghost box sessions as well as my ideas and insights into the working of the ghost box and the entities that used it to communicate with us to Frank Sumption's Yahoo group. My audio and text posts were very well received by the group members as well as Mr. Sumption himself.

After receiving accolades from my fellow group members for my work with the Joe's Box and praise from Frank for my diligent efforts, the idea of the possibility of receiving a Frank's Box had crept into my mind. The Joe's Box was great and would always be my first, but to have a ghost box made by the hands of its creator, well, that was the holy grail at the time.

Some time had passed, and I continued my research with the Joe's Box. Late one evening the phone rang. I picked it up and heard the sound of my friend's voice. He was very excited and went on to inform me that he was to be the next recipient of one of Frank Sumption's coveted ghost boxes. I was happy for him but still could not suppress some feelings of envy at his stroke of luck. Not long after, I received an email from my friend telling me his Frank's Box had arrived. He was overjoyed and a bit anxious about turning it on for the first time. I wrote him back and asked that he contact me as soon as he had finished his first session with it; he did. He admitted that he had been excited and a bit nervous when he approached the ghost box to do his first session. He went on to say that he believed that he had received some communication with it; he also admitted that it would take some getting used to as far as listening to the rapidly sweeping ghost box simply because it sounded and operated so differently than the Joe's Box he was accustomed to. My first question to him was when can I get a chance to hear it? He suggested that we speak over Skype and that he would run the Frank's Box while we were live on Skype so that I could hear it as it actually ran. Later that evening I went down to my computer and initiated a Skype call to him, he answered immediately, we spoke for a few minutes, and he then asked if I was ready for him to turn on the ghost box. Even though I was chomping at the bit to hear the box in operation, I casually said, "Yeah, sure," not wanting to seem like a schoolkid waiting for the recess bell to ring.

As I sat there quietly waiting for the sound of the Frank's ghost box to boom through my computer speakers, my friend asked, "Are you ready?" I replied, "Go." I heard the click of a switch and then a chaotic whirlwind of sound emanating from my computer speakers. Having become used to the way the Joe's Box sounded myself, the Frank's Box sounded a bit strange; it was steady and predominantly uniform and swept the radio band in a linear fashion starting at the beginning of the band sweeping to the end and immediately starting at the beginning again continuously. As I listened, I noticed that the Frank's Box had more static white noise and a higher pitch tone to it.

My colleague directed some basic questions to any

spirit entities that may want to communicate like, "Are there any spirits that would like to speak to us tonight?" We were both able to hear some rudimentary communication like yes, no and some basic words that could be relevant to some of the questions asked. My friend repeated the supposed spirit communication out loud immediately upon hearing it, as did I. It seemed he was hearing a bit more than I was, which I attributed to his being in direct proximity to the ghost box, whereas I was listening remotely through computer speakers. We had the ghost box running on Skype for about fifteen minutes when I blurted out a question from my end of the connection, "If there is an entity communicating, can you say my name?" No more than five seconds later a loud and clear "Bruce" came bounding out of my speakers. My friend and I both shouted, "They said Bruce," at the same exact instant. We allowed the box to run a few minutes more, thanked any communicating entities for their efforts, and ended the session.

The ensuing discussion of the Frank's Box session lasted more than an hour, fueled by our excitement at the relative success of the session. Toward the end of the conversation, I asked my friend if he thought it was possible for me to get one of Frank Sumption's ghost boxes. His reply was, "I don't know. He does not give them away easily." He suggested that I email Frank and ask. The next day I decided to email Frank Sumption. What could I lose? If he agreed to send me a ghost box, great; if not, I would be no worse off than I was already, so I wrote the email. I wrote Frank, introduced myself, briefly explained my experience in paranormal research, and, of course, mentioned my friend's name and rendered all the details of the prior night's session over Skype with his amazing ghost box. I assured Frank that if I were to receive one of his ghost boxes, it would be used for serious research and never for exploitation or monetary gain. I clicked send; the hopes of my future paranormal research career were now traveling the information highway via email. Days passed, which seemed like years, as I checked my email inbox every ten minutes, waiting for a reply from Frank Sumption.

Just as I was about to give up hope and resign myself to the fact that Mr. Sumption had chosen to ignore my email and my request for one of his ghost boxes, I received an email from my friend. I opened the email, expecting to read the usual small talk and the details of his most recent session with his Frank's Box, the first word in the email was "Congratulations." My pulse quickened as I proceeded to read the rest of the email. My friend went on to explain that Frank had contacted him to inquire about me and ask his opinion of my worthiness to receive one of his ghost boxes. He went on to say that he'd informed Frank that I was, in fact, a serious and legitimate paranormal researcher with years of dedicated research into traditional EVP and spirit communication. He also told Frank that in his opinion I would be the perfect recipient of a Frank's Box. What my friend said at the end of the email made my pulse quicken even more, "Send Frank your address. He is sending you a box." As soon as I closed my friend's email, I wrote one to Frank; all the email contained was my full name, address and a thank you. I actually never received a reply from Frank saying that he intended to send me one of his ghost boxes. I later came to know and accept that this was the way Frank Sumption was, and you either took it or left it.

I spent the next week anxiously waiting for the doorbell to ring with a package delivery from Frank. A week went by and then two. I spoke to my friend frequently, but he had no idea why the Frank's Box had not arrived yet. I did not want to email Frank and inquire about the delay, firstly because he never actually contacted me and offered the ghost box, and secondly it would have been pushy of me to do so. It was a Monday night beginning the third week since I had emailed my address to Frank Sumption. I had decided that if the ghost box did not arrive the next day, I was going to contact Frank.

In the morning I drove my wife to work, returned home, and was at the kitchen table, having my third cup of coffee, when the doorbell rang. It actually startled me. I went to the door, amazingly not thinking that it might be a delivery. It was still very early in the day, and for some reason, I felt like package deliveries usually arrived later. I opened the door to see a UPS driver standing there with a cardboard box that looked like it had been used multiple times to ferry items from one place to another. It was scuffed and dented with remnants of old labels and packing tape. My name and address were written on the top with a black Sharpie in big letters. I accepted the package, and even though I knew what it had to be, I still checked the sender's name and address on it just to confirm that it was what I hoped it would be. I carried the package into the kitchen and placed it on the table, my excitement level was off the charts, but I was a little nervous also.

I took a breath and remembered the live spirit communication I had received using just my little manual dial radio and how far I had come with the use of my Joe's Box, which served to alleviate most of the nervousness I felt being at the threshold of operating my own Frank's Box. I retrieved a steak knife from the kitchen drawer and cut the haphazard packing tape barely holding the beaten-up old cardboard box closed. I opened the flaps to see something wrapped in an old dusty towel and surrounded by crumpled newspaper. I removed the newspaper and carefully lifted out the object wrapped in the towel and placed it on the kitchen table. After finally sending the veteran shipping box to its final resting place in my recycle bin, I went back to the kitchen table to unwrap what to me at the moment was the best present I would ever receive. I unwrapped the Frank's Box slowly, removing the towel with surgeon-like care, hoping not to catch any piece of the rare device on the terry cloth of the towel and subsequently damage the ghost box.

As I peeled away the towel, I got my first glimpse of my new Frank's ghost box. It was constructed of plywood and had a myriad of odd knobs and switches on it. There were a few colored wires protruding from inside the box and a makeshift copper wire antenna hanging from it. Each knob and switch was labeled beside it in black Sharpie. It looked like something that was put together by a fifth grader. I prayed that it would perform better than it looked. I decided to let my new Frank's Box rest after its long trip. Even though I had eagerly anticipated its arrival, I was still a bit nervous about actually putting it to the test for the first time due to the high expectations I had set for it.

I emailed my friend and told him I had finally received my Frank's Box. His reply was immediate, asking, "Did you try it yet?" I informed him that I did not and would do a controlled session with it first thing in the morning. The morning came; I dropped my wife at work and proceeded home. When I arrived home, I poured myself a cup of coffee and went down to my lab, where the Frank's Box now occupied a place of honor in the center of my worktable. I sat at the table and wrote a series of five questions that I would ask during my session, checked my digital voice recorder to make sure it had sufficient battery power and no other previous recordings saved to it, took a deep breath, and reached for the power switch on the Frank's ghost box.

The ghost box came to life. I adjusted the volume, selected the AM band, and set the sweep speed. I started the digital voice recorder. The box's sound was nothing like I was used to. The sweep was full of static white noise due to the ghost box's less than stellar radio signal reception. The sweep of the band was a bit choppy and lagged in certain spots on the dial. The overall tone that the box produced was somewhat high pitched; it sounded nothing like the Joe's Box that I had become accustomed to listening to.

I looked down at the scrap of paper containing the five questions I had prepared for the session and proceeded to ask the first question. "Are there any entities that would like to communicate using this device?" I paused, awaiting a response. I was met with only the gibberish of the ghost box sweep. I waited and listened for a few more seconds and then repeated my question. No sooner did I finish my question than a male voice came through the ghost box speaker: "Yes, Mike." The response was somewhat buried within the noise of the box sweep but clear enough for me to hear it live in real time. I asked, "Did you say 'Yes, Mike'?" and I received the response, "Yes." I heard this live also and replied, "Hi, Mike," followed by the question, "Can you tell me who you are?" A few seconds passed without my hearing an answer to my last request, so I continued my session, asking the remaining four questions in the order they were written.

My first live spirit communication session with the new Frank's Box lasted approximately ten minutes. During the performance of this session, I was able to hear a decent amount of what I believed to be spirit communication live as it was delivered through the speakers of the ghost box: the basic yes and no answers, the name Mike three times, and my own name twice. I knew that there was a good amount of spirit communication that I was not able to hear live in real time as I performed the session; this is where recording the live session became invaluable. It not only allowed me to have an audio recording to confirm the communication I believed I heard during the ghost box session but also allowed me to discover any and all spirit communication that was delivered by the communicating entities but missed by me live in real time during the course of the session.

With my first Frank's ghost box session under my belt and the session recording safely saved on my computer, I decided to call it a night and start my step-by-step review of the recorded session first thing in the morning. Following my daily routine, I drove my wife to work and made my way home, poured that much-needed second cup of coffee, and headed down to the lab, settled into my swivel office chair, and switched on the computer. As I waited for the computer to go through its initial paces on startup, which seemed like forever, I thought about the Frank's Box session from the day before, eager to sift through the session recording and discover what I had missed while doing the session live.

The computer finally settled down and was ready for work, so I opened my audio editor and loaded the Frank's Box session recording. Starting the review of a ghost box session recording reminded me of when I was a kid on Christmas morning. I would always have a bunch of presents wrapped under the tree, I always knew I would get what I asked for, but there were always a few gifts that I had no idea about and were a surprise when I tore off the wrapping. Going over a ghost box session recording is like that, you're confident that you will find the spirit communication that you heard live during the session, and then there are the communications you discover that were not heard live, and they are always a surprise. To this day so many years later with literally hundreds and hundreds of ghost box sessions under my belt, I still get that excited feeling at the prospect of finding the elusive spirit communication that escaped my ear during the live session. This session was particularly exciting because it was my first session with a Frank's Box, and I had high expectations for its performance.

I started my recording review and the painstaking procedure of listening and relistening to every sound incrementally, pinpointing what I believed to be spirit communication, isolating it, and making single audio files that could be saved showcasing my question and any relevant spirit responses and/or answers received so they could be saved and documented for reference at any future time.

Because of the significant nature of this particular ghost box session, I really focused on every second of the audio recording, making sure not to overlook a single thing. The recording of a ten-minute session took about four hours of work to review. The end result of my first Frank's Box session was eight single audio files: four made up of my question and a relevant live spirit response; the other four consisted of words that I believed were live spirit communication but did not hold any relevance to any questions I had asked. Taking into consideration the quantity of spirit communication, the quality, and the relevance to my questions posed in the session, I had to give this first session with a device created by the father of the ghost box a C+ grade. If I'm being honest, which I always strive to be, keeping emotions and admiration for the creator of the device out of the equation, I had to admit to myself that for my initial assessment I preferred the Joe's Box. To be absolutely fair, I knew I would have to devote quite a few more sessions to the Frank's Box, so my final personal judgment would come when I believed the Joe's Box and Frank's Box had enjoyed equal time.

Now that I had received my Frank's Box and also had the Joe's Box, after working with them both and experiencing the capability these new devices had to open a doorway for live communication between the physical world and the spirit realm, I made the decision to devote all my efforts in paranormal research to this fledgling field of live spirit ghost box communication. This was truly "the Beginning of a Long Journey."

Chapter 3

The Ghost Box and ITC

A ghost box is a device that is used in the field of paranormal research and investigation. It is designed to receive radio signals from various frequency bands, such as AM, FM, and shortwave. The ghost box is made to sweep across the selected radio band at a set speed, which on some custom ghost boxes can be adjusted by the operator during the live ghost box session. It can be made to sweep in either a linear or random fashion. A linear sweep allows the radio band to be swept in a continual circular motion, starting at the beginning of the radio band, sweeping to the end of the band, and returning to the beginning, continuously repeating the process. A random sweep allows the ghost box to sweep the selected radio band in a random fashion, jumping from one point on the band to another randomly. The box is designed to sweep the radio band at a fast enough pace to break down the received radio broadcast into small fragments consisting of human speech, song, music, and other sounds produced by the radio broadcast, including the inherent white static noise that falls between the radio stations. This cacophony of sounds is referred to as the ghost box sweep and is emitted through the speaker of the device to be heard live in real time by the ghost box operator.

Frank Sumption

The first ghost box was created in the year 2002 by an individual named Frank Sumption. Mr. Sumption was a resident of the state of Colorado and was an avid believer in the paranormal and dabbled in EVP spirit communication. One day Mr. Sumption came across the October 1995 issue of *Popular Electronics* magazine and read an article titled, *Ghost Voices*. The article posed the question, "Are the dead trying to contact us through electronic means?"

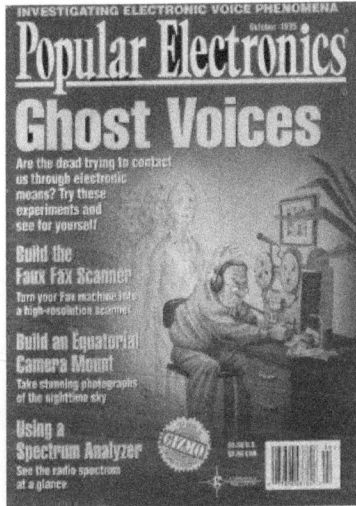

Oct. 1995 *Popular Electronics*

After reading the article, Mr. Sumption, who was very experienced working with electronics, formulated the idea of building a device that could possibly allow a human being here in the physical world to communicate live in real time with spirit entities. Mr. Sumption set about the task of constructing such a device, and in 2002 he succeeded, and the first ever ghost box was born.

As the story goes, Frank Sumption flicked the power switch of the first device he created and heard the fruits of his labor come through the device's speaker. In the midst of the plethora of sounds emanating from the device, Mr. Sumption believed he heard full words of human speech, and he began to realize that the hope of live spirit communication he had for the device he built had come to fruition. Not knowing if he was actually hearing what he thought he was hearing, Frank decided he needed a second opinion, someone who was involved in the paranormal field and would approach his new device and the idea for which it was built with an open mind. That individual was a man named Christopher Moon.

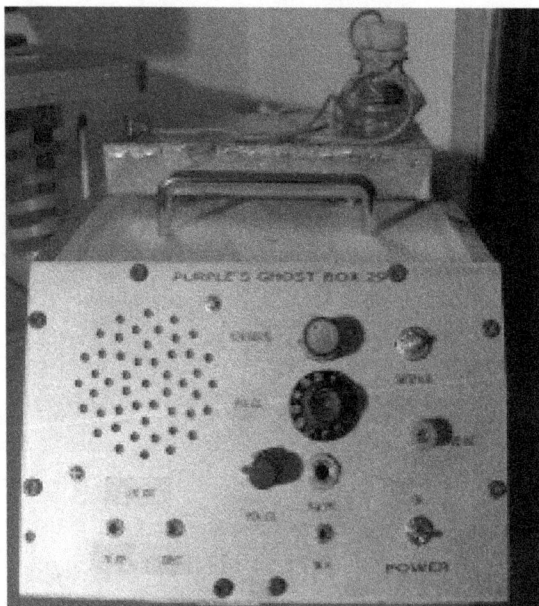

The Frank's Box

Mr. Sumption contacted Chris Moon and set a meeting for him to pay a visit and witness the new spirit communication device in person. Chris Moon arrived at Frank Sumption's home and was escorted to Frank's

workshop, the device was presented, and Frank explained his idea for the box and how it came to be a reality. After a short conversation, Mr. Sumption presented his device and explained how it was designed to work. He hit the power switch, and the device came to life.

As Frank and Chris Moon sat listening to the device spew a continuous stream of random sounds, words of human speech could be heard amidst the mishmash of the device's sweep, intelligible words that seemed to be separated from the rest of the sounds but also a part of them. After a few minutes of listening to the new device, Chris Moon agreed that something extraordinary was happening. Could he definitively say that what he had heard was actually otherworldly entities sending a communication? No, but Mr. Moon did admit that there was something there other than the sweep sounds the device was producing. Chris Moon asked Frank if it would be possible for him to borrow the device for further experimentation, assuring Mr. Sumption that he would take the utmost care of it. Frank agreed to loan the device to Chris Moon on the condition that he would receive updates on Chris's progress and the device would be returned to him at some point. Chris Moon assured Frank that he would comply and that if the device did what they both suspected, it could he would be the one to confirm it.

Frank immediately set to work on a second device, which he had now dubbed "the Ghost Box" or, as it would come to be known, "the Frank's Box." Not long after, Frank's Box number two was completed. Box #2 performed much the same as its predecessor did, although sounding a bit different. Frank would later be known to have said, "No two boxes are the same," meaning although each box was constructed in the same manner with basically the same components, each ghost box seemed to have its own distinct personality, a fact that I can attest to.

While Frank continued to work on the construction of ghost boxes, he received periodic reports from Chris Moon as to his progress with working with the device and the results that were gleaned from it. At this point Chris had no further doubt in his mind that the new device did, in fact, facilitate live spirit communication that could be heard in real time as it was delivered. Frank had also had come to solidify his belief in the ghost box's abilities from his own sessions with it. Now resigned to the fact that his new device was able to accomplish what it was designed to do, Frank Sumption decided to make his new ghost box known to the world. It is not clear exactly when or how Frank introduced his new device, but it is believed that the first public announcement of this unique piece of paranormal equipment came on a Yahoo group dedicated to paranormal research and investigation. Not long after, Frank Sumption created his own Yahoo group dedicated to the ghost box. It was a forum where people could discuss the ghost box and paranormal research and investigation as a whole. Frank posted his progress with the building of new devices as well as his results gathered from sessions with his boxes. Since no one at the time except Frank and Chris Moon had access to a ghost box, the bulk of posts to Frank's Yahoo group were mainly questions, which I believe Frank became somewhat tired of continuously answering.

Frank decided that now with a number of ghost boxes completed, he would choose a couple of individuals he deemed worthy of receiving a Frank's Box, and those individuals would receive one of his boxes on the condition that the Frank's Box would be used for the purpose of research and investigation and that the resulting data and any audio examples would be shared via the Yahoo group. Frank had made a couple of choices and sent out Frank's Boxes to the individuals he chose. After a lucky few from the group had Frank's Boxes, the Ghost Box Yahoo group began to enjoy a flurry of activity. Consequently the word of the new device began to spread through the paranormal community. The Yahoo group enjoyed a boom in membership and many posts daily with questions about this new live spirit communication device. The Frank's Box enjoyed its distinction of being the only ghost box in existence for more than a couple of years, but as with all things, a monopoly on anything is very hard to retain, and inevitably a new model of ghost box hit the scene, which came to be known as the "Joe's Box."

The man responsible for creating this rival to the Frank's Box was Joe Cioppi, a retired engineer with an interest in EVP and the paranormal. The Joe's Box was a reasonable facsimile of the Frank's Box in that it performed the same way. It was a traditional sweeping ghost box that resembled a walkie-talkie.

Bruce Halliday

Joe Cioppi

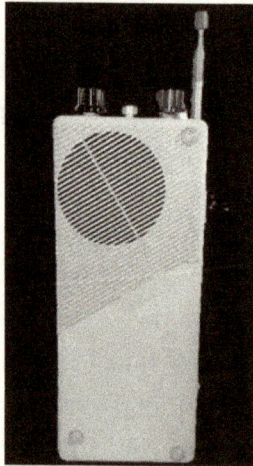

The Joe's Box

    Joe Cioppi had found a set of schematics that Frank Sumption had posted to a website and used Frank's basic design to help create the Joe's Box. My first experience with a real ghost box was with a Joe's Box I purchased from Mr. Cioppi, and it was the device that set my feet on the path to many years of research and investigation into live spirit ghost box communication. The creation of the Joe's Box opened the door of opportunity for anyone who was interested in attempting ghost box communication to own a ghost box. Although Joe Cioppi was a bit of a private man and suffered from health issues, he was willing for a time to build a Joe's ghost box for someone who was willing to purchase it. Joe's career in building and selling the Joe's Box was not long lived due to his increasing health issues and personal affairs. Joe did not manufacture many ghost boxes, his boxes seemed to have some minor inherent flaws, and he was receiving requests for return and repair of some of the boxes he sold. This led to Joe fading out of ghost box building. Subsequently, there are not a lot of Joe's Boxes in existence, and they are a rarity to come across. In November 2007 a man going by the pseudonym "Sum Duc" posted a message to Frank Sumption's Yahoo group saying that he had created a sweeping ghost box from a small Radio Shack digital AM/FM radio by simply snipping a wire on the radio's circuit board. He gave step-by-step instructions on how to perform the procedure and stated that anyone could do it. The man was Bill Chappel, and his simple modification to turn a small radio into a working ghost box gave birth to the RS 12-469 ghost box hack. This small but monumental creation by Mr. Bill Chappel opened the floodgates for anyone and everyone who wanted one to have a working ghost box for under twenty bucks.

Bill Chappel

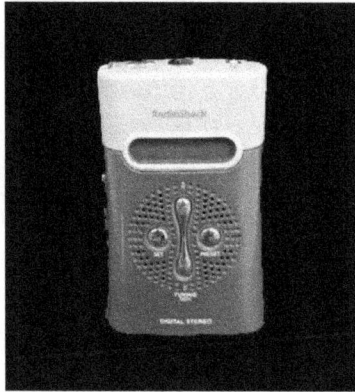

The RS 12-469 Hack Ghost Box

I was driving on the highway, returning home from picking my wife up from work, on the day Bill made the announcement about the RS 12-469 hack box when I received a call from a friend and colleague in the paranormal community. He excitedly explained what Bill Chappel had done and told me he had already made a trip to Radio Shack and purchased his radio and that upon hanging up with me, he would attempt the "hacking" procedure. He went on to suggest I find a Radio Shack and do the same.

I immediately exited the highway in search of a Radio Shack store in spite of my wife's objections. I realized she was tired and eager to get home, but I had to get my hands on this radio. Of course, being the loving and understanding wife she was, she didn't complain much. Within ten minutes of my exiting the highway, I was able to locate a Radio Shack store and promptly purchased two of their model 12-469 portable AM/FM radios, and to my wife's relief, we started home. We arrived home, and although I was chomping at the bit to run down to my makeshift paranormal lab in the basement, I knew my wife and daughter would be hungry and ready for dinner, so I contained my ambition and hurried through the evening meal.

I arrived in my lab and set the two brand-new 12-469s on my workbench, went to the computer, and located the post that Bill Chappel had made to Frank Sumption's Yahoo group explaining the procedure for hacking the 12-469 and turning it into a working ghost box. As Bill put it, "The procedure is simple. Anyone can do it," but still, if you had no prior experience whatsoever with electronics, a simple task could seem daunting. I followed Mr. Chappel's instructions step by step. I removed the radio's back cover to expose the inner circuit board. I searched the tiny circuit board for the the word "Mute," which had a tiny wire soldered at the point of designation. I proceeded slowly and very carefully to snip the wire with a pair of nail clippers, severing its connection to the circuit board. I folded the wire back so that it would not make an accidental reconnection, replaced the radio's back cover, and let out a sigh of relief. According to Mr. Chappel, this was all that needed to be done.

I placed the batteries into my new RS 12-469 ghost box hack, crossed my fingers, and flicked on the power switch. The small hack ghost box's digital readout panel lit up. The radio's band selector was on FM. Next, as per Bill Chappel's instructions, I was to hold down either the up or down tuning buttons to start the 12-469 sweeping the band. I held the radio and my breath and pressed down the up tuning button. I heard nothing, silence. I noticed that the digital station readout was moving continuously through the stations, as would be the case if the ghost box were sweeping, but no sound. I scratched my head, and the first thought in my mind was that I'd managed to screw something up inside the radio during my hacking procedure.

I immediately went back to Mr. Chappel's instructions but could not find anything I had done wrong. I promptly placed a call to my paranormal friend and asked how he'd fared with his ghost box hack, and he informed me that it went great, and his RS 12-469 was performing exactly as a ghost box should. I explained my situation, and what he said next made me feel like a complete idiot. He asked if I was sure that the speaker I attached to the small hack ghost box was working. DUH! How could I have not realized it? The 12-469 radio did not have a built-in speaker and needed an external speaker to be attached. I explained my mistake to my friend and said goodbye to the sound of laughter. I retrieved a small speaker that I used in my EVP research and plugged it into the RS 12-

469. I switched on the power and heard the familiar hiss of static white noise. I took another breath and pressed down on the tuning button. What I heard next was the sweet familiar sound of a ghost box sweep. I exhaled with another sigh of relief as I listened to the new device's sweep.

I turned off the new "Shack Hack," which is what the Radio Shack hack ghost boxes came to be known as, planning on doing a test session with it the next day. The next morning after dropping my wife at work, I found myself approaching the exit on the highway I had taken the previous evening and decided to pay the Radio Shack another visit. I planned on purchasing a few more of the 12-469s; never hurts to have a spare. I entered the Radio Shack and went over to the shelf where I had found the 12-469 the day before. There were four radios left on the shelf, so I decided to get them. As I was plucking these little gems from their resting place, I noticed that directly next to them was a radio that looked identical to the 12-469. I asked the store clerk what the difference was between the two. He informed me that both models were identical except that the 12-469 had no internal speaker, and its cousin the RS 12-470 had an internal speaker. My immediate thought was that if the 12-469 could be hacked so could the 12-470. I grabbed two of them from the shelf, paid for my six radios, and proceeded home.

I stepped into my house and made a beeline to my lab. I set aside the radios I'd purchased with the exception of one new RS 12-470. I sat down at my work desk and proceeded to remove the back cover of the new radio. When I looked at the circuit board inside, there staring me in the face was the word "Mute" in tiny white letters. I took my trusty nail clippers and snipped the designated wire. I replaced the 12-470's back cover, inserted fresh batteries, and switched on the power button. That oh so sweet sound of static came from its small internal speaker. I pressed down the tuning button and held it for a second, and voila, the RS 12-470 began to sweep. What a beautiful sound! Not only did we have a second hack ghost box, but I had created it, sort of; actually, all I did was follow Bill Chappel's instructions on a similar model Radio Shack radio. In reality, it was just a 12-469 with an internal speaker. All that into account, I was still the first to do it, and that felt good.

I decided to run a test session on the RS 12-469 first and then follow it with a test session on the RS 12-470. The live spirit communication session with the RS 12-469 was decent, nothing stellar just the rudimentary spirit communication I was used to. The only real fault I could find with the little hack ghost box was that it emitted an incessant clicking as it swept the dial. This did not hinder the performance or understanding of the spirit communication I was able to hear live, but boy, was it annoying. I gave the RS 12-469 an initial grade of B. Of course, I would have to work with it further to make a definitive assessment.

I moved on to the session with the RS 12-470. I don't want to believe there was any bias involved, but I have to say that the session with the RS 12-470 was quite a bit more productive than the session with the 12-469. I actually heard my name twice, and Mike made his presence known more than once during the fifteen-minute session. This 12-470 session actually gleaned one of the longest messages I had received to date; it consisted of a five-word message that said, "We are here. Help us." I was not able to catch this spirit communication live but discovered it in the review of the session recording. I don't know which was better, getting a full sentence of live spirit communication or not hearing the incessant clicking with the 12-470 that plagued the 12-469.

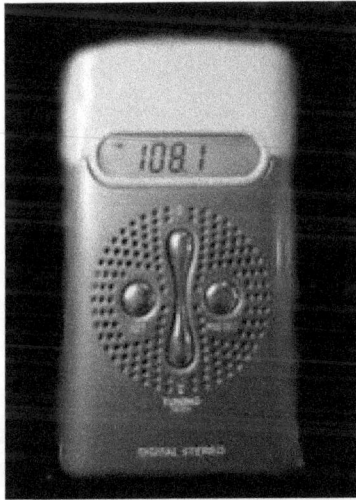

The Radio Shack 12-470

As time went on and more and more people became familiar with the new hack devices and hacked their own ghost box hack radios, different people began to search out and discover other models of small radios that would accept Bill Chappel's hacking procedure, and for a while it seemed like every week there would be a new model of a ghost box hack to hit the scene. Here is a list of most of the ghost box hack radios in order of their debut, the RS 20-125, the RS 12-820, the RS 12-150, the Sangean DT200VX, the RS 12-587, the RS 12-588, and the RS 12-589. There were a few more, but these were the most popular and easiest to hack. There was another small armband AM/FM digital radio that was hacked by me in 2009, the Jensen SAB-55, which I found one day while shopping in a local big-box store.

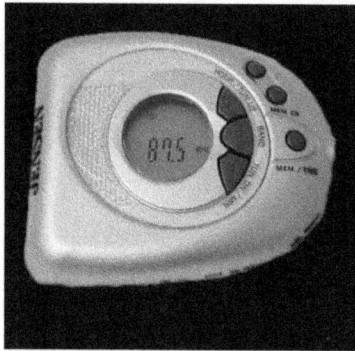

The Jensen SAB-55

This compact radio was very easy to hack and produced a very good sweep. The Jensen SAB-55 became a very popular ghost box hack radio and was used by many paranormal researchers and investigators throughout the paranormal community. The Jensen SAB-55 was featured on a popular paranormal television show, where it facilitated the reception of a significant live spirit communication relevant to the subject of the paranormal investigation that the TV show was based on. The little Jensen SAB-55 went on to be used by custom ghost box builders as the foundation that their ghost boxes were run on.

The MiniBox

With the advent of the hack ghost boxes came a flood of new paranormal enthusiasts. Because the radios used for hack ghost boxes were very inexpensive and simple to turn into a working ghost box, many people were able to try their hand at live spirit ghost box communication. As time passed and many people became competent at live spirit ghost box communication, there arose a demand for new and more sophisticated ghost boxes. The hack ghost boxes were good and did what they were intended to do, but they were limited in their capabilities. The speed of the sweep could not be adjusted, and their signal reception usually left much to be desired. A man named Ron Ricketts announced that he would be releasing a new model of ghost box that would be available for purchase. Ron founded a company named Paranormal Systems and created a manufactured ghost box called "the MiniBox." It was a sleek black professional-looking device that came with a number of features, sweep speed control, signal sensitivity adjustment, and jacks to input a microphone and recording device.

Ron Ricketts contacted me at the onset of his endeavor to build a custom ghost box and asked if I would agree to be a consultant throughout the process of design and manufacture and also beta test one of the prototypes when completed. I agreed and periodically supplied Ron with insights into how the device should run, sound, and perform. When the MiniBox was completed, I received one from Ron Ricketts and was asked to put it through its paces and render my thoughts and evaluation on the new ghost box. I did just that. The MiniBox was an adequate ghost box as far as performance went, and its sleek and professional appearance added to its desirability. The ghost box performed the way it was designed to and was able to facilitate live spirit communication. Its features, such as sweep speed adjustment and signal enhancement, aided in its ability to do so; however for all its features and state-of-the-art appearance, it was finally just a sweeping ghost box. The MiniBox and itssuccesser, "the MiniBox Plus," unfortunately did not enjoy long-lasting success. I would attribute this to the average capabilities of the two devices and the very hefty price tag that came with them.

Some time passed following the introduction of the MiniBox before a select couple of individuals decided to try their hand at custom ghost box building. There were a few individuals tinkering with custom ghost box designs, but none had publicly presented one. In 2010 a colleague of mine in the paranormal field of spirit communication had reached out to one of the individuals who had been experimenting with ghost box construction and the electronic circuitry needed to produce a working ghost box and learned the procedure needed to turn an ordinary radio into a ghost box using electronic additions to the radio's existing circuit board. After some trial and error, my colleague produced a working custom-built ghost box. I was contacted by this individual and asked if I would run the new ghost box through its paces. Of course I agreed and was sent what would come to be known as a "Steve's Box," created by Steve Hultay.

The ghost box I received was labeled "Steve's Box #12" and would become the predominant ghost box that I would use in my research for the next ten years. Steve Hultay would go on to produce different models of custom ghost boxes and is responsible for many of the unique features we find in various custom ghost boxes today. Following the Steve's Box came other custom-built ghost boxes produced by various individuals within the paranormal community. A few had some staying power and performed well, but most were short lived.

Steve's Box #12

The advantages to owning and using a custom-built ghost box are that they can be built with a myriad of different features, and the individual ordering the custom box can interact with the builder and have the box designed to their individual wants and needs. Some of the features offered in a custom-built ghost box are of course, sweep speed control, which I personally consider a necessary feature in a ghost box; also a feature giving the ghost box the ability to switch between linear or random sweep; reverse sweep, which allows the ghost box to sweep the radio band from back to front in a counterclockwise manner; and reverse speech, which is not to be confused with a reverse sweep. This feature allows the ghost box to actually deliver the ghost box sweep in reverse speech like listening to an audio recording in reverse. The premise behind reverse speech is that the human speech received by the ghost box is reversed and that any words and/or phrases of human speech that are heard and captured in normal forward speech are believed to be spirit communication due to the reversal of received radio speech by the ghost box. This reverse in speech helps to eliminate the possibility of what we call "false positives," which are words or phrases of radio broadcast that have escaped being broken down by the ghost box and can be mistaken for spirit communication. Other features that have debuted and become available in custom ghost boxes in recent years are the echo and reverb features. These features do exactly what their name implies, they add echo and reverb to the existing sound being emitted by the ghost box, including the sweep and any spirit communication that may be received. I personally do not have this feature in any of my ghost boxes. My opinion is that the addition of echo and reverb can serve to distort words of human speech, which can then be heard differently than they were delivered by the communicating entity and received by the ghost box operator.

Echo and reverb features in a ghost box have become a subject of controversy within the paranormal community; you either love them or you hate them. One other feature of note is one that has appeared in some custom ghost boxes recently, the "Mute" feature, which gives the ghost box operator the ability to in effect mute the sound of the ghost box sweep by either pressing a button or flicking a switch. The idea behind this feature is that the ghost box session operator can silence the ghost box sweep while asking a question and/or making a statement. This alleviates the operator's need to shout to be heard above the sound of the ghost box sweep and have the sweep sound being heard along with the voice of the operator. It also serves to break down the ghost box session recording into increments that contain the operator's question or statement and the ensuing sweep that may or may not contain relevant spirit communication. I consider this a handy feature but not a necessity. Custom-built ghost boxes are the Mercedes-Benz of ghost boxes, and in my opinion, a custom ghost box, due to its availability of incorporated features, allows the owner operator the best opportunity for quantity and quality of live spirit communication.

I would also like to mention two premiere ghost box builders who are active in the paranormal community today. Their respective boxes have not only found their way into the hands of many, many seasoned researchers and investigators but have appeared and continue to appear on acclaimed paranormal television shows and countless online websites, forums and videos. I consider these two gentlemen to be top in their class as creators, inventors, and innovators in the field of ghost box technology. I'm speaking of

KD Stafford

Austin Maynard

KD Stafford and Austin Maynard, two of the world's most outstanding ghost box builders.

In the past few years, there have been other ghost boxes offered for sale that I call "commercially built ghost boxes." These are different models of ghost boxes that are produced in number, and each individual model is identical to its respective type, unlike the custom ghost boxes, which are hand built and individually unique. Commercial ghost boxes like the P-SB-7 and P-SB-11, the Sbox, and the TAKH TB-1 incorporate a set of basic features found in custom ghost boxes but do not need to be individually requested from a builder of custom ghost boxes with a set of personalized features. They can be ordered online and come as advertised. Two of the commercial ghost boxes, the Sbox and the TAKH TB-1, are virtually identical in looks, operation, quality, and features despite being different models made by different companies. I own the TAKH TB-1 and find it to be an above average ghost box in its features and performance. I have received quite a few high-quality live spirit communications in sessions with the TAKH TB-1.

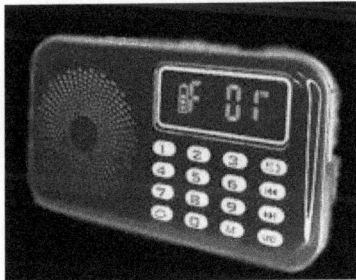

The TAKH TB-1

Bruce Halliday

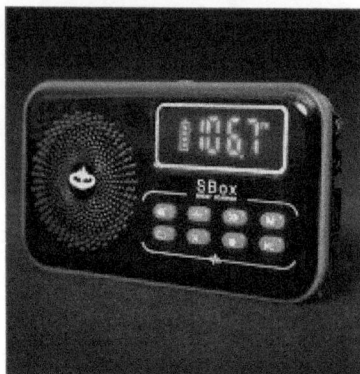

The Sbox

The PSB-7

The PSB-11

Although the basic foundation and intended use for the traditional sweeping ghost box have not changed since the day twenty years ago when Mr. Frank Sumption introduced the world to the first ghost box, there have been many strides in quality, craftsmanship, and features that are incorporated into the modern ghost box we use today. I believe we now enjoy a better quantity and quality of live spirit communication because of those strides. We must, however, always keep present in our minds that without the hard work, dedication, willingness, and the help of our spirit friends on the other side, the ghost box would be nothing but a broken radio.

Live spirit ghost box communication is a method of spirit communication facilitated by an electronic device, i.e., the ghost box; therefore it becomes a part of a larger group of spirit communication methods known as ITC, also known as instrumental transcommunication. What is ITC? The letters "ITC" are an acronym for instrumental transcommunication. ITC is the name that has been given by Professor Ernst Senkowski, a German physicist, for the technique of contacting spirits by electronic means. ITC consists of different methods that are employed by individuals in an attempt to make contact with spirit entities either through visual or audible means.

When ITC was first practiced in the pursuit of making contact with the spirits of deceased human beings, the methods encompassed by the definition of ITC were few. In the early days of ITC, paranormal researchers and investigators employed the basic methods of spirit photography and EVP, electronic voice phenomena. Visual ITC is an attempt by an individual to capture the image of a spirit entity by means of photography. The audible method is an attempt by an individual to capture and/or receive live, audible communication from a spirit entity. ITC in its present state encompasses quite a few paranormal research and investigative methods.

The practiced visual methods of ITC are now accomplished by means of still photography and videography, which allows an individual to capture spirit images by either taking still images with a camera, or taking video footage with a camcorder or even a cellphone.

The audible methods that fall under the umbrella of ITC are more numerous than the visual methods. The basic and most common methods of audio ITC used by paranormal researchers and investigators today are, of course, EVP (electronic voice phenomena), live spirit ghost box communication, and DRV (direct radio voice). There are a few offshoots of these three basic audible methods; however, they are highly experimental and are not as established as the three basic methods of EVP, live spirit ghost box communication, and DRV. Of the audible methods, EVP has been around the longest. In 1959 an individual named Friedrich Jürgenson was recording bird songs. Upon playing the tape of the recording later, he heard what he interpreted to be his dead father's voice and then the spirit of his deceased wife calling his name. He went on to make several more recordings, including one that he said contained a message from his late mother. Later a Latvian psychologist named Konstantin Raudive worked in conjunction with Jürgenson and made over one hundred thousand recordings, which he described as containing communications with spirits of deceased human beings.

The next and arguably the most popular method of audible ITC is live spirit ghost box communication, which is the method of using a ghost box, which is essentially a device that mechanically sweeps the radio broadcast bands such as AM, FM, and shortwave in a rapid fashion, allowing the words, phrases, and sounds of the radio broadcast to be broken down into small fragments of sound theoretically used by a spirit entity to form and deliver communication that is then heard live in real time by the ghost box operator. The first ghost box was created and tested by Frank Sumption in 2002 and has subsequently flourished into the premiere method for spirit communication.

The last but certainly not least of the top three audible methods is DRV, which is the method of receiving live spirit communication in real time by utilizing certain shortwave radio bands and frequencies through a radio receiver. This method allows a spirit entity to use the radio signal and frequencies to form and deliver communication through the receiving device that can be heard live in real time by the session operator. The leading researcher in the field of DRV here in the United States is a gentleman by the name of Ron Yacovetti, who has dedicated himself to the practice and research of live spirit communication with the method of DRV and has managed in a relatively short time to bring DRV into the light as a serious and viable method of audible ITC.

Over the many years that individuals here in the physical world have attempted and accomplished interaction with spirit entities, whether it be through visual or audible means, there have also been reported and documented cases of ITC that would not fall into what we today accept as the "conventional methods" of ITC, if they can be called conventional. I am referring to incidents that entail electronic devices that do not fit the description of the ones I have mentioned here, such as telephones, televisions, computers, text messages, and, yes, even hearing aids. There have been numerous accounts over the years of contact and/or communication from spirit entities through these electronic devices.

One such publicized case that has borne the brunt of much controversy within the ITC community as well as the paranormal community as a whole would be the incident that occurred in 1994 when George Meek, renowned ITC researcher, claimed to have received a telephone call from also renowned ITC researcher Konstantin Raudive, who had been deceased at the point of the phone call for twenty years. The phone call contained verbal interaction between Raudive and Meek; at one point Konstantin Raudive even claimed he had George's deceased wife, Jeanette, beside him. The actual phone call was recorded by George Meek and can be found and listened to on the internet.

There have also been numerous claims by individuals who state they have received messages from spirit entities that were familiar to them on their telephone answering machines. There have been reports of spirit communications received via computer email, cellphone text, and voicemail, and even reports of spirit messages coming through someone's personal hearing aid while the person was wearing it. All of these instances, if they could be verified, would fall under the category of ITC. They are all spirit communications received through electronic means. ITC and especially live spirit ghost box communication are a vital and substantial part of paranormal research and investigation. I would even venture to say that ITC has contributed more to the furtherance of understanding the paranormal than any other field within the confines of paranormal research and investigation. Without ITC our understanding of the paranormal and the spirit realm as it stands to date would be much less advanced.

Chapter 4

Live Spirit Ghost Box Communication, How Does It Work?

"Live spirit ghost box communication, how does it work?" This question is actually a double entendre. The question can pertain to the actual mechanical operation of the device itself, and it can also pertain to how a ghost box is able to render live communication from entities that are not of this physical realm. Let's tackle this question in two parts as it pertains to each aspect respectively. I am by no means a ghost box builder, nor do I have even the slightest working knowledge of electronics. My explanations here are derived from explanations that were given to me by some of the world's premier ghost box builders.

Ok, let's examine how the actual ghost box itself operates and how it is designed to do so. For this explanation, let's use the custom-built ghost box, which is a device that is designed and built by an individual referred to in the paranormal community as a "box builder." The ghost box in spite of all its capabilities is a radio. Its foundation consists of a radio receiving circuit board, speaker, volume control and a receiving antenna; these are the cornerstones from which the ghost box is built. The box builder will commonly start with an ordinary digital radio. Initially, one of three things can be done, the builder can either leave the original radio intact and make electronic modifications and additions to the existing circuitry; he or she can remove the guts of the radio, perform the additional modifications and place the final circuitry in a custom-designed case; or the complete ghost box, including the main circuit board, can be constructed from scratch.

No matter what design the ghost box builder decides on, the key component added to the common radio circuit board is a sweep circuit. This piece of electronic circuitry is what turns an ordinary digital radio into a ghost box. The sweep circuit has a sweep speed adjustment feature already incorporated into it, so when it is added to the ghost box's main circuit board, it immediately allows the ghost box to sweep the designated radio band, and the speed of the sweep can be adjusted. This is the main and most important modification; in addition, of course, you have the speaker and the antenna, which need to be incorporated if the ghost box circuitry is to be housed in a case other than its original manufactured radio case.

I know that my explanation makes the process sound relatively simple; on the contrary, it is anything but. There are many variables and adjustments that go into the production of a ghost box, tuning, voltage adjustment, and the incorporation of custom features such as random sweep, reverse speech, and echo or reverb, just to name a few. Once the builder has completed the ghost box and it is in the hands of the live spirit ghost box communication operator and is finally used for the purpose it was designed, the operator will bring the ghost box to life by switching on the power, choosing his or her preferred radio band—AM, FM or shortwave—start the ghost box sweep function, adjust the sweep to the desired speed, apply and adjust any remaining features to be utilized, and begin a live spirit communication session. The ghost box is now receiving a radio broadcast signal from the designated band, and the sweep feature is breaking down that received radio broadcast into small fragments of sound by sweeping the chosen radio band continuously at a rapid pace. The sound of the ghost box sweep emanates from the speaker of the box, and the live spirit communication session begins.

Now that the first aspect of the question about the ghost box's mechanical operation has been answered, let's move on to the second, "How is it possible for a ghost box to receive and deliver live spirit communication?" The answer to this question is a bit more complicated than the previous one. The answer that I will offer here is based on my personal theories formulated with the help of information that I derived from years of live spirit communication with my spirit technicians and spirit contacts through the use of the ghost box. Many times, in my live spirit communication ghost box sessions, I have posed the question, "How do you as spirit entities send communication using the ghost box?" The numerous answers and responses I have received from communicating entities have culminated in my formulating this accepted theory. When the ghost box is in operation and the request for communication by the physical human operator conducting the session is offered, an entity that is willing to participate in an exchange of communication will focus his or her attention on the ghost box and its sweep of the radio band. Let's use the word "hello" as an example. The communicating entity decides to respond to the ghost box operator with the word hello and needs to deliver this response through the operating ghost box so that the individual performing the ghost box session can receive the communication and have the opportunity to hear it live in real time as it is delivered.

The actions that must be taken by the communicating entity are no easy task, so I have been told by my spirit technicians on numerous occasions. The communicating entity must first concentrate on the plethora of sound fragments that are being produced by the rapid sweeping of the ghost box; the entity must then attempt to locate the fragments of sound within the sweep coming from the ghost box that will allow him to form the word "hello." Once the entity has found the sound fragments needed for the formation of the intended communication, he must now manage to extract those sound fragments from the ever-flowing stream of sound fragments produced by the ghost box sweep. It's sort of like standing on the side of railroad tracks and trying to grab a baseball from a train car on a passing locomotive. Now that the communicating entity has located and gathered the appropriate sound fragments, they must now be formed by the entity into the intended word of communication.

Once the entity has completed these tasks and is ready to deliver the word "hello" as the intended communication, he or she must now send the word of communication to the physical world through the operating ghost box. The entity's communication must now be carefully placed back into the sweep stream and be carried through the speaker of the ghost box to be heard and/or captured in a recording by the individual operating the ghost box session.

In my live spirit ghost box communication sessions, I will ask a question or make a request, and I will then allow ten to twelve seconds for an entity to respond before moving on to the next question or statement. I use this protocol to help ensure that any spirit communication that falls within those parameters will be relevant to the question or statement I pose. If I were to ask the question "How are you doing?" and did not set a time limit for a response, the entity may have only had the opportunity to send the response "good" to that specific question further into the session, and it may have come following an unrelated question or statement by me, which would make the word "good" an irrelevant response to the latest question asked. If I do not hear a relevant answer or response that I believe to be spirit communication to a posed question or statement by me in the set time parameter, any communication heard after that could pertain to the prior question is disregarded. The reason for this explanation of time constraints was to stress the added difficulty the communicating entity faces by having to perform all the tasks necessary to form and deliver communication and to have to perform those tasks and deliver the communication intended within ten to twelve seconds.

Over the course of my live spirit communication research career, I have received quite a few messages from my spirit technicians and other communicating entities reminding me that they do not have an easy task when it comes to delivering live spirit communication via a ghost box. These reminders to me usually come when I start to moan and complain about receiving brief two- or three-word answers and responses as opposed to lengthy spirit messages and/or answers. We as human beings on the physical side of live spirit ghost box communication have the luxury of just speaking our communication to our spirit counterparts aloud, not having to go through the daunting, tedious, and stressful tasks that are necessary for spirit entities to deliver their communication to us. When a physical human being attempts to communicate with entities such as the disembodied spirits of people who were once in the physical life, many things come into play. The ghost box was originally meant to be just a tool to allow us to hear communication from spirit entities live as it is sent by said entities and be heard in real time, as opposed to simply capturing the voice of an alleged spirit on an audio recorder, which then needs to be reviewed at a later time, as with the EVP method of capturing spirit communication, thereby eliminating the live, conscious connection and opportunity for a back-and-forth exchange between beings from different planes of existence. This simple tool has, as time passed, allowed paranormal researchers and investigators dedicated to its use to gather, study, and present evidence and data gleaned from the ability of this amazing device, live spirit communication that has been heard and gathered under many different conditions and circumstances. The ghost box has proved to be an invaluable gift. There are other factors that come into play that allow two-way live communication between physical individuals and spirit entities with the use of a ghost box that transcends this electronic device. I will attempt to explain these phenomena in a forthcoming chapter.

When I think of live spirit ghost box communication and how it works as a whole, it boggles the mind. I have dedicated at the time of this writing almost seventeen years of research and investigation into that very question. I have performed thousands of live spirit ghost box communication sessions in the span of those seventeen years, and to this day every time I turn on a ghost box and receive live spirit communication that consists of direct answers to my specific questions, statements rendered by communicating entities that are accurate and relevant to the topics I present in the given session, the consistent attention I and my efforts receive from spirit technicians I recognize and have formed a relationship with over the years, having the ability to request communication with a specific spirit being and have that spirit come to the forefront and interact with me in an almost conversational manner, and experiencing a communicating spirit entity's joy or sense of humor, desperation or loneliness, fear or confusion, make every minute spent working with the ghost box fulfilling, emotional and unique.

When I ponder the question "Live spirit ghost box communication, how does it work?" one word always pops into my mind: extraordinary! Of all the research I have compiled, all the audio data I have accumulated, and all the hours I have spent interacting and communicating with entities that occupy a different existence than myself, I have to say, as far as offering a definitive answer to the question of how it all works, all I can do is to give the best explanation I can from the experience I have had and the knowledge I have compiled. Live spirit ghost box communication, we can understand its mechanics, we can formulate theories and hypotheses based on actual spirit communication, but for now, I believe we have only scratched the surface. The ghost box and the live spirit communication we are able to receive by using it remain an enigma.

I would now like to address the subject of editing a live spirit communication ghost box recording and why we should not use audio editing filters on it. When listening to some of the live spirit ghost box communication audio that is presented for public review, it is apparent that the individuals who reviewed and edited the live ghost box session recording used noise-reduction filters and/or other types of audio editing filters on the original audio in an attempt to clarify or showcase what was believed to be live spirit communication.

In live spirit ghost box communication, the use of audio filters is a big NO-NO! Audio filters in an editing program will distort the sound of the original audio content and thereby change the pronunciation and sound of any live spirit communication contained within the audio recording, especially noise-reduction filters. These filters do just what the name implies, they remove aspects of the audio in an attempt to "clean up" the sound quality. The detrimental fact is that they not only remove static hiss or white noise but also aspects of sound that make up speech and will subsequently change the sound of any live spirit communication contained in the live ghost box session recording. There are only a couple of acceptable editing techniques for a ghost box recording "clipping," which is removing unused portions of ghost box sweep sound from a selected part of the audio recording so that you can better recognize the live spirit communication without the clutter of unused extra sweep fragments. Volume level—you can raise or lower the playback volume of the audio to help the listener hear it more comfortably. It is also acceptable to lower the volume of the ghost box sweep that immediately precedes and follows what is believed to be live spirit communication so that the spirit communication will stand out from the clamor of the unused part of the ghost box sweep. And finally playback speed, you can adjust the playback speed of the selected audio so that the listener can better follow and understand what the live spirit communication is saying.

There are incidents in every live ghost box session where the communicating spirit entity must deliver the live spirit communication depending on the immediate conditions. When this occurs, the resulting live spirit communication is extremely fast when listened to in the ghost box session recording. This is the result of the spirit entity having to form the live spirit communication in a very short window of availability, having to grab the fragments of sound produced by the ghost box sweep that the entity needs to form the live spirit communication at that point in time. You may ask "Why doesn't the spirit wait for a more suitable time to form and send the communication?" In live spirit ghost box communication, it is essential that the answer to a question or a statement be made at a particular moment in order to be relevant to the question or subject and be recognized as being associated with that specific question or subject. Consequently, the spirit entity, if set on rendering the live spirit communication, will have to make do with whatever is available at that moment in time, and therefore the resulting communication may be delivered in a rapid fashion. Realizing this, the ghost box operator allows for the correction of playback speed in editing in order to have the live spirit communication be better understood; however, if playback speed is altered drastically, it will tend to distort the original audio and may affect the structure of the original live spirit communication. Through trial and error and head-to-head combat with skeptics over the years, I have developed these accepted forms of editing for live spirit ghost box communication recordings.

1. NEVER! use audio editing filters on a live spirit ghost box communication recording.

2. Clipping is an acceptable method of removing part of the unused ghost box sweep fragments that are preceding and following the believed live spirit communication. This unused ghost box sweep tends to distract the listener from hearing the proposed live spirit

communication clearly. It is also acceptable to lower the volume of a small portion of the ghost box sweep that immediately precedes and follows what is believed to be live spirit communication, which will also aid in the understanding of the proposed live spirit communication.

3. Playback speed—carefully adjust the speed of the playback so that the listener can better follow and understand what the live spirit communication is saying.

These three techniques can be used without polluting or compromising the integrity of the original live spirit ghost box communication session audio and therefore allow any live spirit ghost box communication audio to be presented publicly for review with confidence in its quality and integrity.

Chapter 5

How to Perform a Basic Live Spirit Ghost Box Session for Beginners

After working diligently in the paranormal research field of live spirit ghost box communication for some time, I developed a set of protocols for the performance of a basic live spirit ghost box communication session. In this chapter, I will attempt to explain the equipment needed to conduct a basic live spirit communication ghost box session and the performance of a set of basic steps to take that will give the intended ghost box session structure and a solid foundation on which to successfully complete a fruitful live spirit communication session with the use of a ghost box.

Firstly, for any individuals who are interested in trying their hand at live spirit ghost box communication but do not have or want to invest in a custom-built automatically sweeping ghost box, there is an alternative, the manual sweep method; although not as effective in producing superior-quality live spirit communication as the method of using a mechanically sweeping ghost box, it will deliver an adequate live spirit ghost box communication session and allow for live spirit communication to be received and heard. The main difference between a manual sweep ghost box session and one that utilizes a custom-built automatically sweeping ghost box is that a manual sweep session is conducted by the ghost box operator using an average dial-tuned radio and sweeping the designated radio band manually by continually turning the radio tuning knob from the beginning of the radio band to the end and back again in a continuous fashion. Back in the very beginning days of live spirit ghost box communication, the only custom-built automatically sweeping ghost boxes were scarcer than hen's teeth.

Here is the method to perform a manual sweep live spirit ghost box communication session. For the list of equipment needed, please refer to the equipment list below; simply replace "ghost box" with "dial-tuned radio."

The manual sweep method of live spirit ghost box communication could not be simpler; all that is needed is a working radio with a tuning dial, strong fingers, and an open mind. Also, it is important that you document your session. It is very advisable that you record your live spirit ghost box session with an audio recording device; you would not want to have a great live spirit communication session with great communication and not have it recorded and saved. To perform a manual sweep ghost box session, simply make sure your radio has optimal battery strength and you are in an area that gives you the best radio reception and a minimal amount of ambient noise. Try to perform the session in a place that does not have an abundance of electrical devices in operation, as EMF emissions from electrical devices will add static or white noise to your incoming radio signal and interfere with reception.

Prepare your ghost box and set it to your preferred band, either AM or FM. Choose whichever radio band you feel is your best option at the time of the session. It's always a good practice before beginning your session with questions or requests to give a short greeting to any entities that may be listening and willing to work with you in communicating. Turn on your radio and recording device, and start to manually turn the tuning dial from one end of the radio band to the other and back again continuously; make sure you are turning the dial at a fast enough rate in order to minimize the amount of full radio broadcast words that may escape your sweep. As you turn the dial, ask any questions or make any requests you have of the spirits that may be participating in your session and allow a minimum of ten to twelve-seconds of radio sweep before asking your next question; this will give any communicating entity the opportunity to form and deliver the communication it needs to and will allow you time to hear the communication live as it is delivered.

Continue your manual sweep ghost box session in this manner for the time you have allotted or until you are satisfied with your results. An average session usually lasts about fifteen to twenty minutes depending on how productive any given session is. When you are ready to complete your manual sweep ghost box session, it is a good practice to inform your spirit friends that you are going to end the communication session and thank any entities that may have taken part in the session and made the effort to communicate with you and say goodbye. As a practice, I always allow an additional fifteen-seconds after saying goodbye so that any entity that wishes to can return the goodbye.

Stop your sweep and turn your radio off and then your recording device. You have now successfully completed a live spirit communication manual sweep ghost box session!

Let's move on to the standard live spirit ghost box communication session with the use of a custom automatically sweeping ghost box. Here is a list of what you will need to have; these are all the essentials for your live spirit ghost box communication session. You will need:

1. A working ghost box and audio recorder.
2. Adequate power supply for both your ghost box and recorder, either power cord or battery.
3. Headphones or a speaker if the ghost box being used does not have an internal speaker.
4. An area with the best radio reception you can find! Also, an area that is free from ambient noise such as people talking, dogs barking, television, outside traffic noise, etc.
5. A positive upbeat attitude, which is very important for a successful and productive live spirit ghost box communication session.

Those are the essential tools needed to perform a successful live spirit ghost box communication session.

Here now are the basic steps for how to perform a live spirit ghost box communication session in the suggested order for the ghost box operator to follow.

1. Decide what the topic of your session will be and whatever questions you intend to ask before performing the actual session. It is always a good idea to write your questions down so that you can refer to them during the performance of the live ghost box session. As you prepare your question list, speak your intended questions out loud. I believe that spirit entities can hear us as we speak aloud, and this will help your spirit technicians and any potential spirit communicators to get a sort of heads-up and to prepare an answer before the actual session.

2. This step is a matter of personal preference and not absolutely necessary although I do recommend it. I feel that it is better to have it and not need it than to need it and not have it. The protection ritual or prayer is a request to your spirit technicians and any higher powers to guard against any and all negative influences or entities that may try to invade or interfere in your live spirit ghost box session. Spirit technicians are the gatekeepers and guardians of your live spirit ghost box communication session and the connection it creates as you interact with the spirit realm.

3. Make sure your recording device is in working order and turn it on. State your name, the date, the model of the ghost box being used, and the topic of the live spirit communication ghost box session.

4. Turn on your ghost box and select your choice of radio band—AM, FM, or shortwave. The radio band choice is determined by the radio signal reception strength in your location at the time of the ghost box session and also your personal preference. If you are using the AM band and determine it is not receiving enough of a radio signal to supply adequate radio broadcast to the ghost box for a strong sound-filled sweep to supply the communicating entity with enough sound fragments to form and deliver communication, you will have to use FM, which is a much more active band. Do whatever is necessary to get the best incoming radio broadcast signal possible; the better the signal, the better the ghost box sweep, the better the live spirit communication. My personal preference is the AM band, the reason being that it has less clutter noise such as music, song, and harmonics. The AM band broadcasts predominantly talk radio, which I believe makes for better sound fragments produced by the ghost box sweep, which makes it more conducive to the formation of live spirit communication by the spirit entity.

5. With your recorder and your ghost box on and running, say hello and ask for any spirit technicians who are in attendance that will be overseeing the ghost box session, ask for the name of the spirit technician that responds, greet them, and thank them for their help in the upcoming ghost box session. Always remember that all spirits were and still are people only in a different form; whatever respect and courtesy you would extend to someone in the physical world should also be forthcoming when interacting with your spirit technicians and spirit communicators. Always give approximately ten to twelve-seconds for a response from a communicating entity after every question or statement you deliver; this will help to ensure that the spirit communication received is relevant to the question asked or statement made.

6. Ask your first question and wait the allotted time for a response or answer. Listen carefully to try to hear any spirit communication that may be received live in real time as it is delivered. If an answer or response is heard live in real time, always acknowledge it by repeating what you have heard, in the session recording this will be validation that you did, in fact, hear the spirit communication live in real time as the spirit entity delivered it.

7. Continue to ask your questions and receive any and all spirit communication that may have

been sent; keep track of the time the session has been in progress on your audio recorder. I find that a session of approximately fifteen to twenty minutes is sufficient, although a session can run up to thirty minutes before the energy flow between yourself and the communicating spirit entities starts to dissipate.

8. As your session draws to a close, let your spirit technician know that you intend to end the live spirit ghost box communication session, and request that your spirit technician recall any and all spirit entities that may have traveled through an open portal that may have been created by the ghost box in session to our physical world. This will help ensure that any wayward spirit entity will not remain here in the physical realm and be stuck on our side after the ghost box is turned off. I will discuss portals as they pertain to live spirit ghost box communication in a forthcoming chapter. Ask for confirmation that it is clear and OK to close down the session and turn off the ghost box. After this question is asked, you will have to wait for a response that you are able to hear live in real time; a response not heard live in real time does you and the possible wayward spirit entity no good. After the box has been shut down, any open portal will close, stranding the visiting spirit entity. I have never asked for confirmation of it being clear to shut down where I have not heard some sort of response

in real time that it was OK, so wait for the response, and you will receive it. When you get the all clear, thank your spirit technicians and any spirit entities for their effort in communicating with you and say your goodbyes. You can now shut down your ghost box and your recorder.

Congratulations, you have just completed a successful live spirit ghost box communication session! It is now time to review and edit your session. You will need a computer and an audio editing program for this task. There are many free downloadable audio editing software programs on the internet. I always recommend Goldwave to a new researcher. It is relatively easy to learn to use and is free to download. Just type "Goldwave audio editor" into any search engine and follow the links. When you have your audio editing program set up, load the ghost box session recording onto your computer, and review the entire session in the audio editor. The bulk of the spirit communication received and captured by the recorder will be discovered in the review of the ghost box session recording.

These protocols for a basic live spirit ghost box communication session are a guide to afford the novice ghost box operator the best opportunity to achieve live spirit communication with the use of a ghost box and to set a solid foundation that will serve as a basis for future endeavors. Whether the live spirit ghost box session is performed in a controlled environment or conducted as part of a field investigation, experience and knowledge will be gained by the budding live spirit ghost box communication researcher and investigator. They will develop an individual style of their own. These protocols are meant to be a simple foundation on which to build, not a set of hard and fast rules that need to be strictly adhered to. I have many friends and associates within the paranormal community who either work with a ghost box for research's sake, build custom ghost boxes, or incorporate a ghost box into their field investigative efforts; each has some unique quality or aspect that they bring to the field of live spirit ghost box communication. Time and experience will naturally help to mold and shape an individual's technique as far as performing a ghost box session, the type of ghost box that is preferred, the ghost box features utilized in personal ghost boxes, and the manner in which an individual will conduct a ghost box session. Many factors play a part in forming a seasoned live spirit ghost box communication researcher and/or investigator.

Everything that is built, if the builder intends it to be structurally sound, must have a solid and lasting foundation on which it is constructed; this premise also applies to live spirit ghost box communication and the practice of it. I was told once long ago by a very wise man, my grandfather, "If you want to make a delicious cake, you need to follow the recipe, use the right ingredients, and bake it with care and attention." I cannot think of a more suitable parable. For anyone who is taking their first steps into live spirit ghost box communication, if you take these simple basic tried-and-true steps and make them an inherent part of your ghost box session, you will be setting a foundation that will serve you well throughout your journey in live spirit ghost box communication.

Of course, as you develop as a ghost box operator and researcher, you will inevitably want to experiment with the various features that are offered in a custom ghost box. There is only one feature I consider invaluable and should never be disregarded, which is the sweep speed adjustment feature. I consider this to be the only necessary feature and one that should be present in every ghost box if possible. There are a few of the hack radio ghost boxes that will not allow for the sweep speed adjustment feature; beyond that, any box that is capable of incorporating it should have it. Other features, such as random sweep, reverse sweep, echo, reverb, or reverse speech, all have their place with different contributions that will be a part of any success or failure when utilized during a ghost box session; it will be up to the individual taste of the ghost box operator to decide which of these features their personal ghost boxes will have and when and where to utilize them. Knowing when to do so will come with experience and knowledge of the individual circumstances presented during a specific ghost box session.

As any live spirit ghost box researcher or investigator develops, so will their choice of ghost box. With all of this, the basic foundation of performing a successful live spirit ghost box communication session remains relevant and necessary; it will always remain the anchor point to which all their efforts and accomplishments are tethered and will always remain an important ingredient in achieving success in live spirit ghost box communication.

Before closing this chapter, I would like to address the performance of live spirit ghost box communication sessions that are executed in the field at a reported haunted location by paranormal investigators and their teams or by an individual conducting a single ghost box session at an event surrounded by spectators and the proposed protocols that should be observed. Field investigation ghost box sessions that are done on location are predominantly performed in a location that is not completely familiar to the investigator performing the session and has many atmospheric and structural unknowns. Often a location, especially those locations that are large and intricate buildings such as abandoned prisons or medical facilities like asylums or hospitals, has changing conditions from floor to floor or even room to room that may not be conducive to performing the best live spirit ghost box communication session possible. There are a few steadfast conditions that need to be met in order to ensure the quality and success of a ghost box session, such as radio signal reception, minimal noise interference, level of echo and ambient noise in the area where the session is performed, and temperature, which plays a part in battery power and operation of equipment, just to name a few. As paranormal field investigators giving your time, effort, and usually financial expense to investigate a location and gather evidence of any paranormal activity, you will want to ensure that any and all conditions that are under your control are optimized.

When attempting to conduct a ghost box session at a

field location, the ghost box operator prior to performing the actual ghost box session should evaluate all conditions that would or could hinder the optimal operation of the ghost box and recording equipment. A single individual should be designated to be in charge of running the ghost box session. Ensure that the individual is aware of having to control the area around the ghost box session, and they should make a general announcement to ask for the cooperation of any individuals in attendance as far as not talking or offering commentary on what is being produced through the ghost box during the performance of the live session. When a live spirit ghost box communication session is performed at a field location and not in a controlled environment such as a home or designated research location, there are usually a number of individuals present other than the individual operator conducting the ghost box session. During the investigation and performance of the ghost box session, some of the individuals in attendance will have a tendency to yell out what they believe they heard come through the ghost box as spirit communication and do this while the ghost box session is in progress. The result of this is that you have individuals who are present talking or shouting out words and responses; this can cause the communication in the ghost box session to get "stepped on," thereby eradicating any spirit communication that may have been heard live in real time or found in the review of the ghost box session recording, evidence that could have been vital to the validation of the investigation. Also, this type of activity will pollute the session recording, making it very difficult upon review of the session recording to discern what is actually spirit communication and what are spectator voices.

This is very hard to control, as people tend to get excited when they believe they have heard true spirit communication, especially if it pertains to the subject or location of the ghost box session and/or investigation. This is where whoever is conducting the ghost box session needs to be in control of not only the live spirit ghost box session but also the surrounding area and all individuals present who are witnessing the session. The ghost box session operator needs to ask all who are in attendance prior to the session to please refrain from shouting out responses or acknowledgment of what they believe was spirit communication, and that any and all results from the ghost box session will be revealed upon review of the recording and discussed after the investigation is complete. If need be, the operator should explain why they are making this request. The person conducting the session should be the predominant individual speaking out loud unless offering an opportunity for a spectator to speak. If others in attendance would like to pose questions, the session operator should give the individuals the opportunity one at a time to ask the question and then respond to any communication they hear live in real time. The control of the field session will not only keep order during a session but will serve to ensure that any possible communication that can be heard live is or can be recognized in the ghost box session recording.

If, as a field ghost box operator, you follow a few

simple protocols, you will find that your ghost box sessions in the field will glean you better quality and quantity of live spirit communication. I hope I have supplied some basic information that will help anyone who is just beginning or considering giving live spirit ghost box communication a try the basic knowledge to set a solid foundation for further endeavors in this extraordinary field of live spirit ghost box communication.

Chapter 6

Sweep Speeds, What's Better Faster or Slower, Linear or Random

There have been many debates and differences of opinion concerning the "BEST" radio band sweep speeds to be used during the operation of a live spirit ghost box communication session, which would allow a communicating spirit entity the most optimal opportunity to form and deliver live spirit communication and the ghost box operator to hear that spirit communication live in real time. Which is better, a ghost box sweep that is on the faster or slower end of the ghost box's capability? I formulated a simple hypothesis way back in the day, when enough people became involved in live spirit ghost box communication for this question to become an issue.

As the number of live spirit ghost box communication researchers, investigators, and practitioners grew, so did the disagreements between them concerning the speed at which a given ghost box should be set to sweep the radio band in order to facilitate the best opportunity for live spirit communication. This question became an increasing point of contention among the more serious paranormal researchers and investigators. Each individual who operates a ghost box, be it for field investigations, research, or simply for personal and private use, will develop their own personal style of live spirit ghost box communication. Because the basic mechanical operation of pretty much all traditionally sweeping ghost boxes remains a constant, and the basic protocols for conducting a live spirit ghost box communication session follow rudimentary criteria, individual ghost box operators will usually develop their own way of doing things; they will develop certain likes and dislikes as far as the operation of the ghost box. This usually comes in the form of added features such as reverse sweep, echo, reverb or reverse speech, not the least of all of these features and one that I personally consider invaluable in any ghost box is sweep speed control, which gives the ghost box operator the ability to control the speed at which a ghost box sweeps the designated radio band.

The longer an individual works with a ghost box, that individual will start to develop what I call an ear for listening to the sweeping sound that continuously emanates from the ghost box speaker during the operation of a live spirit ghost box communication session. The development of this ability will allow the ghost box operator to better hear spirit communication as it is delivered live by the communicating entity, and in doing so the individual ghost box operator will also become accustomed to a ghost box sweep that operates at a specific speed, which is usually set at the onset of a ghost box session. The ability to adjust the speed of the ghost box sweep has been incorporated into pretty much every traditionally sweeping ghost box, with the exception of some of the hack radio ghost boxes, which are simply modified to run as a ghost box by a minor alteration of the existing circuitry. The hack radio ghost box will run at a predetermined sweep speed dictated by its circuitry and will not have the ability of sweep speed adjustment. This sweep speed adjustment becomes invaluable during the performance of a live spirit ghost box communication session for the simple reason that the conditions during a ghost box session are in a continuous state of fluctuation, and the reception of the radio broadcast signal changes continuously, although most of the time not drastically. This, in turn, can and does alter the quality and quantity of the sound fragments produced by the ghost box sweep and supplied to the communicating spirit entity, which is believed to be used for the formation and delivery of live spirit communication.

The ghost box operator's ability to adjust the ghost box sweep immediately on the fly during a live ghost box session as an attempt to compensate for any degradation or fluctuation of the incoming radio broadcast signal becomes paramount. It enables the operator to retain the most optimal ghost box sweep possible by adjusting the sweep speed to a faster or slower pace, thereby giving the communicating spirit entity the highest-quality ghost box sweep from which to build and deliver the intended spirit communication. A fluctuating or changing reception of radio broadcast signal can also add unwanted static white noise to a ghost box sweep; this tends to overpower the beneficial fragments of sound that make up the optimal ghost box sweep and will hinder the ghost box operator's ability to hear spirit communication live during the performance of the ghost box session. A simple sweep speed adjustment by the operator can help to optimize the sweep and somewhat compensate for the degradation of the radio broadcast signal. When a radio broadcast signal becomes degraded during a live ghost box session, static white noise can drown out and inevitably eliminate a percentage of the sound fragments needed to facilitate live spirit communication; for example, if five seconds of ghost box sweep contained five hundred fragments of sound at optimal performance and for whatever reason the reception of the radio broadcast signal became degraded and lowered the number of sound fragments to one hundred in the same five-second time span, the opportunity for reception of live spirit communication would also diminish. If the ghost box operators were to increase the sweep speed, it would then allow the ghost box to sweep the radio dial at a faster rate, thereby shortening the time span between the sounds of received radio broadcast and delivering more sound fragments per second in the ghost box sweep; theoretically the higher supply of sound fragments would in turn help a spirit entity to form and deliver a higher quantity of communication.

I am a firm believer in the practice of using a sweep speed that is on the slightly slower end, and I do emphasize "slightly," as opposed to an overly fast and more chaotic sweep speed. My personal opinion is that the sweep speed of any ghost box should be fast enough so that no full words or phrases of actual radio broadcast can be regularly heard during the ghost box session, but slow enough to give the communicating entity the most optimal chance at retrieving and using as many sound fragments as is necessary to form and send their communication. Let's break it down. Let's say, for example, an individual spirit wishes to send a specific message; they must have at his or her disposal the right fragments of sound produced by the sweeping ghost box in order to build the communication that is intended. The slower sweep speed will, of course, lend itself to allowing a full word or two of radio broadcast to sneak through. This is the downside of using a slower sweep speed; however, 99% of these stray radio words that escape being broken down by the sweep of the ghost box are readily recognized as radio words and not spirit communication and disregarded by the operator either live when heard or in review of the ghost box session recording. Actual live spirit communication has a completely unique sound and can be discerned from radio words not only by that sound but also by the relevance, content, and delivery of the word, phrase, or sentence. Words and/or phrases of radio broadcast that have managed to escape the ghost box sweep have a very distinctive and physically human sound; they are very structured and uniform in their cadence and tone and delivered in a rhythmic and familiar fashion almost always in the same exact voice. Spirit communication received through a ghost box, on the other hand, is very recognizable by its sound and structure because it is a patchwork of sound fragments that have been harvested and pieced together by the communicating entity. It is, for the most part, foreign to our physical ears and does not have the characteristics of fluid physical human speech. Actual spirit communication can come in the form of a male and female voice combined and have an uneven cadence where the tone and pitch are high and low within the confines of a single word, or it can sound as if there are multiple individuals speaking at the same time. Overall, it is not what we would recognize as natural and fluid human speech.

The slower sweep speed will, for all intents and purposes, deliver as many broken-down sound fragments as possible at a rate that will allow the communicating entity to grasp as many of those sound fragments as is needed to send a particular communication, thus allowing for fuller, better quality and a larger quantity of communication. The opposite is to have a faster ghost box sweep speed where there is a very minute chance of a solid word of radio broadcast infiltrating the sweep of the box—understand I did not say "impossible" but "very minute" because there is still a chance it can happen no matter how fast the sweep speed is. While the higher speed of the sweep cuts down the chance of full radio words coming through, so does it cut down the chances of the communicating entity being able to "catch" the adequate fragments of sound it may need to form the words of communication. Think of it this way, would it be easier to catch a baseball or a bullet? The faster the sweep, the harder it will be for the communicating spirit entity to have available and to be able to utilize what it needs to form live spirit communication.

The proponents of "fast sweep" will tell you that by eliminating the risk of receiving full radio words that can be mistaken for spirit communication, what is received can be thought of as being more reliable as actual spirit communication, which may very well be, but it is still not beyond reproach, given this school of thought the fast sweep speed will definitely decrease the quantity of stray radio signal that is received, but at what cost? Like I said, I am a true believer in a slightly slower sweep speed for the reasons I have stated, and it is in my opinion much more productive to make the effort to discover and eliminate any full radio words you may get and give the communicating spirit entity the ability to send a higher quality and higher quantity of communication than to simply set a fast sweep speed and take whatever words of spirit communication the entity was able to get through while trying to catch that bullet!

When pondering this question, I always remember one particular live spirit ghost box communication session I performed quite a few years ago now. It had started out pretty much like any other ghost box session. The sweep speed indicator knob on the ghost box I was using for this session had increments ranging from 1 to 10. I set my usual beginning sweep speed rate at between 5 and 6 and started my ghost box session. I remember that day the radio signal reception was worse than usual, and the sweeping sound being produced by the ghost box was plagued by an abundance of static white noise, clicks, and pops. Buried in the background and overpowered by this predominant noise were the desirable sound fragments that made up a quality ghost box sweep. By this time in my live spirit ghost box communication research career, I was enjoying a high quantity and quality of live spirit communication, not the least of which was rendered by my spirit technicians Mike and Lisa. I had at this point developed a strong connection and relationship with my spirit technicians and had come to rely on their help and counsel during my live ghost box sessions.

As I often did when I faced a situation like my current one in this particular session, I decided to adjust my sweep speed rate in an attempt to compensate for the poor radio broadcast signal I was receiving. I informed my spirit techs that I was going to increase my sweep speed. Before I was able to reach for the sweep speed adjustment knob, a male voice came through the ghost box speaker, seemingly being delivered above the noise that was infecting the ghost box sweep. I heard the spirit communication live; the communicating spirit entity made a request, "Wait." I heard this spirit communication live as it was delivered and pulled my hand back. I repeated the word wait and asked the question, "Wait for what?" A few seconds passed, and I heard the words, "Not yet." This time the spirit communication came in a female voice. I acknowledged hearing this statement and simply answered, "OK." About twenty or thirty-seconds passed, and in that interval I heard faintly what I believed to be spirit communication. I realized the low faint indication of communication was not directed at me. I did not understand what was being said, but the garbled words surrounded by interfering noise had what I had come to recognize as the sound of spirit communication.

It was later after the session had ended that I came to the conclusion that the faint voices I was hearing were my spirit technicians Mike and Lisa speaking to each other and not directing their speech at me or attempting to have it delivered through the ghost box for me to hear. This specific instance ignited a revelation and sparked an important question in my mind that I would pursue and receive the answer to in future sessions. I will be explaining this phenomenon in a forthcoming chapter.

Back to the story, after the twenty or thirty-seconds passed, I asked, "Can I change the sweep rate now?" and I received the answer, "Yes." I proceeded to adjust my sweep speed rate from 5 to 7 and intently listened to the sound of the ghost box sweep. The sweep at the new speed setting had managed to incorporate a small quantity of additional sound fragments to the sound of the sweep but by no means had eased the problem of the noise interference. I resigned myself to the fact that this would be the condition of this specific live spirit ghost box communication session, and I continued with it, not realizing that I was on my chosen preferred radio band of AM and not having the forethought at that moment to consider that a band change to FM might deliver a better radio broadcast signal.

After a few minutes of struggling to hear even the most rudimentary of live spirit communication, I was becoming increasingly frustrated and knew that it must be equally as frustrating for my spirit techs and any spirit entities attempting to communicate. Just as I was about to end the session and put this low-quality experience behind me, a live spirit message was delivered through the speaker of the ghost box. It was repeated twice in quick succession, "FM, FM." It was like someone had smacked me in the back of my head, and I said out loud, "Of course FM, dummy," referring to myself not the communicating spirit entity. I could swear I heard a laugh come through the ghost box speaker although I was never sure of it. Because the FM radio band inherently has much more broadcast content than the AM band, before switching over to FM, I dialed back my sweep speed to my previous setting of between 5 and 6. I then clicked the band selector switch over to FM and listened to the sweep. Although a bit chaotic and containing more harmonic sound fragments than I liked, the sound of the ghost box sweep was now a hundred times clearer than on the AM band. I was a bit embarrassed that a seasoned live spirit ghost box communication researcher like myself would forget one of the most common alternatives to alleviate a problem with radio broadcast reception during a ghost box session.

I decided now that I and my spirit counterparts had an adequate ghost box sweep to work with, I would continue an already somewhat lengthy live spirit ghost box communication session for a few more moments. I proceeded to ask my spirit technicians Mike and Lisa if they were the entities responsible for sending the pertinent messages and directing me during the ghost box session, and I received the answer "Yes" first from Lisa and then from Mike. I heard their responses live and thanked them for their continuing help. I went on to receive other valuable and relevant live spirit communication in the remaining minutes of that particular ghost box session before bringing the session to a close.

In the review of the audio recording, I was able to discover spirit communication that had been delivered during the time I was on the AM band. The communicating entities, even with the horrendous ghost box sweep conditions, had managed to, with their diligence and hard work, render live spirit communication under the most undesirable conditions. This is a testament to the commitment and ongoing dedication that is shared between live spirit ghost box communication researchers here in the physical world and their spirit colleagues in the spirit realm. This specific example of a particular ghost box session is meant to convey not only the benefit of the sweep speed adjustment feature in a ghost box, but to also show how the adjustment of the sweep speed rate can be used in helping to correct reception and/or radio signal Interference problems that may occur during the performance of a live spirit ghost box communication session.

As I stated earlier, live spirit ghost box communication researchers and investigators tend to develop a personal preference when it comes to the sweep speed rate they utilize during the performance of a live ghost box session; however, those parameters should not be adhered to so strictly that they will interfere with adjustment of the ghost box sweep speed rate in order to compensate for any adverse conditions that arise during the performance of the live spirit ghost box communication session. As for which is a "better" sweep speed rate for a ghost box, honestly, the best sweep speed rate is the one that works best for the individual ghost box operator and the communicating spirit entities based on immediate conditions to allow for the best live spirit communication to be delivered and received during the performance of a live spirit ghost box communication session.

I would now like to broach the subject of ghost box sweep styles, namely linear sweep and random sweep. What is the difference between linear ghost box sweep and random ghost box sweep? Linear ghost box sweep allows the ghost box to sweep the radio dial in a continuous flowing fashion going from one end of the radio dial to the other and returning to the beginning to repeat the process continuously in a circular fashion. Random ghost box sweep will force the ghost box to jump randomly from one point on the radio dial to another, back, forth, middle, etc. in any direction chaotically.

In my opinion, the random ghost box sweep is too chaotic for a communicating entity to be able to grab all of the fragments of sound needed to form the words and phrases of communication and be able to deliver the live spirit communication through a ghost box. When it is possible during a random ghost box sweep, the task must be overwhelming. The theory behind the creation and incorporation of the random ghost box sweep was that it would help to eliminate the possibility of any words or phrases of stray radio broadcast escaping the ghost box sweep and being mistaken for live spirit communication and therefore add to the validation of any live spirit communication presented as evidence. This does not take into account the difficulty it would present to a communicating entity to be able to locate, capture, form, and deliver live spirit communication; in turn, it would hinder the quantity and quality of any live spirit communication attempted by the spirit entity.

Let's look at the linear ghost box sweep as "surfing or skiing." It is my theory, based on my research and experience, that an entity can actually ride the flow of the ghost box sweep to gather fragments of sound produced by the ghost box sweep that are needed by the communicating spirit entity to accomplish the formation of the live spirit communication. My theory is that when the ghost box sweep sound fragments are no longer heard by us as the physical operators of the ghost box, they do not simply disappear, they gradually dissipate, which gives our spirit friends a little more time to grab whatever sweep sound fragments they need to form and deliver the live spirit communication. This I believe only happens with linear ghost box sweep; the radio broadcast signal is not abruptly cut off but allowed to flow continuously in a fluid fashion. Just because we perceive the signal to stop from one station to the next does not mean it doesn't linger past that point and fade away gradually beyond the capability of our human perception. With the random ghost box sweep the entity may attempt to grab a fragment of sweep sound needed to form communication, and then "BOOM," it is abruptly cut off by the action of the random ghost box sweep and jumps out of the spirit entity's reach.

Think of it as a river, the river can either freely flow to

the sea, or it can be abruptly stopped by a dam. If you place a life preserver floating on the river and allowed it to freely go on its way, it would shortly be gone from sight, but even though we could no longer physically see the life preserver, it would still continue to float on that river endlessly until the river reached its destination. On the other hand, if the life preserver were to be placed on the river within sight of a dam, the life preserver would abruptly come to a stop with the flow of the river as it reached the dam, which would stop any further travel of the life preserver. It is the same for the ghost box sweep signal, a linear ghost box sweep will allow the signal to travel a farther distance than we with our limited human hearing can perceive audibly, but with a random ghost box sweep, the abrupt change or continuous interruption of the ghost box sweep does not allow for this free-flowing reception of the radio broadcast signal. The random ghost box sweep does allow a certain minute advantage as far as eliminating a fraction of the possibility of stray radio broadcast escaping being broken down by the ghost box sweep and delivered as full words of stray radio broadcast, but by no means is it a cure-all for such occurrences.

My personal preference is to use a linear sweeping ghost box. It is my experienced opinion that the linear ghost box sweep allows the communicating spirit entity a better opportunity to gather the sound fragments it needs to form and deliver a higher quantity and quality of live spirit communication. The preferences that I put forward here are by no means an attempt to set a standard for the practice of a live spirit ghost box communication session but simply to explain the alternative options available and their pros and cons based on my personal experience. Of course, every live spirit ghost box communication operator, researcher, or investigator should experiment with all aspects of ghost box operation and settle on what works best for the individual.

Chapter 7

Do Ghost Boxes Create a Portal to the Spiritual World

As I stumbled through the first year or so of serious and intense research and experimentation in live spirit ghost box communication, I had an experience that would put me on a path leading to the discovery of the "portal" or "doorway" that a ghost box in session creates between our physical world and the spirit realm. One day I began to experience some intermittent light poltergeist activity in my home such as knocking, lights flickering, small objects falling from my dresser, etc. This activity, which I had never experienced before in my home, started me on a quest to figure out why and how it began to occur, and could the use of a ghost box possibly be responsible? I ran through a list of possible causes in my mind. Was I imagining the activity and attributing coincidence to spirit activity, or did I get a spirit attachment from a location I visited and brought an earthbound spirit entity back to my home? What was the reason for these sudden incidences of what I believed to be paranormal activity? These odd occurrences continued for days; it became apparent that something or someone was trying desperately to get my attention.

After exploring all the available possibilities, the only explanation I could come up with was that my use of the ghost box and the communication it facilitated had something to do with my present situation. My first reaction was that the ghost box may have possibly attracted a wayward spirit entity that had been drawn to the energy the ghost box created by the connection made between our physical world and the spirit world during a live ghost box session. The activity that I was experiencing was completely benign and nonthreatening, so the chances of a demonic or negative presence took a back seat to just a wayward spirit entity who had become lost or confused. I had deliberated about what to do for a short time and decided I would do a live spirit ghost box communication session in my home to try to communicate with any spirit entity that may be present to try to find a reason for why it had taken up residence in my house.

At this time in live spirit ghost box communication research, there were only two models of ghost boxes available, the Frank's Box and the Joe's Box. I was the owner of both but did not use the Frank's Box much, as my area was not conducive to a great broadcast radio signal, and the Frank's Box I owned needed optimal conditions to perform well. I predominantly used the Joe's Box in these early days of ghost box communication; this was a time before even the hack radio ghost boxes were invented.

I set up a quiet time to do the ghost box session

when no one was home. I prepared the Joe's Box and my recorder for the session. I started the session with a single question: "Are there any spirits here in my home?" The question was answered with a loud and clear "YES." I heard the spirit communication live, acknowledged it, and proceeded to do the rest of the session. Now that I had a confirmation that there was in fact a spirit entity present in my home and probably standing right beside me as I performed the live ghost box session, I continued to ask questions now directed solely to my new ethereal house guest. I asked a series of questions that would not require complicated answers but would still serve to render an explanation as to why this entity was in my home, how he got there, and what his intentions were.

My next question pertained to how the entity arrived at my home. I asked, "How did you get in my house?" A few seconds passed, and I heard the answer, "The radio." I heard this live and asked, "Did you say the radio?" The response was, "Yes." It took me a second, but I then surmised that by "radio" he meant the ghost box. Of course, due to the fact that live spirit ghost box communication was still relatively new, and this particular spirit individual was not really familiar with the ghost box or its function, when he observed it, to him it simply looked like a radio. The next interaction from me after this realization was to inform the spirit entity that the device he believed to be a radio was in fact a ghost box and was designed to allow spirit entities like him and physical human beings like myself to communicate and interact with each other live in real time. I assumed he understood my explanation since there were no communications forthcoming to indicate that he did not.

I posed my next question to him, "How did you use the ghost box to arrive in my home?" To this question I received a simple one-word answer, "Door," another puzzling answer. What did the entity mean, what door was he referring to, was it the door to my home? Was this spirit trying to be funny? Was there another door I was not aware of? I let the ghost box run and took a few moments to ponder these questions. There was no way I could formulate an answer, not by the answer of the single word "door." At that moment it occurred to me, why not ask my spirit technicians if they were able to shed some light on this mystery, so I did. I began by calling on my spirit technicians for assistance. I asked if they were able to deliver any more information on my house guest that he himself either did not or could not. I received an immediate, "Yes. Here." My spirit technician was letting me know he was present and able to help.

I asked my spirit technician if he was aware of the spirit entity that was in visitation in my home; he replied, "Yes." I then asked if my spirit tech could give me any information on how and why the visiting spirit was in my home. To that question I received the answer, "Later." I had received this type of response before and took it to mean that the information that I was seeking would not be forthcoming in the current ghost box session but would be explained at a future time. My next interaction with my spirit technician was a request for his help in removing the wayward spirit from my home. To that request I received a positive reply. After a few seconds, I asked my technician, "How do I help this entity leave my home?" I promptly received the answer, "It's done." I heard this live and asked, "Did you say it's done?" to which my technician responded, "Yes." I followed up with, "So the spirit entity that was in my home is gone?" and received the answer, "Yes. Here." I understood that my spirit technician was telling me that the spirit entity that was in my home was now with him in the spirit realm. My mind was racing, there were a thousand questions I wanted to ask, but I decided to respect the fact that I was told further information would come in future live spirit communication sessions. I thanked my spirit technician and bid goodbye to him and my former spirit visitor and ended the ghost box session, which had lasted more than a half an hour.

Much contemplation and the messages I received in my initial ghost box session with my visiting spirit entity, as well as many subsequent live spirit ghost box communication sessions, led me to the conclusion that the wayward spirit entity that had found his way into my home had traveled through a doorway or portal that was being opened when the ghost box was turned on and the live connection was made between our physical world and the spirit world. I performed many live spirit ghost box communication sessions dedicated to the gathering of information on this phenomenon; the information I was able to gather based on the live spirit communication I received during those ghost box sessions led me to the conclusion and ultimate formation of a theory based on the open portal that is created when a ghost box is in operation.

The encounter I experienced with the spirit entity that was in my home began during a live spirit ghost box communication session. When the ghost box was turned on and the live session began, the energy connection between our physical world and the spirit world commenced; this connection was and is the catalyst for the opening of a portal or doorway between our world and theirs, creating an opening through which a spirit entity can travel. During the course of the live ghost box session, an entity utilized this "portal" to travel from the spirit realm to our physical world, which was unknown to me at the time. Without my being aware of this occurrence, I concluded the live spirit ghost box communication session and turned off the ghost box, thereby literally slamming the door shut and stranding the wayward spirit in my home. The benign paranormal activity that I was experiencing was that spirit entity's way of alerting me to his presence in an attempt to garner my help in returning him to the spirit world where he belonged. Thankfully at the time of this incident my spirit technician was aware of the situation, and once I had reinitiated a live ghost box session and inadvertently reopened the portal, my spirit technician was able to retrieve the wayward spirit entity from my home and guide him back through the portal to where he belonged.

This portal or open door is always necessary; it allows for the mutual connection and melding of physical energy from the ghost box operator and spirit energy, which in turn makes the exchange of live communication between worlds possible. The portal is created whenever a ghost box is turned on. I had also learned that the doorway is never unattended. There is always a spirit technician that is in attendance and that monitors everything that is happening during a ghost box session; that includes any passage through this portal back or forth. I have spoken publicly many, many times on this topic, and I always recommend that a protection ritual or prayer be done before initiating a live spirit ghost box communication session and a closing procedure be done before the session is completed and the ghost box is turned off. The "closing" procedure simply consists of the ghost box operator asking the attending spirit technician to retrieve any wayward entities that may have traveled through the portal during the session and have them go back across to the spirit side. Always ask for verbal confirmation from the technician that it is safe to close the ghost box session and turn off the ghost box. This may take a few attempts, as it is necessary for the operator to hear the confirmation from the spirit technician live in real time to know it is safe to close the session and turn off the ghost box. This is just a basic explanation of my theory on the open portal a ghost box creates; it is based on my longtime experience and research and the live spirit communication I have received from my spirit counterparts.

The open portal or doorway that is created during the performance of a live spirit ghost box communication session can be utilized to serve another purpose. This additional purpose entails the rendering of assistance by the live ghost box session operator to a spirit entity or entities that are requesting help. In the practice of live spirit ghost box communication research and investigation, it is not uncommon for a ghost box operator during the course of a live ghost box session to receive a request by a communicating spirit entity for assistance. Sadly, this cry for help is not always heard live in real time by the operator during the performance of the live ghost box session. However, when the plea for help from a spirit entity in need is heard live in real time during the live ghost box session, it is the duty of the operator conducting the session to try to render any and all assistance he or she can. Needless to say, because the ghost box operator is a physical human being, and the interaction between the operator and spirit entity is limited to verbal interaction facilitated by the ghost box, the assistance that can be rendered by the ghost box operator is limited by the constraints of that unchangeable situation.

A request for help from a spirit entity can consist of different needs and circumstances on the part of the requesting spirit entity. Firstly, the ghost box operator, upon hearing the plea for help live and acknowledging it, must attempt to determine whether the communicating spirit entity is earthbound or delivering the live spirit communication from the spirit realm. Once this is determined, the ghost box operator will basically know what type of assistance the spirit entity is in need of. If the live spirit communication for help is being received from a spirit entity that is sending the communication from the spirit realm, the situation that the help is needed with can and usually does consist of a spirit entity that has very recently made the transition from the physical life to a spiritual existence and is scared, confused, disoriented, and may not realize that they have died. It can also be that the spirit entity is consumed with thoughts of some earthly business left unsettled at the time of their death, or the missed opportunity to say goodbye to friends or family. When the ghost box operator is confident that this is the case after receiving verbal confirmation by the communicating spirit entity, the operator can offer a short explanation to the spirit entity of his or her having left the physical life and how it is now on a new journey as a spirit being. The operator can offer comfort to the spirit entity in the form of calm and reassuring verbal interaction.

If the issue that is tormenting the spirit entity consists of unspoken words or messages to a loved one or friend, the ghost box operator can pursue gathering information and any messages that the spirit entity needs to deliver in an attempt to relay said messages to the intended parties; however, this is a tricky matter and warrants serious thought by the ghost box operator before attempting a resolution.

More often than not, this interaction between the ghost box operator and the spirit entity asking for help will help to give the spirit entity the help he or she needs to orient themselves, accept their situation, and begin to move forward with a basic sense of confidence. If the ghost box operator determines that the live spirit communication is being delivered by a spirit entity that is earthbound, that is a horse of a different color and entails a completely different approach by the operator to attempt rendering assistance to the wayward spirit entity. If it is determined by the ghost box operator that the requesting spirit entity is earthbound, the assistance by the operator calls for him or her to perform what is called a "crossing over session."

The crossing over session is basically a deliberate action on the part of the live ghost box operator to attempt to help the wayward spirit entity to cross over from the physical world to the spirit realm. This is accomplished by verbal interaction between the ghost box operator and the communicating spirit entity. The operator is usually assisted in this task by the attending spirit technician or technicians that are overseeing the particular live ghost box session. The spirit technician will be integral in the actual process of the wayward entity's crossing from one plane to the other. I will not go into detail here about the crossing over session. I will cover this subject in detail in a forthcoming chapter. However, I will say that as with the distressed spirit entity that requests help in a live spirit communication from the spirit world, the earthbound spirit entity requiring assistance in crossing over will be plagued by the same emotional and stressful feelings; he or she will be lost, confused, scared, disoriented, and oftentimes in a state of panic. The ghost box operator should follow the accepted protocols for this type of situation and render any and all assistance possible.

Chapter 8

Chasing Ghosts, Phantom Communication While Editing a Session Recording

There is a practice that many if not all live spirit ghost box communication operators do when reviewing and editing a ghost box session recording. I call it "chasing ghosts." This practice is when a ghost box operator literally dissects and digs into the inaudible or unintelligible parts of a ghost box session recording in an attempt to uncover what they believe to be spirit communication that is not otherwise apparent upon listening to and editing the ghost box session recording. The "phantom" communication is either distorted by other sound fragments, buried in static noise, stepped on by the operator speaking over it, or simply garbled sound that can be misinterpreted for live spirit communication. 99% of the time, the action of chasing ghosts is a fruitless effort. These phantom communications may or may not be valid communication. Whether they are or not, the quality is so poor that no matter what amount of editing is done, said communication will be of such poor quality that there is a very, very slim chance that anyone who listens to it will hear what is described by the operator.

When "chasing ghosts," the reviewing operator will get an initial impression of what they believe they are hearing and focus their attention on that specific piece of audio, then begin the editing process. The operator will listen to the chosen audio of the believed spirit communication numerous times with an already preconceived idea of what they believe they are hearing, therefore reinforcing the belief that the audio actually contains that spirit communication. The operator will then proceed to edit that portion of the recording in an attempt to clean up the abundance of noise and uncover the suspected spirit communication.

At this point, the human mind and senses of the operator will play tricks on him or her. After repetitively listening to the selected audio numerous times, the operator will actually begin to believe they are hearing the nonexistent spirit communication and proceed to create an audio file containing the segment of the ghost box recording and retain the audio file as research data. Commonly upon listening to the audio file at a later date, the operator will often not hear the spirit communication they initially believed existed. Most of the time they will hear nothing but an audio clip that contains blurbs of gibberish buried in white static noise. This being the case, after the operator has already posted the file for public review, now if the operator who captured, edited and described the communication in the file can no longer discern it, then how can anyone else be expected to? This happens quite often in live spirit ghost box communication. I would say that this phantom or ghost audio makes up a fair amount of the audio evidence that is publicly posted today by ghost box operators. Of course, there are varying degrees of quality of these audio files. Some fall into the quality level of being able to be heard after the file description is read, some have to be listened to numerous times in order to be heard as described, then there are the audio files that no matter what the circumstance, the listener will walk away scratching their head, saying, "What did that say?"

The best way to combat "chasing ghosts" is to only select and develop files that contain live spirit communication that is readily apparent in the review of the session recording, and that is relevant to the question asked or topic of the live spirit communication session. If the spirit communication consists of more than a single word, the combined words should be coherent and compatible with each other. This will produce an audio file of high quality that will present a strong validation for being actual live spirit communication and will be hard to dispute as being a stray radio broadcast signal, gibberish, or pareidolia. The technology we possess today in the way of ghost boxes allows for the reception of a good percentage of quality, loud and clear live spirit communication.

I have spoken to many ghost box operators who state they discover some of their most important communication from "chasing ghosts," and if it were not for the attempt, the important communication they believe was found in the recording would have been lost to them forever. This is not a valid argument for "chasing ghosts." Audio files that are derived from this type of editing attempt are never reliable, either in their quality or content, and cannot be relied upon to give the operator confidence in the live spirit communication they believe they hear. I am not trying to say keep only the class A+ spirit communication and do not bother to listen to the rest, always assess any and all suspected communication, but do not allow yourself to fall into the trap of chasing those ghosts. Unless we can present a certain degree of audio evidence that is of a certain quality and understandable to all who listen to it, we cannot instill confidence in those who review the audio that it is in fact actual spirit communication and not just a trick of the ear or mind. In other words "communicate with the spirits, don't chase them."

We must also remember that live spirit ghost box communication is inherently difficult to hear due to the manner in which it is derived. I can safely say that I believe I have more time accumulated listening to live spirit ghost box communication, during live sessions and in session recordings, than any other living human being. I have performed live ghost box sessions and reviewed their subsequent audio recordings almost daily for the past seventeen years, give or take a day or two. My point is that if it is a daunting task for a seasoned ghost box operator to recognize, hear, and understand live spirit ghost box communication, how much more difficult is it for someone who is a novice or simply listening to an audio example posted for public review. I understand that every individual who captures any class of live spirit ghost box communication is eager and excited to share their evidence, myself included; what I would like to stress is that when a ghost box researcher derives a piece of audio evidence, consider the overall quality of the live spirit communication and the audio example as a whole. Try to listen to the audio that is to be presented for public review objectively, put yourself in the average person's place, and consider what it will sound like to that individual who has little or no experience. I always try to follow this rule of thumb, "It is better to present one audio example of live spirit ghost box communication and have it heard by the majority of listeners as you yourself hear it, than to present many audio examples that only a very few may hear." In the case of examples of live spirit ghost box communication audio files, quality far outweighs quantity.

In my early days as a live spirit ghost box communication researcher, it would take me many hours of tedious and painstaking scrutiny in the review of a live ghost box session recording derived from only a ten-or-fifteen-minute live spirit ghost box communication session. This undertaking would glean me a fair share of individual audio files that contained examples of what I believed to be live spirit communication. If my efforts resulted in the accumulation of twenty audio files from a single live ghost box session, there would be maybe five examples of live spirit communication that were capable of being heard by anyone who listened to them. The remainder would consist of audio examples that were, let's just say subpar. Nevertheless, I would proceed to post all the audio files for review by any and all individuals interested in examining them. Consequently, after such a posting, the majority of responses I would receive were less than complimentary. At the time I was still relatively new to live spirit ghost box communication; as a matter of fact, at that time live spirit ghost box communication research and investigation was in its infancy. The fact was that there was no real information about live spirit ghost box communication other than what I and maybe one or two other individuals were documenting and contributing; no one really knew when reviewing examples of live spirit communication audio what they were listening to. Therefore, any audio evidence presented for public review had to be of the highest quality and capable of being understood by anyone listening to it. I finally realized that the majority of the audio examples of live spirit ghost box communication I was presenting were of inferior quality and that this was due to my practice of digging out low-quality, barely understandable audio examples of what I believed was live spirit communication when editing a live ghost box session. This turned out to be an epiphany and led to my not only stopping the practice of "chasing ghosts in a live ghost box session recording" but also formulating and publishing a solid theory on the subject.

In this chapter, I would also like to address another subject that pertains to the review and editing of live spirit ghost box communication sessions. When I refer to this practice, I title it "Audio recording a ghost box session is a must. Video is not enough." It covers the practice by ghost box operators to only video record a live spirit ghost box communication session as opposed to also capturing a stand-alone audio recording of the same ghost box session. From the time it has become possible to record decent video on your cellphone, paranormal researchers and investigators have used this medium to record all manner of alleged paranormal evidence, whether captured on location at an investigation or making a video of a paranormal occurrence in the home and also videotaping a paranormal experiment or attempt at capturing some paranormal activity, be it visual or audio or both. Since my chosen field of study in the paranormal is predominantly live spirit ghost box communication and has been for close to two decades, now I will focus on that particular field of paranormal research and investigation for this explanation. Please note that what I comment on here is my own personal opinion based on my years of experience and is not by any means meant to be proposed as the end-all fact of how things should be done or to chastise anyone else's method of doing things. It is meant to merely give my opinion and explanation based on my experience.

Over the years I have watched literally hundreds of cellphone videos created by individuals who were performing live spirit ghost box communication sessions, either at a field location or in the controlled environment of their home, and have found myself many, many times commenting on the video with descriptions of spirit communication I heard in the video that the operator of the ghost box session was not aware of. I have come across the same occurrence in many videos; the producer of the video, usually the individual conducting the ghost box session, would label in the video description and/or state in the video any believed spirit communication that was heard live during the actual ghost box session. That is not where I personally find fault with video recordings of live spirit ghost box communication sessions. It's not that you cannot hear the reported spirit communication as the operator did or that the audio and video presented are of inferior quality, it is that the individual who performed the live spirit ghost box communication session used the video recording device as the sole means of documenting and recording their evidence. The problem with this is that when the video of the ghost box session is reviewed by the person or persons who performed the session and recorded the video, they will review that video and in essence relive the actual ghost box session they performed. You may say, "Yes, they have an accurate video recording that allows them to document and review every detail of the ghost box session they performed. What's wrong with that?" Let me explain, there is absolutely nothing wrong with filming a video of a live spirit ghost box communication session. As a matter of fact, it allows any individual who subsequently watches the video to witness the live spirit ghost box communication session as if they were there live when it was performed, which is what makes the ability to so effortlessly produce a video so amazing.

Please do not misunderstand me. I am not trying to discredit or undermine the use of video in live spirit ghost box communication. Far from it, the point I am trying to convey here is that the video recording of a live spirit ghost box communication session is not enough on its own for the ghost box operator or researcher to be able to review and discover any and all spirit communication that was missed being heard live during the actual ghost box session. Through my experience and research in live spirit ghost box communication, I have come to formulate that we are only capable of hearing approximately 20 to 25 percent of the total live spirit communication received in any given ghost box session, live in real time as it is delivered. The majority of the communication produced in a live spirit ghost box communication session is found in the review of the ghost box session recording. When the individual only reviews the video of the live ghost box session, as I stated earlier, they are in essence reliving the same exact session that they experienced live as it happened and therefore are subject to the same auditory input that they were during the actual live session, which means they are still missing the bulk of the live spirit communication that was delivered in the video as they did in the live ghost box session. Of course, with video, it can be replayed as many times as desired, which is somewhat positive for a review of the ghost box session; however, what I am attempting to convey here is that video should not be relied on as the sole medium for review of a live spirit ghost box communication session. I always try to stress that it is fine to video a live spirit ghost box communication session, but the operator or researcher should also employ a digital audio recorder and record the session separately as a stand-alone audio recording. This would allow for the best of both worlds, the live spirit ghost box communication session can be relived and presented as a video, and the individual will also have a detailed audio recording that can be loaded onto a computer and reviewed systematically in small increments and in detail in an audio editing program, so as to have the ability to discover and hear any and all live spirit communication that was delivered during the live spirit ghost box communication session, but not readily apparent when reviewing only video footage of the live ghost box session.

It is an injustice to both the individual who conducted the live spirit ghost box communication session and an even bigger injustice to the spirit entities that labored to form and send the live spirit communication to allow any spirit communication that might have been found through a meticulous review of both audio and video data to go undiscovered and subsequently lost. I shudder to think of how many live spirit communications have gone unheard due to the lack of detailed review of the ghost box session data, spirit messages that may have been of substantial importance and significance, not only to the individual researcher or investigator but to paranormal research as a whole and possibly mankind. I personally would not want to have the nagging thought in the back of my mind as to whether I missed something that should have been heard. We must always remember that the spirit entities that communicate with us during our live spirit ghost box communication sessions have a very hard task to perform. It is extremely difficult for a spirit entity to form and deliver live communication through a ghost box. We must do our best as responsible researchers and live spirit ghost box communication operators to make the effort to discover as much of that communication as possible so that the efforts of our spirit friends do not go unheard. Believe me, I will be the first to say that the correct review of an audio recording from a live spirit ghost box communication session is nothing less than daunting, tedious, and time consuming, but I will also be the first to say, in my opinion and experience, it is a necessary task and should never go undone. Consider the alternative; the chance of losing something that is possibly irreplaceable and valuable far outweighs the amount of effort to secure it.

Chapter 9

The Difference Between Live Spirit Communication And Stray Broadcast Signal

From the day that the first ghost box and its intended use were announced publicly, live spirit ghost box communication has had staunch opponents, individuals who no matter what type of evidence or explanation is given refuse to acknowledge the ability of the ghost box to facilitate live spirit communication. Every individual I have ever spoken to who is a nonbeliever in live spirit ghost box communication has offered the same reason for their disdain of the device and its purported capabilities, "You're mistaking words of radio broadcast for live spirit communication," which they follow up with, "The device receives and utilizes live radio broadcast to deliver alleged spirit communication that can never be validated. There is too much of a chance of mistaking words of radio for spirit communication." I wish I had a buck for every time I heard those statements; I would be a rich man. The majority of these naysayers have never heard a live ghost box in session let alone tried one for themselves. Their negative opinion was formed the moment they first heard of a ghost box and the premise for which it was created.

Most people who dismiss something out of hand without any investigation into it usually know very little about the subject and base their negative opinion on the initial thought that they had when hearing about it for the first time. I must confess that the very first time I was told about a ghost box and what it was intended for, I immediately dismissed the idea. The difference is that very shortly after, whether it was my inquisitive nature or divine intervention, I decided to approach the ghost box and its proposed abilities with an open mind and discover through the gathering of knowledge if the device and its methods were viable. Thank goodness I did because it became my life's work. In this chapter, I will attempt to explain the difference between words of stray radio broadcast that may escape the ghost box sweep and actual live spirit communication.

In a perfect scenario, a ghost box would go through a whole live spirit communication session without picking up any amount of stray radio broadcast, but we all know that these boxes are far from perfect! The way to recognize the stray words of radio broadcast is to be aware of whole words, sentences, and/or phrases that have escaped the sweep of the ghost box and have not been broken down by it. These stray words of radio broadcast will be recognizable by being distinctly familiar as normal physical human speech. Physical human speech has a very distinctive sound. It is uniform and tonally the same in its makeup; it utilizes set tones and patterns of harmonics and sound. What I mean by "uniform and tonally the same" is that when we hear words come from the box that are spoken in a fluid tone, are spoken in the same voice, and are uniform in their delivery, as you would hear normal spoken physical human speech, you can pretty much mark it down as stray radio broadcast. When we hear actual live spirit ghost box communication, it is an almost, let's say, patchwork of syllables that form the words from different fragments of sound. They can differ in volume, speed, and even be made up of male and female voices within one word or phrase. This is what allows us to differentiate between what is live spirit communication and what are words of stray radio broadcast.

A ghost box will utilize whatever radio broadcast signal it receives and sweep the dial at a set rate whether it is set to sweep in a linear or random fashion. The signal being constantly in flux due to changing conditions will allow for certain broadcast signals to surge in strength. Let's say, for instance, 1160 on the AM dial gets a sudden burst of extra energy, allowing the signal to increase in strength by 50%; this will, in turn, deliver the stronger signal to the receiver of the ghost box, which may cause the individual radio station to overlap the previous and the following dial settings on the radio band. For example, you will get a single signal over the 1150, 1160, and 1170 settings on the dial at the same time instead of just a single signal on the 1160 setting alone. This will sometimes give you the same signal over three stations as opposed to one, hence creating a lingering signal for triple the amount of time it would normally have been received. This may cause the ghost box to spit out a word or two of stray radio broadcast. This happens very rapidly during the sweep of the ghost box and will tend to cause the hiccup that allows the ghost box to deliver a full word of radio broadcast, which in turn can be mistaken by the ghost box operator as live spirit communication. This cannot be helped; it is an incident that is unfortunately inherent in live spirit ghost box communication. If the ghost box operator stays vigilant and trains himself to recognize the difference between stray radio broadcasts and live spirit communication during the performance of a ghost box session, the instances of mistaken live spirit communication can be kept to a minimum.

In order for a ghost box operator to become adept at recognizing the difference between stray radio broadcast and live spirit communication, it will take time, experience, and constant vigilance on the part of the operator. This skill does not develop overnight. When it comes to the short one-syllable words like "yes, no, or hi," it becomes much more difficult to discern whether they are stray radio broadcast or spirit communication. These small single words, if actual live spirit communication, will carry a distinctive sound, which will only be recognized by the operator with a trained ear for listening to live ghost box sweep. The one-syllable words that are actual live spirit communication will have a raspier and ethereal sound, they will tend to be askew in tone, be not uniform, and they will sound unnatural to the human ear, but like I said, they are difficult to pinpoint and take a seasoned operator to readily recognize them. The lengthier spirit communication that comes in the form of two or three or more word phrases is a bit easier for the operator to recognize. For example, if the ghost box operator hears a three-word phrase during a live spirit ghost box communication session, like "Hello, I'm John," if the phrase is a stray radio broadcast, it can be determined in a number of ways. First, was the phrase relevant to a question or statement made by the ghost box operator? If not, the phrase becomes suspect. Second, was the phrase delivered in a structured and uniform manner, pitch, tone, and in the same voice? If so, the phrase becomes more suspect. Third, did the words in the phrase contain any other sound such as hiss or harmonics? If not, there is a 99% chance that the phrase was a stray radio broadcast and not actual live spirit communication.

As I mentioned earlier, stray words of radio broadcast that escape being broken down by the sweep of the ghost box and are subsequently heard by the ghost box operator during the live ghost box session is an inherent problem that comes with live spirit ghost box communication. As researchers and investigators, or even casual ghost box users, we must strive to train ourselves and develop the skill necessary to be able to recognize those words of stray radio broadcast when they do manage to creep into our live spirit ghost box communication sessions.

As a ghost box operator, a good way to develop an ear for catching the annoying stray radio broadcast when it does appear is when reviewing a ghost box session recording and discovering what is believed to be a stray radio broadcast, isolate the specific words or phrases, and save it as its own audio file. Do the same with a word or phrase that you believe is actual live spirit communication. Set aside time to compare and study the two audio examples. Listen to the audio clips consecutively, play the two audio clips back-to-back, and listen to the difference in the way the words sound, how they are formed, the cadence in which they are spoken, the tonal structure, the aspects of pitch. Is it high and low within the same word or phrase? Are the words delivered in a fluid form, or are they choppy and sound as if they are pieced together from different fragments of sound? Does the word or phrase sound as if there are both male and female voices combined? Do the words have a hiss or static sound incorporated into them? Performing this exercise will help you to train your mind and your ear to discern the difference between what is a stray radio broadcast and what is actual live spirit communication during a live ghost box session as well as in the review of a ghost box session recording. This ability will not be immediate; it takes time, practice, and experience in listening to a live ghost box sweep as well as developing the instinct to recognize stray radio broadcast from live spirit communication during the performance of a live spirit ghost box communication session.

If, as live spirit ghost box researchers and investigators or simply ghost box operators, you take the time to address this issue, not only will it alleviate frustration and confusion during a live ghost box session and session recording review, but it will also allow for more confidence in the validity of your research and live spirit ghost box communication evidence. You will be secure in the knowledge that you have compiled and presented what you believe to be the best examples of live spirit ghost box communication for public and peer review. Remember, as individuals in any chosen field of research, investigation, or practice in the paranormal, your presented evidence, research data, and theories will always come under scrutiny and skepticism by some. This holds especially true for the field of live spirit ghost box communication, partially due to the inherent possibility of the pollution of stray radio broadcast captured during the performance of a live spirit communication ghost box session that can be mistaken for and presented as evidence of actual live spirit communication. Every live spirit ghost box communication researcher or investigator who has presented evidence for public review has at one time or another had the validity of their presented evidence questioned. The only way for an individual to defend the integrity and validity of a presented example of live spirit ghost box communication is to always be prepared with the knowledge and ability to explain the evidence example in question. This will take confidence, not only in the presented evidence in question but also in the researcher's own ability to render a specific, knowledgeable, and coherent answer to any queries made concerning a specific piece of evidence. This confidence is only attained through the dedication of the ghost box researcher in developing the knowledge and experience that is needed in a field of paranormal research and investigation that has more than its share of opposition.

I personally make it a rule to review all live spirit ghost box communication evidence that I intend to present for public and peer review numerous times before actually presenting it. There is a phenomenon that occurs all too frequently in live spirit ghost box communication that entails a ghost box operator, or any individual for that matter, listening to a live spirit communication example. Oftentimes a live spirit communication is heard live in real time during the performance of a live ghost box session and is understood by the ghost box operator when heard. Following the live ghost box session, the operator will review the live ghost box session recording with the live spirit communication that was heard during the session still fresh in their mind. The ghost box operator will remember approximately where in the live ghost box session the live spirit communication was heard and stay vigilant, waiting for it to arrive in the ghost box session recording. When the specific believed piece of live spirit communication finally presents itself in the ghost box session recording, the ghost box operator finds himself hearing the remembered live spirit communication either partially or completely different than what was heard during the live ghost box session. If the ghost box operator was to present an audio file of the live spirit communication with the description of what he believed he initially heard and the audio example did not actually contain that specific live spirit communication or a partial form of it, and it was scrutinized by a skeptic or opponent of live spirit ghost box communication, the integrity of the audio example could be brought into question as well as the integrity of the live spirit ghost box communication researcher him or herself. I myself have fallen victim to this situation on occasion due to a momentary lack of diligence during the review of a live ghost box session recording.

The phenomenon of hearing live spirit communication differently not only occurs from live ghost box session to recording review but can also occur with an established audio example file that has been saved and stored. The ghost box operator can listen to the audio example of live spirit communication, save it, and store it as evidence for future review or presentation, go back and listen to the exact file that has not been touched for an indeterminate amount of time, which could be up to months or even years, listen to the audio example, and hear something completely different than he or she remembers and totally contrary to the description documented with the audio file.

It also happens that the ghost box operator will hear no live spirit communication at all upon review of the audio example. There are a few theories floating around that address this very phenomenon. There are individuals who believe that the cause of this occurrence stems from a simple mistake on the part of the ghost box operator in hearing the believed live spirit communication incorrectly either live during the live ghost box session or in the review of the ghost box session recording, a simple and easy explanation. There are other individuals who believe that the spirit entity that initially sent the live spirit communication had decided to change the live spirit communication they originally intended to deliver and altered the recording of it directly on the recording medium. There are still others who believe that the spirit entity is able to change the live spirit communication at any point after it is delivered, including when the live spirit communication is stored on a computer hard drive as an audio example file.

My personal theory and belief is spirit entities are capable of energy manipulation; this includes but is not restricted to electromagnetic energy, static energy in the form of white noise, the energy produced in and by radio frequency, and physical human energy. Because these energies in one form or another are incorporated into all aspects of live spirit ghost box communication and the devices we use in the performance of it, including the recording devices that are used to capture live spirit ghost box sessions, the computers that we store audio data on, a spirit entity can manipulate the live spirit communication at any stage of its existence from delivery through the ghost box up to the point it is stored as an audio file on a computer. Given this ability to manipulate the already delivered communication, spirit entities can and do at times alter and even destroy live spirit communication that has been documented and preserved by the ghost box operator as audio files. This action by a spirit entity is what will lead to an individual who examines the audio examples at a later date to hear the original live spirit communication differently than it was heard at the time of its reception, or even hear nothing at all. A live spirit ghost box communication researcher, investigator, or operator, if keeping this phenomenon in mind, will not scratch their head when reevaluating a previous live spirit communication that sounds completely different from what was originally heard.

Chapter 10

Different Aspects of Listening to Live Spirit Ghost Box Communication

The first aspect of listening to and distinguishing live spirit ghost box communication, either during the performance of a live ghost box session or in the review of a ghost box session recording, is *"Do not listen for single letters or random numbers during a live ghost box session."*

When I first started my research into live spirit communication with a ghost box, there was literally only one other individual doing controlled live spirit ghost box communication sessions and documenting the data and any audio evidence gathered. I had very limited experience in performing live ghost box sessions and an even more limited ability when it came to listening for and recognizing what was actual live spirit communication, not only during a live ghost box session but also when reviewing the audio recording of a live ghost box session. In those early days, I found myself intently listening for every single sound of human speech that was apparent to me, single letters, random syllables, and numbers. I would do this during live ghost box sessions, but it would become more intense during the review of a live ghost box session recording. I would focus on everything that sounded to me like human speech no matter how tiny the sound was. This became a very tedious and daunting task. Every time I heard a number or letter that stood out above the flowing garble of the ghost box sweep sound, I would stop and focus my attention on it, asking myself, "Could that be spirit communication?"

A fifteen-minute live ghost box session recording that should have taken and would now take me two or three hours to review, including the isolation, cleanup, and saving of individual audio files of actual live spirit ghost box communication, at the time took me triple that amount of time. Needless to say, this became not only tedious but also frustrating and boring. Finally, after some time had passed and I started to gain more and more experience, it dawned on me, and I realized that I had literally been wasting my time and that of my spirit counterparts by allowing each and every inane sound produced by the ghost box sweep to garner my attention. After giving the subject much thought, I finally decided to train myself to be aware of this action and to avoid doing it in future ghost box sessions and ghost box session recording reviews.

This is a common mistake made by most individuals who are taking their first steps into live spirit ghost box communication. They tend to listen for every intelligible sound produced by the ghost box during a live ghost box session as well as in the session recording. These sounds will consist of individual vowels, consonants, numbers, and inherent sounds that come with the live radio broadcast. These are sometimes mistaken by the novice ghost box operator as being live spirit communication or a part thereof. The live ghost box sweep, when in operation, will contain a continuous abundance of singular sounds created from the fragmented radio broadcast signal produced by the sweeping of the radio band by the ghost box. This sweep will contain vowels, consonants, bits of music, song, and pops and clicks, all enveloped in the inherent static white noise that is ever present, derived from the space that falls between radio stations. These are not recognized as being communication, as they are part of the makeup of the raw sweep, but all are utilized by communicating spirit entities in the formation of live spirit ghost box communication.

Numbers are also heard singularly. Individual numbers can be considered actual live spirit communication, as they will sometimes signify dates, ages, quantities, etc. Numbers are usually only recognized as valid live spirit communication when relevant to a statement or in direct answer to a question such as "Can you tell me how old you were when you died?" with the possible response being, for example, "Eight." You may also get an answer of, say, "Forty-two," for example. Another instance could be "How many spirits are here with me?" and the response may be,

"Two." These would be valid live spirit communication if in direct response to the questions asked. The main thing we strive for in live spirit ghost box communication is to be able to hear as much valid and relevant communication as possible consisting of full words, phrases, or even sentences.

Messages or responses that we recognize to be live spirit communication are full words in answer to questions and/or the subject matter being proposed in the particular session. Live spirit communication can also come in the form of a message that is independent of the topic and/or question but is recognized as being live spirit communication by its being highly unlikely to be heard over public radio broadcasts. Notice I did not say impossible to be heard on public radio broadcast but highly unlikely; for example, the message we receive quite often is "Help me." This can and does come at any given time during a live ghost box session and is heard by most operators very often. Another would be "I'm dead." These phrases when heard live by the ghost box operator are likely to be actual live spirit communication simply because they are direct statements or requests made apparently to the ghost box operator performing the session and not likely to fit into the common banter heard on a radio station. Live spirit communication of this type can and is usually validated by spirit communication that will follow it, which is in conjunction with the previous phrase or message. This being said, there is still the possibility, no matter how slight, that the ghost box delivered stray words of radio broadcast that escaped the ghost box's sweep, so the suspected live spirit communication must still be analyzed by the operator in the review of the session recording to confirm its authenticity.

The communication we do not catch live during the ghost box session will be discovered in the review of the ghost box session recording. Of course, it goes without saying, no one should ever do a live spirit ghost box communication session without recording it. Even with the review of the recording, not all communication will be recognized or understood. What a novice ghost box operator should concentrate on is doing short simple sessions with the ghost box, stick to simple questions that require only simple yes or no answers and possibly names or short two-or-three-word phrases. This will afford the novice operator the best opportunity to hear the spirit communication live and to develop an "ear" for hearing live spirit communication, which will lead to hearing and understanding more intricate communication as the ghost box operator gains experience.

The point I am attempting to stress is to pay attention to the full words you are able to hear and not single letters. When numbers are heard, make sure that you as the ghost box operator validate their relevance to the question or topic at hand. This will hone the skills of the live spirit ghost box communication operator and help build a solid foundation on which to advance knowledge and experience. Even after seventeen years dedicated to the field of live spirit ghost box communication, I still find myself in awe and wonder of every live ghost box session I do. Each ghost box session is different and holds its own unique attributes. Every day I find myself learning and gaining more experience.

The second aspect of listening to live spirit ghost box sweep, either live or in the review of a session recording, goes hand in hand with the former subject, and I consider it a negative habit. When I explain this particular action by a ghost box operator to anyone, I tell them, "Don't anticipate live spirit communication in a ghost box session." This action is committed by the ghost box operator predominantly during the performance of a live ghost box session. This action by live spirit ghost box communication operators and researchers is not a conscious effort on their part, but an unconscious practice and a byproduct of the human mind. Live spirit communication anticipation occurs during the performance of a live ghost box session. I, of course, am a firm supporter of anyone who applies the dedication it takes to be a successful live spirit ghost box operator to attempt to receive and understand live spirit communication; however, there are many, many examples I see, both audio and video, where the operator claims to hear relevant answers and/or statements received during a live spirit communication ghost box session that pertain to the topic of the session, the location where the session is being performed, or a specific entity they are attempting to communicate with, and the presented evidence is described by the operator either verbally or written as a text overlay on the video presentation, but when viewing or listening to the presented evidence, it is very clear that the described communication that the operator reports hearing live or even in the review of a session recording is in actuality not accurate or does not convey anything coherent at all. This situation is a product of live spirit communication anticipation and plagues many live spirit ghost box communication sessions. Let me also say that this is not a conscious effort on the part of the ghost box operator but a trick of the human mind.

Spirit communication anticipation occurs when a live spirit ghost box communication operator performing the live communication session anticipates hearing the answer to a specific question or statement that pertains to the location they are in or a specific entity they are trying to communicate with. The human mind is extremely rigid when it comes to order, and the ghost box operator during the live session has already set the predetermined answers to his questions or information that he is seeking in his mind subconsciously; therefore in the inherent chaos of a ghost box sweep or the overpowering hiss of white noise, etc., the operator will unconsciously anticipate the answers to submitted questions or the information on a location or individual, and any audio that may come through the device that sounds similar to, or oftentimes just a blurb of noise that happens to contain the same amount of syllables as the expected response, will be mistakenly heard by the ghost box operator as the correct answer or pertinent information.

We actually make ourselves believe we hear what we expect to hear. Once that is firmly embedded in the individual's mind, it becomes hard for them to hear anything different or even nothing at all. This not only leads to misinterpreting the existence of actual live spirit communication, it serves to distract the operator from hearing any other live spirit communication that may have in fact come through at that specific time. So much valuable spirit communication is missed and lost due to this occurrence. This not only happens during live communication sessions but can also occur in the review of a live spirit communication recording; the same principle applies. Subconsciously in our minds, we ask a question during a live spirit communication session and hope for a direct answer to that question, so we anticipate an answer. Inevitably in the operator's mind they have received the live spirit communication that they were expecting, thereby validating not only their efforts but the live spirit communication they believe was received. The only way to combat this trait, because it is basically a subconscious act, is to approach every live spirit ghost box communication session with the awareness that there is a great possibility for live spirit communication anticipation and to be aware throughout the live ghost box session of its occurrence. The ghost box operator must stay focused during the live ghost box session and listen to all audio being received without looking for that predetermined answer or detailed message.

In the great majority of live spirit communication sessions, there is a certain amount of real live spirit communication. The operator must be dedicated to attempting to hear any and all communication whether it pertains to a question, topic, location, or not. We will never be successful in eliminating 100% of this fault, but we can minimize it by being aware of its existence and focusing on our task as live spirit ghost box communication operators. This, of course, also applies to the review of any and all live spirit ghost box communication recordings, be they audio or video. Please understand that the explanation of this occurrence was by no means an attempt to infer that there are live spirit ghost box researchers, investigators, or operators out there who intentionally perpetrate this occurrence in order to sway the opinion of any individuals who may review any presented evidence, be it audio or visual. It was strictly meant to bring awareness to an existing affliction that can plague live spirit ghost box communication.

The third aspect of listening to and discerning live spirit ghost box communication I would like to cover in this chapter I call "the difference between astral and earthbound live spirit ghost box communication." It describes the differences between live spirit communication that is delivered through a ghost from spirit entities residing in the spirit world as opposed to live spirit communication that is received through a ghost box from a spirit entity that is in direct proximity to the ghost box in session here in the physical world. There are noticeable distinctions between the live spirit communication we receive from astral entities in the spirit realm and live spirit communication that comes from spirit entities that are earthbound here in the physical world, such as those encountered during a paranormal investigation conducted at a field location.

I have discovered that in order for us to receive any

live spirit ghost box communication at all, there must be a mutual exchange of energy between the ghost box operator here in the physical world and energy that comes from the communicating spirit entity. I believe that the ghost box in operation creates an open portal or doorway between our two worlds. This portal allows for the exchange and combining of both energies, physical and spiritual. This energy connection makes it possible for a communicating spirit entity to be able to manipulate the energy needed to structure the sound fragments that are produced by the spirit entity to form and deliver live spirit communication. This combination of spirit energy and physical energy via that connection gives the live spirit communication produced by an entity communicating from the spirit realm a distinct makeup and sound. It is recognizable as astral live spirit communication by this unique sound. Live spirit ghost box communication that is delivered from a spirit entity that is in the spirit realm is usually lower in volume and more incorporated into the ghost box sweep. It has, when heard live, an ethereal quality and tends to be delivered containing more of a hiss. This type of live spirit communication is indicative of being astral in nature.

The second type of communication is that of an earthbound entity, whether it be in visitation, earthbound, or grounded. A spirit that is in attendance here in the physical world and in proximity to the ghost box session being performed. This earthbound spirit entity is either attracted to the open ghost box session, or the live ghost box session is being performed in a location where the spirit entity is present. This communicating spirit entity is therefore only capable of utilizing the ambient energy that is surrounding the running ghost box and able to manipulate that energy to draw from the ghost box sweep the necessary sound fragments needed to form and deliver its live communication. The earthbound entity's ability to perform this task is akin to the traditional EVP theory in which a spirit manipulates surrounding energy to form communication and place it onto a recording device, only in this case the spirit is using that ambient energy to manipulate the ghost box sweep and deliver live spirit communication through the ghost box. This direct use of existing earthly energy allows the spirit entity to form stronger and more distinguishable communication that is audibly different from the astral communication formed and delivered by a spirit entity from the spirit world. I call this "earthbound ghost box communication," and it can be recognized by traits common to this type of live spirit communication.

Earthbound ghost box communication has an even more distinct sound than that of its counterpart, astral ghost box communication. The earthbound form of live spirit communication carries readily recognizable traits such as being louder in volume, the impression of being delivered apart or above the sound of the ghost box sweep, being more gruff or coarse sounding, and usually pertaining to the location that is being investigated by the ghost box session operator, or the circumstances surrounding said location and/or conditions and causes leading to the communicating spirit entity's departure from physical life. I believe this is due to the two different types of energy being used. There are individuals who might say, "The communication is formed with the same sound fragments no matter how they are manipulated." This is true, but I believe that the addition of spirit energy to the physical energy of the ghost box operator and the hybrid energy it creates has a direct effect on the structure of the audio frequency and sound fragments utilized by a spirit entity communicating from the astral plane and therefore creates the distinct sound and tone of the received astral ghost box communication. Even with the distinct differences between the two types of live spirit communication, it may at times require an experienced ear to discern the difference.

The fourth aspect of listening to and discerning live spirit ghost box communication I would like to explain is "the explanation of a harmonic live spirit communication," what it is, and how and why we receive it. Harmonic live spirit communication is the occurrence of receiving a live spirit communication through the use of a ghost box that is in a singing or melodic fashion. This type of communication occurs when the communicating spirit entity has only fragments of music or fragments of a song delivered by the ghost box sweep available to them at the exact moment they need to form the words and phrases of communication.

Through experience, I have learned that a communicating spirit entity is aware that they need to deliver a response to a question or statement made by the ghost box operator in a given amount of time. After a certain amount of time, which is determined by the individual running the live ghost box session, passes following the question or statement that is posed, either the communicator doing the session will go on to the next question, or the length of time between the operator's question and the communicating spirit entities response will negate the relevance of the live spirit communication to the preceding question or statement made by the operator. I have found that 99.9% of the spirit entities that deliver live spirit communication will deliver answers or statements to any given question, request, or statement made by the ghost box operator and will do so within ten to twelve-seconds of the posed question, request, or statement. In order for the communicating spirit entity to accomplish this and not have their message, response, or answer simply disregarded or unrecognized by the ghost box session operator as being a direct response or answer, they need to form the communication with whatever fragments of sound are available to them within the allotted time parameters. In the event that the ghost box finds itself sweeping a series of stations that are broadcasting music or both music and singing, the communicating spirit entity finds itself with two choices: create and send the communication from the music fragments that are available, or simply disregard that particular interaction. Remember this decision and resulting action on the part of the communicating spirit entity needs to be enacted in a split second.

So on the part of the communicating entity, the series of actions for communicating a "harmonic" communication are to hear the ghost box operator's question or request, decide on a response, formulate and gather the energy needed to deliver the live communication, seek out the available fragments of sound to form the words of communication, decide if the sound fragments available are capable of forming the words of communication they need to send, place the fragments in the correct order to enable the communication to be audible and understandable to any physical beings listening, and finally use the energy to deliver the live spirit communication correctly through a device that is scrambling all the sound that it produces. The communicating entity must do this in a certain amount of time in order for it to be heard and recognized as relevant live spirit communication pertaining to that particular interaction. WHEW! I'm going to hate it when I make my transition to the spirit realm and I have to do that in order to communicate with a ghost box operator attempting to speak with me!

The final aspect of listening to live spirit ghost box communication comes in the form of an odd and uncommon occurrence that can come at any point in a live spirit ghost box session. I am referring to the occurrence of "pre-cognizant live spirit communication." What is pre-cognizant live spirit communication? Quite a few years ago, while practicing live spirit ghost box communication, I began to notice incidents during a live ghost box session and in the review of a ghost box session recording that I was receiving live spirit communication answers to questions that I had not asked yet. The first few instances caught my attention, and I realized that there was something happening that I could not quite put my finger on.

As I continued my live ghost box sessions, I stayed

alert for any occurrence of this incident. Because I had a heightened awareness regarding this occurrence, it did not take long for me to catch the next example of it. I made a mental note of where it occurred in the live ghost box session so that I could locate and examine it in the review of the live ghost box session. I began the review of the session and fast-forwarded to the point in the recording where I remembered hearing the oddity occur and isolated that portion of the recording so that I could examine it. At this time I do not remember exactly what the live spirit communication consisted of, so for the purposes of this explanation I will use the example "There are five." As I played the section of the live ghost box recording, I heard the live spirit communication "There are five." The communication was clear and easily understandable. I knew that the spirit entity who delivered the communication meant it to be in the form of an answer. However, I had not asked any question leading up to that point that would warrant the answer of "There are five." Up to that point I had been considering a line of questioning that was directed at obtaining information regarding any spirit entities that may have been present at the location of the live ghost box session but did not verbalize any specific questions pertaining to that topic. My first question that would have been at the onset of my attempt to gather information about spirit entities that may have been present at my location would have been "Are there any spirit entities here with me now?" to which a specific and relevant live spirit communication answer would have been "There are five." I did not make the connection of the live spirit communication I heard and my intended topic and questions at the moment during the live ghost box session, so I proceeded to address the topic of spirit entities that may have been in proximity to my live ghost box session. My first question on that topic came approximately fifteen to twenty-seconds after my hearing of the lone live spirit communication, which was "If there are any spirit entities here around me now, can you let me know you are here?" to which I received the answer "Yes. Here." My next question was, "Can you tell me how many spirit entities are present?" to which I received the answer, "Five." This is where I had the aha moment.

What I have learned from that incident and many incidents like it henceforth was that a spirit entity is capable of, for lack of a better term, reading our minds. I don't mean reading our minds in the literal sense; what I am referring to is the ability of a spirit entity to have knowledge of a question or statement that is intended by the live ghost box operator to be rendered, but has yet to be verbalized by him or her. This can result in the communicating spirit entity delivering an answer or response to the unspoken question or statement before it is orally submitted by the ghost box operator. I have formulated a theory as to how this occurs, accepting that the live ghost box in session creates an energy link between the ghost box operator and the communicating spirit entity that acts as a type of umbilical cord, allowing the free exchange and melding of the two energies. It is my belief that a spirit entity involved in the live ghost box session and that is a part of this free exchange of energy can and does receive the ghost box operator's cerebral energy. This reception of what is basically the ghost box operator's thoughts can be received by an interacting spirit entity; therefore any information in the form of a question or statement that is existing in the mind of the ghost box operator and has yet to be verbalized by him or her can be accessed by the communicating entity and acted upon before the actual question has been asked or statement made, allowing the spirit entity to deliver a specific response to an unspoken question and/or statement.

Many of these incidents are not recognized by the live spirit ghost box operator simply because this phenomenon is not at the forefront of the ghost box operator's thoughts during a live ghost box session or even in the review of a ghost box session recording. If the ghost box operator hears a live spirit communication either in the live session or the recording and it is not directly associated with an already asked question or statement, the operator will usually mark it down to random live spirit communication and move on, not realizing or anticipating that the live spirit communication that was irrelevant to a previous question may be the specific answer or response to a future one that is completely relevant. This type of oversight is very prevalent with individuals who are new to live spirit ghost box communication, simply due to the lack of experience. However, it is also common among seasoned live spirit ghost box communication researchers, investigators, and operators due to oversight or lack of focus in the performance and review of a live ghost box session. My advice would be to try to keep this phenomenon in mind during a live ghost box session or review of a session recording. The question or statement you believe may have gone unanswered or ignored may have very well received a valid and relevant live spirit communication response. It simply came before the question or statement and not after.

Chapter 11

Which is Better AM or FM band For Live Spirit Ghost Box Communication

I often get the question:

"What is better for receiving live spirit ghost box communication, the AM or FM band?"

I have worked with virtually every model of ghost box from an original Frank's Box to present-day custom-built ghost boxes constructed by some of the world's leading ghost box builders and everything in between. First, let me say at the onset that my personal preference as to a particular radio band as far as live spirit ghost box communication is concerned is the AM band. I have come to this preference through countless hours of work and research in live spirit ghost box communication. I would like to mention that a custom-built ghost box and even a couple of the commercially available ghost boxes allow for the use of shortwave bands as well as the AM and FM band that can be utilized for live spirit ghost box communication; however, the shortwave bands are not commonly used for live spirit ghost box communication sessions due to their sparse amount of broadcast, so I will not be including them as a contender here.

I would like to attempt to explain the reasons for my preference for the AM band over the FM band. Let me say initially that both bands are capable of producing what is needed for a communicating spirit entity to form and deliver live spirit communication. Both the AM and FM bands provide adequate radio broadcast signal needed by the ghost box to be broken down into tiny fragments of sound, which in turn are used by a communicating entity to build words and sentences of intelligible, audible speech that can be heard and understood live as it is sent through the ghost box in session. In the field of live spirit ghost box communication, there are staunch proponents of both the AM and FM bands respectively. Every individual who has more than casually worked with a ghost box has certainly developed a preference for one over the other. I know live spirit ghost box communication researchers and operators who will argue the merits of one particular radio band over the other to the death; it's akin to die-hard sports fans who are loyal to one team and support that team no matter what.

In my experience, which has inevitably formed my opinion and preference for the AM band over the FM band for use in live spirit ghost box communication, the AM band, no matter where you access it, lends itself to broadcasting predominantly "talk radio." The majority of what you will find on most AM radio stations is speech related—sports, news, religious and political broadcasts all done in a speaking voice—in other words, the absence of singing and music. Don't misunderstand; I am not saying that the AM radio band is completely devoid of any harmonic content, but I have found that the majority of content on the AM band consists of speech.

Let me explain why this is important to live spirit ghost box communication. Way back in the infant days of live spirit ghost box communication, I was one of the original individuals who formulated and tested the theory that the live spirit communication we receive through a ghost box is formed and delivered by an entity utilizing fragments of sound produced when the ghost box sweeps the radio band at a fast enough speed to effectively break down the content of radio broadcast into tiny fragments that are then used by the communicating entity to build and form words and sentences that are delivered through the speaker of the ghost box, enabling us to hear the communication live in real time. It is my belief that because the AM radio band consists of mainly speech broadcast, it provides a better ghost box sweep that is made up of fragments of actual human speech as opposed to fragments consisting of harmonics and music notes.

Think of it this way, if you were attempting to make fried eggs for breakfast, you would, of course, break the eggs into the pan carefully, trying your best not to break the yolk so that your end result would be an intact fried egg. You would certainly not put the eggs into a bowl and scramble them and expect at the end to be left with whole fried eggs with their yolks intact. It's the same principle for live spirit ghost box communication. If you want the end result to be intelligible speech, you would supply the best ingredients you can for that result, which are sweep fragments consisting of speech. You would not supply music and harmonics and expect the result to be plain human speech without being harmonic in tone or delivered in a singing voice. The AM band, because it consists of mainly speech broadcasts, supplies the ghost box sweep with the best ingredients a communicating spirit entity would need to deliver live spirit communication in speech form.

There is a theory that I do subscribe to, which is that a communicating entity can and does use harmonics as part of the structure of the communication they form and deliver. However, I also believe that a communicating entity will utilize the static white noise that falls between broadcast stations as well as other blips and clicks that may work their way into the broadcast signal. I do not believe that a radio broadcast band such as FM, which offers predominantly music and song, is conducive to supplying the best ghost box sweep for a spirit entity to form intelligible live spirit communication.

I must say, however, in support of the FM band that there are times when the conditions during a live spirit ghost box communication session require the operator to switch between broadcast bands in an attempt to receive an adequate supply of radio broadcast to fuel the ghost box sweep. Because a ghost box operates on an incoming radio broadcast signal and said signal fluctuates continuously depending on conditions, at times it becomes necessary for the ghost box operator to switch back and forth from the AM to FM bands. I would also like to say that I do use the FM band during certain live spirit ghost box communication sessions and have over the years received outstanding communication derived from a live spirit ghost box communication session using the FM band. The FM band is an integral part of live spirit ghost box communication and can never be totally dismissed, but given the choice, I will opt for the AM band over the FM band whenever possible.

There is another radio band that is sometimes utilized by live spirit ghost box communication operators; this is the shortwave radio band. The shortwave radio band operates on the frequencies between the AM and FM bands. It does not broadcast, music, instrumentals, or Sunday sermons. It is predominantly used as a means to communicate over long distances such as internationally. There are a few ghost boxes available today that incorporate the shortwave bands. There are some ghost box operators who will occasionally utilize the shortwave radio bands during a live spirit ghost box communication session, but this is not a common practice. Most ghost box operators will stick to the AM or FM radio bands as their staple for live spirit ghost box sessions. I personally do not work with the shortwave radio bands in my live spirit ghost box communication research. I find that there is very little activity on the shortwave bands and not nearly enough to produce an adequate ghost box sweep for a spirit entity to draw from to form and deliver live spirit communication. The few times that I did experiment with the shortwave radio bands for a live spirit ghost box session, I was able to receive a few words of what I believed to be live spirit communication; however, those few words consisted of small one-syllable words such as "yes, no, or hi." The ghost box sweep produced with the shortwave radio band as its foundation was almost entirely made up of static white noise. There were instances of sporadic verbal sweep, which I assumed were produced when the ghost box picked up a random shortwave transmission, but those were few and far between.

There is also an inherent risk that comes with using the shortwave radio band during a live spirit ghost box communication session. Live spirit ghost box communication is forever being scrutinized by opponents and naysayers of the field. Because the shortwave radio band receives incoming signals that consist of a single usually private individual transmitting speech over its airwaves in a personal one-on-one conversation with another single individual using the shortwave radio band, any live spirit ghost box communication evidence examples presented will immediately be dismissed by the naysayer as being speech derived from transmitted conversations. Opponents of live spirit ghost box communication in the past have even gone as far as to say that the live spirit ghost box operator had deliberately solicited an individual to transmit specific content over the shortwave radio band that would be received by the live ghost box operator and consist of direct answers or statements that would be proposed by the ghost box operator as being actual live spirit communication. The legitimacy issues faced by the live spirit ghost box communication researcher, operator, and investigator are greatly compounded when and if the ghost box operator utilizes the shortwave radio band in his or her live spirit communication ghost box sessions.

Speaking of opponents and naysayers of live spirit ghost box communication, I would like to add to this chapter some of my insights and opinions on individuals whom I refer to as "hard-nosed skeptics." Hard-nosed skeptics, the "Scrooges" of the paranormal research world! Hopefully, all will be visited by the "the Spirit of Paranormal Existence" someday! Hard-nosed skeptics fall into two categories: individuals who are a practicing part of the paranormal community as researchers and/or investigators who dismiss and denounce live spirit ghost box communication for various reasons. Then there are the individuals who skirt the fringes of the paranormal community, neither researchers nor investigators but self-proclaimed experts who lunge at every opportunity to try to discredit and disrupt any and all attempts at an explanation or presentation of evidence in favor of the existence of spirit beings and paranormal activity. In my opinion, and this is only my opinion as a paranormal researcher, the individuals who are what I refer to as hard-nosed skeptics are not your ordinary run-of-the-mill open-minded skeptics who will look at a subject respectfully and unbiasedly even though their personal beliefs are contrary to the claims of the subject. I am referring to the closed-minded individuals who have no respect for others' opinions, ideas, beliefs, or statements. The HARD-NOSED SKEPTIC is the one who will shoot down any subject or practice that does not immediately sound logical to them or coincide with their personal beliefs. These individuals usually have no basis of information on which to draw; it always seems that they have not taken the time to gather any substantial information on the subject at hand but feel it is necessary to give their negative and scathing judgment on a topic or piece of proposed paranormal evidence that they have little or no knowledge of.

I will be using my sixteen years of experience and knowledge in my chosen field of paranormal research, live spirit ghost box communication, and over twenty years of experience as a whole in paranormal research and investigation as the basis for my opinions as well as countless interactions with hard-nosed skeptics over those many years. I have stated that I was one of the original people to make the data gathered from live spirit ghost box communication available to the public for review. A large part of the data that is presented publicly by paranormal researchers and investigators consists of audio files that capture the live spirit communication that is claimed to have been received by a ghost box operator during the use of a ghost box for live spirit communication. In this, I refer to any and all persons who are actively involved in live spirit ghost box communication and present their audio examples and research findings for public and peer review.

From the beginning days of live spirit ghost box communication research, the public posting of audio and written data led to an awakening in the paranormal community as to the existence of the possibility of a ghost box operator here in the physical world having the ability to receive and understand words and messages live in real time as they were being delivered from the spirit world. Of course, anything new will be taken with a grain of salt by all who are steeped in the tried-and-true methods of spirit communication learned and practiced without contention for decades in the field of paranormal research and investigation. The method of EVP for audible spirit communication was, up until the birth of live spirit ghost box communication, the sole method for the capture of spirit voices, and it was practiced by paranormal investigators and researchers for many, many years. It was considered to be one of the cornerstones of paranormal research and investigation.

As I said, with anything new, and live spirit ghost box communication fell nicely into that category, people will immediately dismiss it for the lack of understanding, knowledge, and personal experience. The discomfort of having to think about an alternative to what was the only game in town for a long time was dismissed out of hand with bias. Live spirit ghost box communication was ripe for this negative train of thought and dismissal. It was a method that reportedly received spirit communication live using a radio signal as the foundation to facilitate said live spirit communication, which admittedly carried the inherent chance of stray words of radio broadcast escaping the ghost box sweep and being mistaken for spirit communication. The immediate opinion of the majority of people involved in the paranormal community who had even heard of ghost boxes and their intended use was that there was much too much room for pollution and false positives by receiving human speech from the core radio source, and therefore it was deemed unreliable and unacceptable and should be dismissed as a viable form of spirit communication.

I have to admit that I myself fell into that category upon my first introduction to the ghost box. I held the same opinion as most in the paranormal community: "It's bull, and it doesn't work. It's nonsense." Until I was baptized by my first manual sweep ghost box session that consequently led to my sole dedication to that field. I explained this in detail in a previous chapter of this book, so let me get back to the topic at hand. In every form of things unknown there are individuals who will glean only particular aspects and minute parts of the whole and then fill in the "unknown" portions of the equation with what they personally believe. This holds true to all things that cannot be seen, heard, smelled, tasted or touched. Anything that falls outside the realm of these five senses must, according to the hard-nosed skeptic, not exist. There are countless things in the universe and on this planet and in our realm of existence that cannot meet the criteria of all five of these human senses and some not any. There are countless examples of this just in our basic knowledge of how we exist and what exists around us. The specific anomalies would be way too many to mention here, and the resulting combinations of any or all of the accepted senses would be infinite. The hard-nosed skeptic is just that, hard-nosed and closed-minded; I would even go as far as to say ignorant. Now, I do not use that term to describe someone who is lacking in intelligence, but the individual who is lacking in the open-minded attempt at trying to understand things that are not readily understandable.

Let me explain. The majority of skeptics whom I have come into contact with and have had to face in a debate on certain topics pertaining to different aspects in the paranormal and my chosen field of live spirit ghost box communication are for the most part open-minded and at the very least will have a working knowledge of the subject they endeavor to breach. Most skeptics will enter a discussion taking the "con" position to the opposite individual's "pro," and the debate will carry points from both sides. Many times these debates lead to the same conclusions that they started with, and no ground has been gained on either side. But what has been accomplished is that each side learned more about the opposing side's point of view and what leads to that point of view, resulting in each party walking away with a little better understanding of the facts presented and hopefully a healthier respect for the others' opinions and efforts in supporting and presenting them. This is what I refer to as a "healthy skeptic," and they are in my opinion a welcome part of the paranormal community. They give the field balance, "without darkness there can be no light," and vice versa. Without skeptics there are no points to prove or have disproven, only agreed-upon conjecture and theory. Nobody benefits from always being in agreement.

Of course, it is nice to have your opinions and ideas agreed with but not very motivating or fulfilling. Now we come to the "Scrooges" of the paranormal skeptic community. The individuals who will attach themselves to a subject or field of study that they "attack" blindly for only the simple reason that they can! They are like hyenas that prey on the weak animal in a herd or the newborns that are relatively defenseless due to their being new to the world and lacking the strength and experience to protect themselves fully. These hard-nosed skeptics will take any topic or field of study and use whatever opportunity presents itself to take pen in hand or spew negativity and accusation about the given subject, the majority of the time being completely ignorant of the facts or taking the effort to at least gather basic knowledge of the subject they seem so determined to ruin.

I have recently encountered such hard-nosed skeptics and have read their rhetoric and found myself yet again in a heated debate over the lack of facts presented, requesting the basic information they gathered to come to their conclusions; of course, no such evidence was produced. This has been repeated over and over again in my experience over the years. This type of unsubstantiated claim, or some may say attack, is a typical one for the hard-nosed skeptic. They jump in, throw a punch, and then run away, never staying long enough to finish the fight. I guess because that one punch is all they have, and it is always pretty weak at that!

In recent years I was asked to be a featured guest on a paranormal radio show to discuss my research, theories, and findings in the field of live spirit ghost box communication. The show was to be about one and a half hours in length. If memory serves me right, it was around forty-five minutes into the show when the hosts decided to take questions from the listeners via telephone calls. The first couple of calls rendered basic questions that did not entail lengthy answers or explanations, and then a call came through from a male audience member. His demeanor seemed confrontational from his first words. After saying how he had always enjoyed listening to the show, he followed with, "I don't understand how you can have a guest who talks about such nonsense." He went on to say that "everyone" knows that spirit communication, especially with a ghost box, was fake and that any and all evidence presented was fabricated by people like me. The show hosts moved to hang up the call and end the negative interaction when I stopped them and explained that I would like to speak with the gentleman. I asked the man to elaborate on his accusations of fake and fraud. He went on to state emphatically that there was no way anyone could produce an electronic device that would allow spirits to talk to someone here in the physical world, and that anyone who claimed that was a fake and a liar. He spewed out a few more like-minded sentences, and when he finished, I asked, "Is that your professional opinion?" His answer, "I don't have to be a professional. I have a brain." I responded with, "Ok, you have a brain, agreed; we all do. Let's see if you can wrap your brain around this." I proceeded to ask the gentleman a question and informed him that if he were able to answer it, I would leave the show and the paranormal forever.

My question to him was this:

"Can you tell me the odds of my doing a live spirit ghost box session at a specific point in time using a ghost box that runs on the reception of public radio broadcasts and that is designed and built to sweep the radio band and break that radio broadcast down into tiny fragments of sound that are for all intents and purposes simply gibberish to the naked ear, then have that ghost box render full words of human speech that deliver answers to specific questions I have asked within seconds of my asking, and to have my name mentioned numerous time in a very short period of time during that session? While you are at it, calculate the odds of a radio broadcasting specific answers to my questions and mentioning my name numerous times and having those instances received by me in full human speech while the ghost box turned the radio broadcast into small unintelligible fragments of sound, and have this all happen at the very moment I was conducting a live spirit communication ghost box session."

When I finished my question, I offered the hard-nosed skeptic on the other end of the telephone line time to retrieve a calculator and figure out the odds of that happening. A few seconds passed, and the only response that came from the negative caller was, "It's still all bullshit." The next thing that was heard was the sound of his slamming down his telephone receiver. Although the listening audience could not see it, the radio show hosts both had big smiles on their faces as they sat shaking their heads. A few more calls came in congratulating me on how I'd shut down the disgruntled caller.

My intention was not to "shut down" either the hard-nosed skeptic caller, or anyone else for that matter, or to make him seem ignorant or foolish. The question I posed to him was an attempt to supply him with food for thought, something that may have ignited a spark that would allow him to actually research information and data regarding the subject that he so adamantly denounced. I found that over the years when faced with a staunch skeptic whose mind was made up, no amount of explanation, recorded data or proposed evidence would or could dissuade a hard-nosed skeptic from his condemnation. I must say, however, that there were a couple of hard-nosed skeptics whom I had come up against that I actually got to admit to some of my points, which to me was a victory in itself.

Back when live spirit ghost box communication was in its infancy, there were limited means of online interaction —forums, Yahoo groups and Myspace, which was still relatively new—and paranormal investigation and research had not yet enjoyed the boom that occurred with the advent of paranormal television shows like *Ghost Hunters*, so the likelihood of encounters between skeptics and believers was not an everyday event. Don't misunderstand me, there were skeptics, there were always skeptics, but not as prevalent as they are today. With the birth of social media platforms like Facebook, Twitter, and Instagram, the connection between individuals in the paranormal community became much easier and more prevalent, but so did the interaction between paranormal researchers and investigators and hard-nosed skeptics. A skeptic could join a paranormal Facebook group or follow a paranormal researcher on Twitter and was free at any moment to leave a scathing negative comment or tweet, which would then more times than not ignite a back-and-forth fray that would more often than not become derogatory on both sides. I can only speak for myself here, but I have discussed this topic with quite a few paranormal colleagues who are of the same mind on this subject. As I stated earlier, skepticism can be a healthy and beneficial thing, it drives us to pursue the truths that can quell some of the rhetoric skeptics arm themselves with. I have no problem with a healthy debate on any topic, especially one that I am passionate about. It's the hard-nosed skeptics, the ones who lurk on the fringes of the paranormal community and in the shadows of the social media platforms, who are simply waiting for an opportunity to strike and spew negativity and accusations for the simple reason of being able to do so and create drama and chaos.

This becomes an ongoing problem for some individuals in the paranormal community who are involved in presenting their evidence and evaluations on social media platforms, especially if the data presented is of a highly controversial nature. People will endure just so many negative confrontations before becoming silent and even giving up their pursuit of paranormal research and investigation. I have known individuals who were practicing researchers for years who threw in the towel and quit the paranormal field, not being able to deal with the stress of having to continually justify themselves and their field of study. I myself made the decision to remove myself and my research from the public arena and continued my research and investigation in private for almost ten years. Those were the days when the internet was like the Wild West, the days of anything goes. Today, thank goodness, we enjoy administrators and moderators on social media forums, and the problem of negative confrontations is kept to a minimum, and still with those safeguards in place, there are still individuals out there who will attack and berate someone when the opportunity presents itself.

When I returned to the public eye and became active again on social media and in the public paranormal community, I found that things had changed for the better, and for the most part people involved in the paranormal community, serious researchers like myself, and serious investigators can interact side by side with people who may have a casual interest in the paranormal or just a healthy curiosity, the majority of whom support and encourage one another, learn from and teach one another, and basically coexist in harmony. Don't get me wrong, there are still skeptics out there, hard-nosed and passive, but for the most part, the Scrooges will only get so far before they are either silenced or removed completely.

I think I have covered pretty much all I can on this subject, so at the risk of ranting on about the inept attempts of hard-nosed skeptics, which would only become redundant, I will end this chapter by saying that everyone and anyone who has an opinion is entitled to it as long as it can be presented in an intelligent, respectful, and open-minded manner, which would leave the "BAH HUMBUG" out of legitimate discussion or difference of opinion.

Chapter 12

One and Two Word Live Spirit Communication, Is It Relevant?

As the technology of live spirit ghost box communication stands at this point in time, we are only receiving on average around two-to-three-word live spirit communications during any given ghost box session. On rare occasions when conditions fall exactly right, it is possible to get a five-or-even-six-word sentence, but those are the exceptions to the rule. In my whole seventeen-year career practicing and researching live spirit ghost box communication, I have received relatively few live spirit communication messages that were more than seven or eight words in length and only a handful that have surpassed that number. For example, the yes, no, and short two-to-three-word live spirit communications are what make up the meat and potatoes of live spirit ghost box communication. Is it possible to receive full sentences of live spirit communication using a ghost box? Of course. I myself have received live spirit communication in full sentences that have contained over ten words. That being said, those instances of full-on sentences of live spirit communication are the exception to the rule. Given the state of ghost box technology at this time and the conditions needed for that type of live spirit communication to happen, let's just say it does not occur every day.

This should not be discouraging. There is a wealth of information to be gathered by just receiving the simple but direct and relevant one- and two-word answers of live spirit communication to your questions. For example, if you were to ask the question "Can you please bring my father forward to speak with me?" and received the answer "Yes" live as the spirit entity delivered it, you would most likely follow it with the question "Dad, are you there?" and again you were to receive the answer "Yes," you would most likely then ask something like "Can you tell me your name so that I know it is you?" and you receive the response "George," which was the correct name you were looking for, this would constitute excellent validating and relevant live spirit communication. These are all simple questions that gleaned one-word answers but gave you all the information that you needed or wanted to feel confident that you did indeed communicate with the entity that you intended to contact. This is just a basic example that can be applied to any ghost box session.

The short one-or-two-word answers are the ones you will be more apt to hear live as they are delivered by the communicating entity, which is the main goal of this field of live spirit ghost box communication. Every researcher, investigator, and ghost box operator should strive to actually hear as much live spirit communication as possible live in real time as it is delivered. Hopefully, as the technology advances, we will be able to develop a ghost box that will allow for the reception of more complex and detailed live spirit communication, but for now, we have to be very grateful for the live spirit communication we are receiving. The fact that we are receiving communication from entities that are not of this physical world in itself is a gift and a miracle.

I have come to find that the more often you perform live spirit ghost box communication sessions and the more experienced you become at doing ghost box sessions, the stronger the energy bond becomes between you and your spirit counterparts. This will also help to facilitate better and clearer live spirit communication. My longtime experience in this field and the frequency with which I do live ghost box sessions has allowed me to enjoy a very high level of live spirit communication both in quality and quantity, which I firmly believe can be achieved by any person with the focus and dedication to put in the time and effort needed to build experience and knowledge in the field of live spirit ghost box communication.

I must touch on a certain aspect that is associated with this particular subject. I have had this question posed to me on many occasions by skeptics of live spirit ghost box communication as well as fellow researchers and operators. Because the practice of receiving live spirit communication is achieved with the use of a ghost box, which is essentially just a radio that has been altered so that it will sweep the radio broadcast bands continuously, how do you know that what you are receiving is not just stray words of radio broadcast that escape being broken down by the sweep of the ghost box? Let me first say that there is no way to prove beyond a shadow of a doubt that some of what we as live spirit ghost box communication researchers and operators claim is actual communication from spirit entities is just that.

The reason this particular topic is so relevant to the suggestion that we are hearing stray words of radio broadcast as opposed to actual live spirit communication is that the one-syllable words we tend to receive most often—the yes and no responses, single names, and one-or-two-word answers—are the ones that have the highest chance of escaping the ghost box sweep as stray words of radio broadcast. That being the case, it becomes the basis for any argument against the actual reception of live spirit ghost box communication. At this time in paranormal research and investigation as a whole, we are not yet capable of delivering irrefutable evidence that can be submitted as solid fact, and therefore any and all paranormal evidence can be scrutinized and dismissed by skeptics and naysayers. However, we as paranormal researchers and live spirit ghost box communication researchers, investigators, and operators are not defenseless to counter these skeptics' claims.

In live spirit ghost box communication, we, as operators and researchers, perform live spirit ghost box sessions that are largely comprised of topics and questions that are designed to glean information from our spirit communicators, such as names, dates, aspects of death and the spirit world and their existence in it, specific details of a communicating entity's physical life, specific places, etc., just to name a few. More often than not, a live spirit ghost box researcher or operator will receive specific, relevant, and validating answers and/or statements that pertain only to the questions asked or topics posed by the ghost box operator conducting the session. These relevant and pertinent live spirit communications are delivered through the ghost box in an acceptable time proximity to those questions, which means they are received within seconds of the operator's inquiry. Can we prove that what we are hearing is emphatically live spirit communication from an entity not of this world? No, but I would hate to be the person who had to calculate the odds of a stray word or words of radio broadcast escaping the rapid breakdown of the ghost box sweep and being the correct and relevant answer to the operator's questions delivered within seconds of the question being asked. I don't think there is a computer let alone a person capable of calculating those odds.

In this chapter, I would also like to explain the ability for a live spirit ghost box operator to receive live spirit communication not only delivered from communicating spirit entities in the spirit realm but also from a communicating spirit either grounded or in visitation here in the physical world that could be in direct proximity to the ghost box in session or at a distant remote location. I often get asked the question "Is live spirit communication from different locations possible?" I had discovered way back at the beginning of live spirit ghost box communication research that the spirit technicians that we have come to rely on for assistance and guidance during our live ghost box sessions are the "gatekeepers" and conduits of a live spirit ghost box session and the live spirit communication that is delivered through the ghost box to our physical world. Through experience and research as well as information given to me by my spirit counterparts during live spirit ghost box communication sessions, I believe the live spirit communication we receive can be derived from different locations and possibly even different dimensions, and that spirit technicians act as liaisons between us and the communicating spirit entities. If there is an entity that wishes to communicate that is, for instance, "Earthbound" and not in proximity to a ghost box in session, if need be, a spirit technician will help facilitate the live spirit communication in both directions to us from the entity and vice versa.

There are many individual spirits and other entities that wish to communicate, and they do tend to all speak at once, and this tends to have the communication overlap as it would here in the physical if a number of people spoke all at once. I believe this also is a major factor in our disability for understanding much of the live spirit communication received that would otherwise be heard and understood if it were singular and separate from any other spirit communication being attempted at the exact same moment. I know that the spirit technician also acts as a conduit, sort of a spirit communication antenna. The spirit technician's energy connection that is melded with the physical energy of the ghost box operator running the live ghost box session will automatically feed the live spirit communication and/or manipulated energy through the spirit technician and subsequently through the ghost box without the spirit technician being directly responsible for the manipulation of the sweep fragments to form the live spirit communication. Think of the spirit technician as a fuse in a fuse box. If he or she is removed, the connection is broken, and no live spirit communication can flow. I have learned that live spirit communication is possible by the combination of spirit and physical energy that allows for the manipulation of the ghost box sweep sound fragments to form live spirit communication that is audible to the physical ear. Remove one aspect from the equation, and the live spirit communication is not possible.

All factors combined make up what is needed to facilitate live spirit communication. This combination of factors also makes it possible for separate spirit entities in different locations and circumstances to communicate simultaneously. There may even be spiritual energy relay stations like broadcast towers that carry the communication energy from different locations to a central point where it can be distributed and transmitted by the ghost box into audible physical speech that we can understand.

Throughout my years of live spirit ghost box communication research, I have received solid validating spirit communication from entities that not only reside in the spiritual realm but also from entities that were grounded, stuck, or in visitation here in our physical realm. I have received communication from entities that were in distant locations, entities that were in specific locations that gave specific information pertaining to their identity and location, which was validated and confirmed by evidence gathered by paranormal investigators who had previously obtained said evidence from the same locations, thus validating the information that was received in a controlled ghost box session I had conducted literally thousands of miles from the purported locations. This data and evidence led me to formulate my theory and belief that live spirit ghost box communication is capable of producing live spirit communication not only from spirit entities communicating from the spirit realm but also from earthbound entities that are not in proximity to the live ghost box in session that is receiving said live spirit communication. This is only possible with the diligent help of our spirit technicians, who oversee and help to facilitate live spirit communication between physical human beings and spirit beings no matter where they are.

Some time ago I had a very extraordinary experience with this type of occurrence. I was contacted by a friend and colleague who is in the paranormal investigation field. He informed me that he was contacted by another individual who had performed a live spirit ghost box session and reportedly received live spirit communication from an entity that claimed to be residing in an abandoned mental asylum that was located many hundreds of miles from where this individual had conducted the live spirit ghost box communication session. My friend had been contacted due to the fact that he had investigated this particular location in the past and had publicly presented evidence he had gathered during his investigation. My friend had a question and a request for me. His question was, "Can someone perform a live ghost box session and receive live spirit communication from a spirit entity that was not in direct proximity to the ghost box in session?" My answer to him was, "Yes, absolutely." He then went on to explain the details that were given to him by the person who had contacted him. According to this individual, they had been performing an impromptu live spirit ghost box communication session in the home of a friend who was supposedly experiencing some poltergeist activity. The individual proceeded to perform the live ghost box session in an attempt to garner live spirit communication from any spirit entities that might have been present in the home.

As the live ghost box session progressed, the individual claimed to have received live spirit communication from one particular spirit entity and was able to secure information from said spirit entity through the live spirit communication they were receiving via the ghost box. The communicating spirit entity gave his name, year and circumstances of his death, and the location where his death occurred. As the ghost box operator continued to pose questions to the communicating spirit entity, he was able to determine that the entity lost his physical life in a mental asylum that had since been abandoned, and informed the ghost box operator that he was still in residence there. When my friend heard the ghost box session operator's story, he recognized the name of the abandoned asylum and the name that the spirit entity had given during the live ghost box session, as well as other details delivered by the spirit entity. That is when my friend decided to contact me and solicit my help.

When I confirmed that it was possible for a live spirit ghost box operator to receive live spirit communication from an entity in a distant location, I went on to explain to him how this type of incident occurs. I explained that with the help of the spirit technicians who work with live spirit ghost box communication operators in every live ghost box session that is performed, it is possible for a spirit entity that is not in proximity to the ghost box in session and can be any distance away from the set location to have words and messages delivered through the ghost box in session. The spirit technician simply acts as a relay, receiving the spirit communication from the wayward entity and in turn delivering that spirit communication live through the intended ghost box in session. My friend completely understood the premise and then asked if it would be possible for me to do a controlled live spirit ghost box communication session from my location and attempt to contact the same spirit entity that had communicated with the ghost box operator who reported the incident to my friend. Of course I agreed, not only because I would not deny my friend a favor but because this was a great opportunity for an experiment that would have multiple validations from a number of different individuals.

I set a time and date to perform the requested live spirit ghost box communication session. I received information from my friend that only included the name and location of the abandoned mental asylum and the date that the original live spirit communication ghost box session was performed by the original operator. I did not possess any knowledge of the name, date, or circumstance of death of the specific spirit entity that delivered the live spirit communication in the original ghost box session. Having a limited knowledge of relevant information that may be delivered by the spirit entity would help to ensure the validity of any correct answers and/or information delivered to me during my live spirit ghost box communication session. I began the live ghost box session and solicited the aid of my longtime spirit technicians and friends Mike and Lisa, who have been with me in literally every live spirit ghost box communication session I have done throughout my career. I apprised my spirit technicians of the situation and received confirmation from them that they would do their best to help facilitate the long-distance live spirit communication. The spirit entity that I was attempting to communicate with was allegedly residing in an abandoned asylum that was hundreds of miles from the location where I was performing the live ghost box session and was not able to manipulate the energy surrounding the ghost box in order to use the live ghost box sweep to form and deliver the live spirit communication. It was up to my spirit technicians to contact the target spirit entity, establish a connection, receive any communication sent by the wayward spirit entity, and then deliver it to me through the live ghost box in session.

I asked my spirit technicians if they were ready and if I could proceed with the ghost box session. I received a loud and clear, "Yes." I was very confident that this particular live spirit ghost box session would be successful due to the fact that I was enjoying very good radio signal reception, and the ghost box sweep contained a minimal amount of static white noise. I proceeded with my first question, "Is the spirit entity at the asylum available to communicate with me today?" I waited a few seconds and did not hear a reply. I repeated the same question, but still, no response. As I was about to ask my spirit technicians if there was a problem, I received the response, "Yes. Here." I heard this live and acknowledged it.

I posed my second question to the distant spirit entity. "Is this the spirit that is in the abandoned asylum?" Within seconds I received the answer "Yes" and then immediately "Yes" again. This type of double response was not uncommon, so I did not pursue an explanation for it, I simply accepted the yes. The responses and answers I was receiving through the ghost box were delivered in both male and female voices and were recognizable to me as having the sound of ethereal live spirit communication that was derived from spirit entities who communicated from the spirit realm and not here in the physical world. This reassured me that the live spirit communication being delivered to me through the ghost box was being relayed to me through my spirit technicians Mike and Lisa, hence the double "Yes" communication. Most likely Mike and Lisa decided to send the answer from the wayward spirit entity at the same time; hey, it happens.

My next question to the spirit entity was a request for his name, full name if possible; if not, one name would suffice. This request for his name had to be made three times before I was able to hear a live response. I would come to find in a review of the session recording later that the name was delivered after the first time I asked; I just did not hear it live at the time. The spirit entity had delivered a single name. I was to find out later that it was his surname. My next series of questions pertained to the spirit entity's location. I was able to hear two out of the three responses live in real time, and I knew that the location name was the correct one, which bolstered my confidence in my communicating with the correct spirit entity.

By the conclusion of the live spirit ghost box communication session, I had received answers from whom I believed was the spirit entity I had intended to contact, receiving the date of his transition from physical to spirit form and the circumstances that perpetuated that transition. After thanking both the wayward spirit entity who communicated with me and my spirit technicians for their exemplary help in this live spirit communication session, I turned off my ghost box and looked forward to the forthcoming review of the ghost box session recording.

Since the live spirit ghost box communication session had lasted only sixteen minutes, the session recording review was not lengthy, only lasting about four hours. This

I attribute in part to the high quality of the ghost box session and the minimal amount of noise it contained. When my ghost box session recording review was completed, I had gleaned a total of nine individual audio files. Each file contained my question or statement and the subsequent relevant answers or responses of live spirit communication. I promptly forwarded said audio files to my friend and awaited his response. I received a phone call from my friend not long after sending the evidence I had gathered. He expressed his amazement at the quality of the live spirit communication and informed me that out of the nine live spirit communications received, two could be construed as relevant but were not exact, and the other seven were spot on, delivering specific and correct answers pertaining to the spirit entity involved: the name, location, time and circumstances of death.

This particular situation and its outcome are a perfect example of the capability of receiving live spirit ghost box communication from spirit entities whether they are communicating from the spirit realm or earthbound and communicating from a location that is not in proximity to the location where the live ghost box session is being performed.

Chapter 13

Reverse Spirit Communication in a Ghost Box Session

This information can be helpful to novice as well as experienced live spirit ghost box communication operators. The novice ghost box operators are probably not aware of this, but spirits do use the ghost box sweep to deliver live spirit communication in reverse speech. Sometimes the ghost box sweep provides radio broadcast fragments of sound that may only allow a spirit entity to form live spirit communication in a reverse speech form instead of what we consider as normal forward speech. When we listen to a recording, we listen to it as the recorder captured it, in a forward or normal speech pattern, but all audio captured with an audio recording device, including live spirit communication captured during a live ghost box session, has a reverse side. Since our spirit friends on the other side are not articulating words in human speech using physical vocal cords or human phonetics, they utilize whatever fragments of sound are made available to them by the ghost box sweep at the precise second that they need it to communicate a relevant answer or to form a phrase that will be recognized by the ghost box operator as being associated with the question that was asked or the topic of the live ghost box session.

In order for us, as physical human beings, to accept a live spirit communication as being relevant and validating to the question or topic at hand, we must receive that live spirit communication in close proximity to our question or statement. If the live spirit communication is sent at an interval that is further than approximately ten to twelve-seconds following our request for communication, we may miss it altogether or fail to associate it with our question or statement because it was received later than appropriate for the ghost box operator to connect it to the preceding question or statement. Therefore when an entity is in search of the sound fragments needed to form a particular live spirit communication, they will utilize any fragments of sound they can. Sometimes these fragments of the ghost box sweep only afford the entity the chance to form the communication in a reverse speech manner so that the opportunity for a relevant answer or statement of live spirit communication is not lost. When you get a live spirit communication but cannot quite make it out, something that has the unique sound of a live spirit communication but is not understandable, just gibberish, simply reverse the playback in the audio editor and you will possibly get a coherent message or answer in forward speech.

I have many audio examples of this reverse live spirit communication phenomenon, which is actually very common. I even have audio files that have half the live spirit communication played forward and the remainder of the communication delivered in reverse speech. This is a phenomenon that would and could never occur with physical speech. Human pronunciation of speech and the arrangement of phonetics and syllables would not allow for a sentence spoken by a physical human being to be heard backward.

Communicating spirit entities are not only capable of delivering live spirit communication in either forward or reverse speech but also in forward and reverse combined. I have examples of a live spirit communication audio where the spirit entity has rendered two different pieces of live spirit communication both forward and backward at the same exact point in the recording. If the audio of the live spirit communication contains three words of communication and that exact piece of audio recording is played forward, it will say, for example, "Hello, I'm here." When the piece of audio is reversed and played back, it will say, "I am Tom." These two examples contain completely different words or phrases when played forward and backward. Some audio examples affected by this phenomenon contain the same exact word or phrase when played backward and forward, which would be an impossibility for physical human speech. This is a perfect form of validation for a claim by the presenting ghost box operator that the live spirit communication was in fact delivered by a spirit entity, not of this physical world, and is actual live spirit communication. So check your audio files in reverse before discarding an unintelligible piece of audio that you suspect may be live spirit communication. You can also check your good files; you never know if there is a continuing or extra message on the flip side.

The next aspect I would like to cover is what I call "the act of missing live spirit communication in a ghost box recording." Let me attempt to explain why we sometimes miss some of the live spirit communication that is of lesser quality when reviewing a ghost box session recording as opposed to the more apparent loud and clear live spirit communications that stand out during the performance of a live ghost box session and in the subsequent session recordings. There are a couple of factors that come into play here.

1. The operator or listener is relatively new to live spirit ghost box communication and has not had time to develop an experienced ear for listening to a live ghost box sweep during a ghost box session or become familiar with the review of the ghost box session recording.

2. The spirit communication that is missed is of a lesser quality than the spirit communication that is immediately apparent. The missed spirit communication is either too low in volume, delivered too fast amidst the ghost box sweep, or too shrouded in static white noise or ghost box sweep chatter to stand out enough to be recognized and therefore goes unheard.

3. This factor is I believe the most likely culprit. It occurs when the ghost box operator reviewing the live ghost box session recording had based the ghost box session on a specific topic and

hears him or herself asking questions during the live ghost box session while reviewing the recording. The ghost box operator remembers hearing certain live spirit communication being delivered after a specific question and remembers acknowledging that by repeating the live spirit communication that was heard during the live ghost box session. Upon reviewing the live ghost box session recording, the ghost box operator does not hear or recognize some of the live spirit communication that they remember hearing during the performance of the live ghost box session. This results in the ghost box operator reviewing the recording and subconsciously concentrating on and expecting to hear only the live spirit communication that is remembered by them as being relevant to the questions asked or the topic of the ghost box session that was performed. This concentration on the part of the ghost box operator will allow them to miss any live spirit communication that did not directly pertain to a specific question or topic of the live ghost box session. The ghost box operator will only tend to hear and accept the live spirit communication they believe should be there. This does not happen 100% of the time, but does occur on a fairly regular basis. The only way for a ghost box operator to diminish this occurrence is to stay aware of any and all live spirit communication from the beginning to the end of the live ghost box session recording, thus helping the ghost box operator not to miss any of the live spirit communication that may be there. This may take listening to the ghost box session recording a few times and reviewing the recorded session slowly and carefully in small increments. I recommend that the ghost box operator also listen to any isolated audio files produced from said ghost box session immediately before posting them for public or peer review. Sometimes the lapse between creating the audio file and presenting it will give the operator a different perspective on it, which will allow the operator to hear something they may have missed in the initial review of the live ghost box session recording.

My explanation of this occurrence may sound like the explanation of the act of "chasing ghosts" that was given in an earlier chapter. Chasing ghosts is a saying I once used to describe the act of digging out whispers and non-apparent pieces of spirit communication that are inaudible and unintelligible to most ghost box operators and the average person listening to the presented audio file of live spirit ghost box communication. I have said and firmly believe that any spirit communication that is not loud and clear will most likely be missed by the novice ghost box operator or the average person listening to the audio file and therefore will not coincide with the audio file description of the live spirit communication it is purported to contain, which the creating ghost box operator has presented. When we miss live spirit communication in a ghost box session recording, it is most likely due to not paying close attention to the total content of the recorded ghost box session. If we stay aware of this, we can discover live spirit communication that otherwise may have been lost for lack of concentrating on the whole instead of the sum of the parts of a ghost box session recording.

Here is another subject I would like to cover that I call "non-intentional live spirit ghost box communication." Non-intentional live spirit communication, what is it? It is live spirit communication that is received through the ghost box during a live session that was not a deliberate act by a spirit entity to form and deliver a specific answer, statement, or message while interacting with a ghost box operator during a live ghost box session. The non-intentional live spirit communication is the result of eavesdropping, for lack of a better term. Think of it like this, let's say there was an individual in a crowded room communicating with an individual in another location by way of a walkie-talkie. The individual operating the walkie-talkie did not speak but held down the transmit button on the device, allowing the individual receiving the transmission to hear conversations and talking that occurred in the area where the transmission was taking place, thereby allowing the receiving person to hear communication that was not directly intended for him to hear, background speech. When we think about live spirit ghost box communication, we tend to take for granted that the live spirit communication we receive during a live ghost box session is always intended by a spirit entity to be delivered directly to the ghost box operator performing the live session. It would be logical then to believe that a spirit entity that was not conscious of the ghost box, or how to use it, would not be the spirit entity forming and sending live spirit communication or be aware that their words were being delivered through a ghost box to a person in the physical world. I believe that no live spirit ghost box communication session can or does occur without having a spirit technician present to oversee the proceedings; therefore if we entertain the idea of non-intentional communication, then we must be open to the possibility of the spirit technician being unaware when this type of live spirit communication is received during the performance of a live ghost box session. Some individuals in the field of live spirit ghost box communication will argue that only an open portal or open connection is necessary to receive live spirit communication through the ghost box, and that a spirit technician is not an integral part of the communication process. I wholeheartedly disagree.

When I refer to "non-intentional communication," I am attempting to convey that the source of the live spirit communication is not aware of any opportunity to communicate and is not intentionally manipulating any supplied sound fragments from a ghost box to form and deliver live spirit communication that is being received during a live ghost box session. If the point is made that only an open portal or connection is needed for the non-intentional communication to be sent and the presence of a spirit technician is not necessary, I would have to agree with that assessment. A spirit technician is not necessary for the reception of non-intentional live spirit communication during a ghost box session. However, I do not agree that a spirit technician is neither present nor necessary for a live spirit ghost box communication session overall. The spirit technician's task is to control and oversee any and all interaction between spirit entities and live spirit ghost box operators during the performance of a live ghost box session. The spirit technician's focus falls on the spirit entities that are attempting to communicate directly with the ghost box operator performing the session. It is my belief that non-intentional live spirit communication is not spirit communication at all but words, phrases, or statements that the ghost box operator happened to catch during the live ghost box session, whose source is most likely spirit entities that are speaking to each other in proximity to the open connection that is created by the ghost box in session. It's sort of like when you are sitting at a table in a restaurant and you can hear parts of the conversation being had at an adjacent table. It's not part of the private conversation at your table and is not a focal point for you, but you still are able to hear parts of the conversation from the adjoining table.

The instance of "non-intentional communication" may be accomplished when a spirit entity who is in proximity to the open connection created by the ghost box session simply speaks a word, phrase, or sentence without the intention of sending a communication through the live ghost box. This action creates a form of energy that in turn serves to bend or shape the audio frequencies and wave patterns that are being received by the live ghost box in session. This signal is combined with the spirit energy as the two flow freely back and forth between the physical and spirit worlds via the connection that the ghost box creates. As the spirit entity speaks, the combined energies would then be returned to and delivered through the ghost box as live spirit communication during a live ghost box session. This would occur without the specific intention or even the knowledge of the spirit entity that spoke the communication.

This subject started me thinking. Since I realized the possibilities involved in non-intentional live spirit communication, I began to wonder if in fact our communicating friends were not just manipulating sound fragments produced by the sweep of the ghost box, but the possibility of there being two separate methods of forming live spirit ghost box communication available to them. Depending on the circumstances at the time the live spirit communication is being formed and sent, it may be possible that the live spirit communication is formed by a combination of methods consisting of not only radio fragment manipulation from the ghost box sweep, but "adjustment" and/or "bending" of audio frequencies as well. Audio frequency is the foundation of all sound. This bending method may occur due to the type and content of spirit energy that is prevalent during a live ghost box session. The energy that is generated by the spirit may have the capability to manipulate frequencies and/or non-spirit energy on a subconscious level. Let's entertain the possibility that by the act of subconscious thought on the part of a spirit entity, said spirit entity becomes capable of emitting energy that can independently manipulate the energy that it is encountering from the ghost box in session, and therefore has the capability of creating sound in the form of speech that is delivered to us through the live ghost box and has been sent by an entity that had no conscious knowledge of using the live ghost box to communicate.

These two methods of forming communication may be capable of being used separately or in tandem depending on the awareness of the spirit entity. This could possibly explain both types of communication formation, direct intentional live spirit communication and non-intentional live spirit communication. The entities that are sending intentional communication may have both separate methods and/or a combination of the two methods available to them to form and send the live spirit communication. The entity that is sending non-intentional communication may be unconsciously utilizing only the "frequency bending" method of live spirit communication formation and subsequently have that spirit communication delivered live through the live ghost box in session. Since we can only speculate on how a nonphysical spirit entity is able to produce a voice or if they can even speak as we understand the concept, we tend to associate a spirit's speech with the way we understand our physical form of speech and the way we form and deliver it between ourselves as physical beings. We cannot know how a spirit entity communicates with other spirit beings; we can only rely on the knowledge we have accumulated through research and experience as to how they use a ghost box to form and deliver live spirit communication in the form of human speech so that we as physical beings can hear and understand it.

The final aspect of this chapter that I would like to discuss is what I refer to as "Why do some hear the same audio example of live spirit communication differently?" There is a very common occurrence that takes place when a number of different individuals listen to the same exact audio example of a live spirit ghost box communication at the same exact time. I will attempt to explain my theory as to why this phenomenon takes place.

The traditional sweeping ghost box and its predecessors operate on the same basic principle; whether it is a custom-made box, a commercially manufactured box, or a simple hacked radio, the basic operation is the same. The ghost box is designed to automatically sweep a designated radio band, be it AM, FM, or shortwave, continuously. It can be made to sweep in a linear fashion, which sweeps the radio dial from one end to the other in a forward circular motion, going from the beginning of the band to the end and back to the beginning repeatedly. The ghost box can also be made to sweep the band in a random fashion, which allows the sweep to jump from one point on the dial to another randomly. The ghost box can also be designed to produce an effect where the incoming radio broadcast signal is received by the ghost box and transformed into reverse speech so that all incoming radio broadcast is received as if spoken in reverse before it is broken down into fragments by the ghost box sweep. The accepted theory is that an entity not of this physical world can utilize the fragments of sound produced by the ghost box to produce coherent audible words and phrases of human speech that can be heard live by the ghost box operator in real time during the performance of a live spirit ghost box communication session. Many if not all individuals who practice live spirit ghost box communication and record their live ghost box sessions will produce either video and/or audio files of what they determine to be the best-quality examples of the live spirit communications that were received, and subsequently present them for review by other individuals either privately or publicly. This is where the aforementioned phenomenon of different individuals hearing the same exact audio of a live spirit ghost box communication differently comes into play.

Because of the way a ghost box works and the way it is believed entities deliver live spirit communication through the ghost box, the live spirit communication that is received is delivered as a patchwork of human speech being composed of many different individual fragments of sound gathered and constructed by the communicating spirit entity. This live spirit communication is delivered through the ghost box as intelligible human speech. The words and phrases of live spirit communication, although discernible as human speech by our physical hearing, are nonetheless lacking in the quality and content of actual human speech that would be present if being spoken by someone in physical form. Because of the manner in which the live spirit ghost box communication is constructed and delivered by the communicating spirit entity, it loses the inflection, nuance, and most of the time the emotional content that gives verbal communication between physical human beings the capability to almost be unconsciously understood by any and all listening. This inherent shortcoming in the live spirit communication that is formed and delivered during a ghost box session by communicating spirit entities is therefore without the content of physical human inflection, pronunciation, and delivery.

A good portion of live spirit communication that is reviewed as recorded audio, and even that which is heard live during a live spirit ghost box communication session, can be heard differently by one or more individuals listening to the specific audio example. For example, if the live spirit communication presented in an individual audio example consisted of the words "Yes, I am here" and that phrase of live spirit communication was heard by four or five individuals at the exact same time, it is possible that all will hear what is proposed by the presenter of the audio example and all listening hear the same phrase; however, the odds are that one or two or even more will hear the audio example of the live spirit communication differently. Some may hear it partially the same, and some may hear the entire phrase differently, or any combination thereof.

When two physical individuals interact in a conversational manner, there are a plethora of factors that come into play that construct the verbal interaction between physical human beings, not only the tone, inflection, emotional content, and deliverance of the human speech, but also facial expression and body language. Sadly, the majority of these are absent from the live spirit communication we receive from spirit entities during a live spirit ghost box communication session and subsequently in the audio recordings of a live ghost box session. I usually go with my initial interpretation of the spirit communication I heard either live or in my review of the session recording. If and when I am presented with an alternative interpretation by an individual who has reviewed an audio example of live spirit communication I have presented, I will always consider the alternative and reevaluate the live spirit communication in question.

In listening to live spirit ghost box communication, whether it is during the performance of a live ghost box session or in the review of a live ghost box session recording, the ability to discern what is live spirit communication from what is stray radio broadcast signal or simply gibberish that sounds like it could be live spirit communication takes a trained ear. This trained ear can only be acquired through experience in listening to and working with a live ghost box in session. Whenever I offer an explanation of what I mean by "an ear for live spirit communication," I use this analogy. I liken the novice ghost box operator to an apprentice piano tuner. The novice piano tuner starts his or her career with little or no experience and has little knowledge, if any, of what a perfectly tuned piano should sound like. The budding piano tuner will seek knowledge from a seasoned and experienced piano tuner as well as arm himself with the tools he needs to accomplish his task, such as a metronome and a tuning fork. When he first starts out, he must rely on whatever knowledge he has managed to accumulate and the tools he will use to ensure that he does a satisfactory job and that the piano he works on will be in tune at the end of the job. The professional piano tuner with years of experience tuning all types of pianos achieves his desired result without the use of any tools. He is armed with confidence, knowledge, experience, and most importantly, an "ear" for listening to the piano and recognizing when it is in perfect tune. The professional piano tuner did not start out with the knowledge, confidence, or ear he uses in the mastery of his craft; they were acquired through years of practice and dedication. In time the novice piano tuner will lay down his tools and rely on his own experience and developed ear for recognizing the correct notes.

I would like to add a story here that pertains directly to the subject of hearing communication differently or not at all. There have been times that I have clearly heard a live spirit communication during the performance of a live ghost box session. Upon review of the live ghost box session recording, I would reach the part of the recording where I remembered hearing the live spirit communication, and I would either hear something partially or completely different or even hear nothing but the chatter of the ghost box sweep. This would leave me scratching my head.

One incident of this type stands out clearly in my mind, not because it is different than any other incident of hearing live spirit ghost box communication differently, but because I still feel the sting of embarrassment that came with it. I had been contacted by a well-known individual in the paranormal community and asked if I would like to be a featured guest on a paranormal radio show that aired on the internet and enjoyed a major following. This was about six or seven years into my live spirit ghost box communication research career, I felt confident, and I have to admit a tiny bit cocky in my ability as a researcher and practitioner of live spirit ghost box communication. Hell, I was one of its original pioneers, so I agreed to do the show.

One of the radio show hosts emailed me prior to the airing and asked if I would choose one of my audio file examples and send it to him so that it could be played on the live broadcast. I agreed without forethought or hesitation, and this is where I made my big mistake. Instead of doing my due diligence and reviewing the selected audio file before submitting it, so confident in my evidence and research, I just forwarded the audio file to him without a second thought. I had particular confidence in this one audio file. To the best of my knowledge at the time, it contained one of the highest-quality live spirit communications I had ever received. The audio file contained a very specific question by me that entailed a very specific answer. Following the question was a second or two of low ghost box sweep and then a very specific live spirit communication answer that was completely relevant to the question I had posed. Following that, my voice could be heard stating that I had heard the spirit communication live and acknowledging that the answer I received was completely correct and relevant to my question. Like I said, I had all the confidence in the world that this audio example of live spirit ghost box communication would be a jaw-dropper when played during the live radio broadcast.

The radio show aired at eight p.m., and I believe it was on a Saturday night. The show began, and the two hosts went through their opening ritual. I sat at my computer, listening and waiting for the host to introduce me. Like I said, I was confident and secure about my knowledge, experience, and the audio example of live spirit communication I had submitted, but still, I did have some butterflies in my stomach. After all, I was about to be the featured guest on a major radio program listened to by a vast audience.

The time came for the host of the show to introduce me and bring me on live. The host gave a brief detail of who I was and what my accomplishments were in the field of live spirit ghost box communication and introduced me. The interview started off with the usual pleasantries, and as with every other show I had done before, I gave an explanation of how I got started in the paranormal research and investigative field, including how I had discovered and dedicated all my research efforts to live spirit ghost box communication. The radio show, because it was internet based, had a live chat board associated with it where listeners could post comments and questions live. One of the two hosts would monitor the chat room activity and render any questions or comments from listeners at the appropriate time. The show was going smoothly, and I had settled into my comfort zone discussing different aspects of live spirit ghost box communication as well as the paranormal as a whole.

The radio show was intended to be one and a half hours in length, and we were around the thirty-five-minute mark. Up to this point the show had been peppered periodically with questions and comments from listeners via the chat room, and all had gone smoothly for the most part. I had noticed, however, that there were one or two individuals who had posed questions that could be considered on the confrontational side but nothing overt and nothing I could not handle. The show reached the halfway mark, and the hosts announced a five-minute break. During the break, the hosts and I could speak to each other, but the audience heard only music that played while we were on the five-minute break.

When we returned from the break, the hosts announced that they would be playing an audio file of one of the live spirit communications I had captured during a live ghost box session. They asked me to explain what the audio file contained and the circumstances surrounding it. Of course, I had the utmost confidence in this audio example and talked it up like it was the pinnacle of live spirit ghost box communication and was an example of irrefutable actual live spirit communication. The host announced, "Ok, here we go." He stated the description of what the live spirit communication contained in the file was believed to say and proceeded to play the audio file. A second went by, and my voice could be heard addressing a spirit entity and asking a question. Like I said, the question associated with this particular live spirit communication left no room for a vague answer; the answer, to be valid, had to be specific. Everyone listening knew this because I had made a point of stating that fact while setting up the file to be played. As the audio file played, you could hear me finish my question, and then as I sat there expecting this phenomenal live spirit communication response to come booming over the air, all that was heard was the gibberish of the ghost box sweep, which contained a few garbled words that could be mistaken for some attempt at speech. In essence, nothing even resembling human speech was there.

As the audio file continued for what seemed like an eternity, finally my voice could be heard with an excited acknowledgment of the stellar live spirit communication I had just heard. The audio file came to an end, and there was a couple of seconds of silence as I waited for the response of the two show hosts. Of course, being gracious and professional, the two hosts both said, "Wow, great"; then one of the hosts said, "Let's hear that again," hoping that this time would be different. He again uttered the description of what the live spirit communication was supposed to be and replayed the audio file. At the time I think the second rendering of the audio file sounded worse than the first. I must admit I was stunned. I knew what this file had contained; I had listened to it countless times before. I was actually at a loss for words but tried my best to retain my composure. After the repeat playing of the audio file, one of the hosts said graciously, "Yes, I think I heard part of what was described," and turned to the other host, who awkwardly nodded and said, "Yeah, I think I did too." All three of us knew full well that the only intelligible speech in that audio file was my question and final acknowledgment. Being good hosts and professionals, they did not ask me to comment any further on the audio file or its performance and attempted to move on, but no such luck.

Immediately following the double presentation of the audio file, the chat room lit up with activity. Of course, the radio show hosts could not ignore their devoted listeners and were pretty much forced to address their questions and comments. At this point, we were just about at the one-hour mark with a half hour of show remaining. One of the hosts announced that it was time for a break, and upon return, I would take questions and address comments from the chat room. This break was not scheduled. I knew this because I had listened to previous shows in preparation for my appearance. The show's usual protocol had only one break mid show. As soon as we were in the break, one of the hosts said to me, "Bruce, you sounded a bit flustered after we played the audio file, so I thought it might be a good idea to take a break so you could take a few breaths before we address any questions or comments from the chat room." I thanked the two hosts and told them that I had listened to the same audio file that they and their whole audience did and that I did not hear a thing in it that resembled even remotely what could be considered live spirit communication. Before they could respond to me, I thanked them for their consideration and the way they handled the situation and for taking the unscheduled break. I assured them that the questions and comments from the audience when we returned, although some may be uncomfortable, would not be a problem. I also asked that they not cherry-pick any of the questions or comments rendered but to bring them forward so that I could address them. They agreed.

The radio show went back live, and the hosts made a few generic statements and then announced that I would now take questions and comments from the chat room. One of the hosts said, "Ok, Bruce, here is the first question." He gave the name of the person asking the question and then proceeded to state the question posted to the chat room. The first question, of course, pertained to the audio file. I remember these questions vividly, as I do almost every detail of the whole experience, not just because it was an embarrassing incident, but because it was also the first time I had to explain the occurrence of hearing a live spirit communication differently or not at all, and have to do it in a live setting to so many people. The initial question from the listener was "Did you hear the live spirit communication that was described in the audio file live while you were doing the ghost box session?" I did not need time to think about my answer. The truth was, yes, I did, which was the answer I gave. After my answer, the show host asked if I would like to explain. Of course, I did. I went on to explain that at the time of the live ghost box session, I had heard loudly and clearly the live spirit communication that was described in the audio file that was played.

For the next few minutes, I fielded a few more similar questions and a couple of statements, all pertaining to the audio file and its lack of content. All were respectful and non-confrontational, and then the show host, before offering the next comment from the chat room, said to me, "Bruce, I know you asked us to allow you to address all questions and comments. I have one here that is a bit confrontational." I told the host that I would absolutely address it. The host proceeded to read the comment from the chat room, which said, "How could you claim to be an experienced ghost box researcher and describe a piece of your audio evidence stating that it was loud, clear, and unmistakable when the audio file that we heard obviously contained nothing but the noise from the ghost box and no type of speech at all besides your own?" Although stated a bit harshly, I could not argue with the listener's statement. What he said about the audio file example was true. I did, however, take issue with his questioning my experience and validity as an experienced live spirit ghost box researcher. Because this was an internet radio show and all the questions and comments were processed through a chat room, there was no opportunity for a live interaction between the listener and myself, which afforded me the opportunity of a detailed explanation without interruption. I proceeded to explain my theory of how individuals can hear different things when listening to a live spirit communication audio example and how it sometimes occurs that the live spirit communication can disappear from an audio file altogether. The listener accepted my explanation although I'm sure with a grain of salt. The explanation of my theory must have made sense to most of the listeners because comments in the chat room began to pop up stating things like, "Oh yeah, that makes sense" and "Hmm, I never realized that." There were actually quite a few individuals who were live spirit ghost box communication operators who said they had experienced this phenomenon and appreciated the theoretical explanation.

The radio show came to a close after I was able to do some damage control. The hosts thanked me and said even with the hiccup of the audio file, it was a great show and I would be invited back, which I was numerous times. Needless to say, the incident with the audio file on the radio show had left me red faced, to say the least, but this is the nature of live spirit ghost box communication. For all its pitfalls and inconsistencies, it is still a great gift, and I feel privileged to be a part of it.

Chapter 14

Who Are Spirit Technicians, and What Do They Do?

"Spirit technicians" or "techs," who are they, and why are they there? Back at the very beginning when live spirit ghost box communication was in its infancy, I started to do multiple live ghost box sessions daily when I started to realize that the same one or two names would come up numerous times in every session, the names Mike and Lisa. After hearing these two names consistently, I decided to dedicate a number of live ghost box sessions to find out who they were. After quite a few sessions, I was able to piece together all the live spirit communication I had received and came to the conclusion that Mike and Lisa were spirit entities in the spirit realm that aided me in my live spirit communication ghost box sessions. I would come to know Mike and Lisa as the two spirit entities that would always be there to work with me and aid me in my efforts. They helped to facilitate the live spirit communication, and attempted to bring forward any specific spirit person I may have been trying to contact, safeguarded against negative entities or energy that may try to infiltrate the live ghost box session, and also protected the doorway or portal that was inevitably opened when a live ghost box session was being performed.

After formulating this theory of who these special spirit entities were, I performed a series of live spirit ghost box communication sessions in order to try to ascertain the spirit technicians' specific functions and if they needed to be present during every live ghost box session without fail. I found out through the live spirit communication I had received during those ghost box sessions that, yes, they were in essence supervisors, moderators, and keepers of the gate as it were, and that a spirit technician would always be present when a live ghost box session was being performed.

The name "technicians" and my theory of who they were and why they existed stuck and is pretty much widely accepted in the field of live spirit ghost box communication as well as in the paranormal community as a whole. As more individuals began to come into live spirit ghost box communication, Mike and Lisa became technicians to many. After the advent of the hack radio ghost box, live spirit ghost box communication became so flooded with new people interested in doing live spirit communication just going out and getting Radio Shack radios, hacking them, and doing live ghost box sessions. That is when it became necessary for our spirit friends on the other side to enlist the aid of additional spirit technicians in order to cover the load of new live spirit ghost box operators performing live ghost box sessions. This may be the reason why so many new live spirit ghost box operators say that they do not know who their technician is and ask "Do I have a spirit technician?"

Because of the number of live ghost box operators today, there are few permanently assigned spirit technicians. Many are assigned to oversee whatever live ghost box session is in progress and in need of a spirit technician. I call these "facilitating techs" because they do not have a live spirit ghost box communication operator whom they are permanently assigned to. I consider myself one of the lucky ones. I believe that because of my pioneering in live spirit ghost box communication, I still enjoy my close friendship with and the help of my original two spirit technicians, Mike and Lisa, as well as a close association with a few of the more seasoned techs, Tom, Dave, and Peter. All live spirit ghost box communication operators, researchers, and investigators can rest assured that whenever you initiate a live spirit ghost box communication session, there is and always will be a spirit technician present to help and protect you. If you are curious as to which spirit technician you have overseeing a live ghost box session you are performing, just ask, and if possible, you will receive a name. You can then verify if, in fact, they are a spirit technician by asking. Spirit technicians are present to help and protect us as we attempt to interact and communicate live with spirit entities, and I have always found them to be friendly and willing to identify themselves. Always keep in mind that spirit technicians are our friends and have only our safety and best interest in mind as they perform their difficult tasks.

Here is a subject that goes hand in hand with the

previous one. "Spirit technicians and strengthening your bond with them." To address the question of "bonding," do we bond with our spirit technicians? Yes, absolutely, when an operator performs a live spirit ghost box communication session, there is a mutual exchange of energy. There is physical energy that is emitted by us as the physical operator of the ghost box, and there is also spiritual energy that is emitted by the communicating spirit entities we are receiving live communication from, especially the energy connection that is formed between the ghost box operator and the attending spirit technician. These two energies combine to allow for two-way live spirit ghost box communication. I believe that without this energy connection, it would not be possible to perform live spirit ghost box communication. The exchange of energy tends to strengthen over time. The more live ghost box sessions the operator performs, the more the two energies are allowed to develop and grow stronger. This I have found leads to a higher quantity and quality of live spirit communication, a stronger ability to hear spirit communication live in real time during a ghost box session, and a better understanding of the live spirit communication we are receiving and who is delivering it. The bond that I have forged with my spirit technicians Mike and Lisa over the years has continued to strengthen, which has led to the development of a relationship, a friendship. I have come to consider Mike and Lisa as spirit companions whom I have come to rely on for my protection and level of success in live spirit ghost box communication research.

I guess you can refer to a spirit technician as a sort of

spirit guide, but I believe these to be two different types of spirit being. A spirit guide is accepted as an entity that will associate itself with a certain physical individual and will help and protect that specific individual in all paranormal situations. It could and probably does follow the chosen individual in all situations and locations, and can aid in many different things, whereas a spirit technician is a spirit entity that I have only encountered during the performance of a live ghost box session. I believe that the spirit technician's primary task is to protect and help the live spirit ghost box communication operator during the performance of a live ghost box session.

I frequently get asked, "Is it possible to strengthen your bond and connection with your spirit technicians?" The answer is, "Absolutely," through the activity that involves their assistance and protection, live spirit ghost box communication. The bond between a ghost box operator and a certain spirit technician will grow and strengthen with the advent of live spirit ghost box communication sessions. This is possible due to the mutual energy exchange between the operator and the spirit technician, by asking for and accepting their help, protection, and guidance during live ghost box sessions. Think of it as you would a friendship here in the physical. A friendship grows and becomes stronger with time, caring, mutual respect, interaction, and consideration offered mutually during time spent together. These same instances will help the ghost box operator to build and strengthen the bond between themselves and the spirit technicians. In turn, this strengthening of the bond will help to raise the quality of live spirit ghost box sessions and the quantity of the live spirit communication received during the performance of a live spirit ghost box communication session.

The worst mistake that can be made by a ghost box operator and researcher is to disregard or ignore your spirit technicians, which is an all too common occurrence. If you were in the company of a friend, would you ignore them and act as if the friend was not even there or that they were insignificant? To do so would be very insulting and disrespectful and most likely lead to the termination of the friendship. Always acknowledge your spirit technicians during a live ghost box session and let them know you appreciate the work that they perform and the protection they provide for you during your live ghost box sessions. Remember, spirits are people too.

Finally, I would like to explain something that is vital to the success of live spirit ghost box communication but is often overlooked, misunderstood, or simply disregarded. I call this subject, "Respect and consideration are vital for good live spirit communication as well as paranormal research and investigation." Now I would like to address the subject of the way we as live spirit ghost box communication operators, researchers, and investigators conduct ourselves when interacting with the spiritual entities that we contact, interact with, and exchange communication with. First, let me say that this topic does not only concern the field of live spirit ghost box communication but paranormal research and investigation as a whole; however, I will direct my comments here in conjunction with live spirit ghost box communication, as that is my chosen field of expertise.

We, as live spirit ghost box communication operators, being physical human beings, tend to have the ingrained subconscious concept that whatever we cannot see, smell, touch, taste or hear is detached from us and therefore does not seem real. As paranormal researchers and investigators, on the other hand, we approach, investigate, and study ideas and situations that go against that ingrained subconscious concept with an open mind and curiosity that leads us to interact with entities and beings that are not of this physical world, entities that do not readily adhere to those five physical senses we so blindly rely on. Can we see spirit entities? Yes, given the right conditions and circumstances. Can we hear spirit entities? Yes, given the right equipment, conditions, and circumstances. We can also on certain rare occasions even smell a spirit entity or feel temperature changes that are theorized to be in conjunction with the presence of a spirit entity. BUT! If as seekers of evidence and interaction with entities not of this physical world, we are lucky enough to see, hear, smell, or get a chill from an encounter with a spirit entity, the paranormal occurrence we experience does not really meet the inherent criteria of what constitutes those five basic human senses. The paranormal encounter we may be subject to is usually fleeting and open to doubt and interpretation that does not adhere to the solid and unwavering conditions that we believe are necessary to quantify those five rigid physical senses.

To put it in a nutshell, do we as paranormal

researchers and investigators believe that spirit entities exist and that we do have encounters and even coherent and sentient interaction with them? I believe the vast majority of individuals involved in the paranormal community do. This is not counting the rare few individuals who are involved in the paranormal community explicitly to prove those spirit entities and paranormal occurrences do not exist, and can be explained away or debunked by logic and science. For those of us who believe and dedicate our time, effort, and thought to obtaining evidence that helps to further the belief and acceptance of spirit entities and an existence beyond this physical world, my comments here are for you.

As dedicated paranormal researchers and investigators, we have a responsibility not only to ourselves but to the paranormal community as a whole, especially to the entities that we interact with and intentionally seek out and establish communication with. As live spirit ghost box communication operators, or paranormal investigators as a whole for that matter, we are the individuals who seek out, initiate, and supply the means for live contact and communication between ourselves as physical beings and entities that are not of this physical world. In doing so we place ourselves in the position of ambassadors and liaisons between the physical world and the spiritual realm.

I know that there are varying schools of thought on what type of entities we can and do communicate with. For example, some believe we interact with alien beings from other worlds, and some believe we communicate with beings from other dimensions, just to name a couple. Most of us in the paranormal community are open to the possibility of communication and interaction with all types of entities and beings. Then there are some who believe we are only in contact with or interact with entities who are the spirits of deceased human beings who once lived in the physical world and had human lives. I myself believe that we are capable of and do communicate with all types of entities, and some of the evidence I have gathered with live ghost box communication lends validation to that theory. However, I also believe that the majority of our communication and interaction in paranormal research and investigation is derived from contact with the spirits of deceased human beings. It is also my experience and belief based on countless live spirit communication sessions with the use of a ghost box and literally thousands of responses, messages, and answers to questions that have cemented my belief that spirit entities do retain all the feelings, emotions, and intelligence that they developed, accumulated, and experienced while in their physical life. These attributes remain as much a part of the spiritual individual in their spiritual life as they were in their physical existence; therefore, YES, they can and do get insulted, slighted, agitated, and disgruntled. They are subject to fear, love, confusion, jealousy, hate, and the whole myriad of emotions that we in the physical world as human beings experience.

There are those who would say, "Well, there is no way we can prove spirits have emotions and logical thought." To that I must concede there is no way at this moment in time for us as paranormal researchers and investigators to PROVE beyond a shadow of a doubt that is the case, but I can produce hundreds of documented audio examples of live spirit ghost box communications with spirit entities who can personally attest to those traits still being a very real part of that entity's existence. I have communicated with the spirit of loved ones, family, and friends who have crossed to the spirit world and have received live spirit communication messages containing verbal expressions of their love for me and their desire to see me again when I make my transition. I have had countless communications from entities expressing their happiness or sadness, confusion or fear. All of these live spirit communications and interactions have formed and solidified my theories and beliefs. I have two spirit friends whom I call technicians, their names are Mike and Lisa, and they have been with me and aided me in my live spirit ghost box communication practice and research since virtually the day I first turned on a ghost box. I consider them to be not only colleagues but dear friends whom I have come to rely on and have an affection for, and they let me know that those feelings are mutual.

This explanation thus far leads to one very simple but profound point. Any and all individuals who are involved in paranormal research, communication, or investigation will inevitably find themselves in situations where they are interacting with a spirit entity, especially those of us who are dedicated to the verbal exchange of live communication with spirit entities. We must always keep in mind, first and foremost, that we are dealing with the disembodied spirits of former people and not just a random voice in the dark or the fleeting glimpse of a figure. We are interacting with human beings, simply in a different form. Who, as I explained, still have all the emotional and intellectual characteristics that those of us in the physical carry. It simply comes down to the old adage "Do unto others as you would have others do unto you." If you were to interact with a person here in the physical, an acquaintance, friend, loved one, or even a stranger you met on the street, you would afford them the common respect and courtesy that we as human beings have come to rely on as part of a civilized society. When you are in the process of conducting your live spirit ghost box communication session or in the field at an alleged haunted location doing an investigation, keep these simple human qualities in mind as you go about your paranormal research or investigative efforts. Respect, courtesy, and consideration. Always remember a little common courtesy goes a long way.

Chapter 15

Can We Get EVP Messages During a Live Ghost Box Session

Is it possible to capture a traditional EVP (electronic voice phenomena) spirit communication during a live ghost box spirit communication session? The answer is YES.

First, for those of you who are not completely familiar with the method of traditional EVP spirit communication, let me explain the accepted theory on how it is believed to be accomplished. Traditional EVP is captured when the communicating entity manipulates the ambient energy, white noise, and sound that is in proximity to a recording device to form and place words and phrases directly onto the recording medium, be it a digital recorder, tape, cellphone, or even a video camera. A traditional EVP session is conducted by an individual who activates a recording device and allows the device to record while asking questions or making statements. It is an accepted theory by most EVP practitioners that the spirit entity that places the communication during the EVP session is in direct proximity to the recording device being used;

therefore spirit communication from an entity that is in the spirit realm and not in the location of the EVP session and recording device would not be capable of delivering communication as a traditional EVP. A communicating entity will manipulate the energy and ambient sound around the recording device to form the spirit communication and place it directly onto the recording device. Traditional EVP spirit communications are not heard live by the individual conducting the EVP session but discovered later in a review of the session recording.

Also, traditional EVPs are inherently more difficult to discern than the spirit communication captured by, say, a live spirit communication ghost box session. Due to the foundation of white noise, ambient sound, and energy that an entity will use to form and place the EVP spirit communication, a traditional EVP will tend to be more hidden in white noise and therefore more difficult to hear and understand. Live spirit ghost box communication is typically much easier to hear clearly and understand than that of traditional EVP due to the fact that it is largely composed of pieces of actual human speech and therefore does not contain the overabundance of static white noise that a traditional EVP will have. However, it is also believed that the communicating spirit entity can and does also utilize the static white noise inherent in radio broadcast signals, especially those that come from the areas of the radio dial that are between stations and receive no signal. It is believed a spirit entity can use this static noise to help form parts of the live spirit communication that is delivered during a live ghost box session. It is strongly suggested and advised that anyone performing a live spirit communication ghost box session use a recording device to record and capture any and all live spirit communication that was not only heard live during the ghost box session by the ghost box operator, but also any live spirit communication delivered through the ghost box during the session that may have been missed by the ghost box operator.

It has been established over many years of live spirit ghost box communication research that we are only capable of hearing around 25% of the actual delivered spirit communication live in real time during any given ghost box session, which leaves the majority of any live spirit communication that may have been delivered unheard by the ghost box operator during the live ghost box session. That is why it is imperative that any live spirit ghost box communication session be recorded so that the bulk of the live spirit communication that was not heard by the ghost box session operator will have been captured by the recording device and discovered during a review of the live ghost box session recording.

This is where the question of the capability of receiving traditional EVP spirit communication during a live spirit ghost box session comes into play. As I have said, it is possible to receive traditional EVP spirit communication during a live spirit ghost box communication session. Let me explain my theory as to why it is possible. As I explained in describing traditional EVP, the spirit communication is delivered by the communicating entity using the ambient white noise, energy, and sound in proximity to a recording device to form spirit communication and place it directly onto said recording device. That occurrence is exactly what happens when a ghost box operator receives a traditional EVP during a live spirit ghost box communication session. The traditional EVP spirit communication is not being produced by the spirit entity using the ghost box, it is being formed and placed directly onto the recording device that is being used at the time to record the live ghost box session, and therefore is not capable of being heard live but is discovered when the ghost box operator who performed the live spirit ghost box communication session is reviewing the recording of the live ghost box session. It also lends credence to the theory that the spirit entity that delivered the traditional EVP was not communicating from the spirit world or a remote location but was in direct proximity to the live spirit ghost box session and the recording device being used to capture the live ghost box session.

A traditional EVP that is captured in the recording of a live spirit ghost box communication session and discovered upon review of the ghost box session recording is usually immediately apparent in the fact that a traditional EVP capture has a very different and distinct sound that is apparent and set apart from that of a live spirit ghost box communication that was formed and delivered through a ghost box. As I explained earlier in my description of traditional EVP, because it is comprised of mainly white noise and ambient sound and is not delivered through the speaker of a ghost box, it tends to be, for lack of a better word, "hissy" and overpowered by the sound of white noise. EVP spirit communication has a distinctive-sounding quality, whereas live spirit communication formed and delivered with the use of a ghost box, although it may still sound a bit noisy and slightly hissy, can be readily distinguished by its similarity to actual human speech. This is due to the live spirit communication being composed of bits and pieces of actual human speech. When a ghost box operator is lucky enough to capture a traditional EVP during a live spirit communication ghost box session, it is a rare bonus to their efforts as researchers and investigators.

Here is another aspect of live spirit ghost box communication that is of importance. This subject addresses the question of "Presenting live spirit ghost box communication examples to aid in law enforcement or missing person cases, should we?" When we examine the subject of presenting a live spirit ghost box communication in the form of an audio file or recording in an attempt to aid in the furtherance of a criminal investigation and/or missing person case, this is the steadfast rule that I follow as a live spirit ghost box communication researcher and why. When it comes to presenting live spirit ghost box communication audio files to any type of civil authority investigating a crime or pursuing a cold case, a family, or an individual who is in the position of having someone missing or in danger, my rule is to never present any messages, answers, or statements that are received as live spirit communications with the use of a ghost box as a possible clue, lead, or information in such situations. You have to remember that ordinary people who are not familiar with the paranormal or paranormal research and investigation, which is about 99.9 percent, will upon being presented with anything that is even remotely connected with any unorthodox methods or is considered to be paranormal in nature will most likely view it as "hocus-pocus," and the person presenting it is almost always considered to be eccentric or a few cents short of a dollar. There are law enforcement agencies that will in certain situations solicit the help of well-known psychic mediums on occasion in an attempt to garner a lead in a case that is at a dead end, but those instances are extremely rare. I believe that they are only considered due to the fact that psychic mediums have been around and publicized for hundreds of years and are basically more apt to not be looked upon immediately as a joke or some type of farce. Most people when presented with the word "psychic" or "medium" will be somewhat familiar with the term and what it means and therefore be somewhat more accepting. Imagine going to a law enforcement agency or the distraught family of a victim of supposed foul play or a missing person and saying, "Excuse me, but I have information about the case and/or whereabouts of the individual." When asked where and how you came to have this information, you explain that, "A spirit told me while having a conversation through an altered radio." Even explaining the theory and process in a clinical manner will have you immediately dismissed as eccentric and disregarded by the average person and/or civil authority.

I personally made the mistake in my early days of live spirit ghost box communication research of contacting an individual who publicized a family member who was missing and asking for help in locating them. I did a live ghost box session based on the person in an effort to discover their possible whereabouts. I received a live spirit communication that stated, "Under a log," followed by another live spirit communication that said, "In the water." I presented the audio files containing the live spirit communication messages in an e-mail with an explanation of how I received this information. I was immediately dismissed and asked never to contact those individuals again. Three months after presenting the audio examples, the missing person's body was discovered snagged by a dead tree lying at the edge of a lake. Needless to say, I was never contacted by anyone with a confirmation of my information and probably was dismissed so thoroughly that they never even recalled the information I had presented to them.

After this initial incident, I made up my mind that I would in the future refrain from presenting any audio examples and/or information gleaned from a live spirit ghost box communication session to anyone other than fellow live spirit ghost box researchers and/or individuals active within the paranormal community. I believe that someday live spirit ghost box communication will come to the point where we can and will use it successfully in conjunction with public agencies and even judicial agencies to aid in resolving criminal cases and missing person investigations, but that is a very long way off. We, as live spirit ghost box researchers and investigators, need to continue to strive for the day when that can become a reality, but for now, we must be satisfied with our belief that the work we are doing in live spirit ghost box communication as well as all paranormal investigation and research is not only beneficial, but necessary meaningful and respectable.

This next subject is one of utmost importance. It is an act perpetrated by the live spirit ghost box communication operator. "Never leave a ghost box on and running unattended." Throughout my career in the field of live spirit ghost box communication, I have repeatedly heard ghost box operators say, "I just left my ghost box on and running," "I left the ghost box running and recorded it," or, "I turned the ghost box on and went about my household chores." In my opinion and from my experience and also live spirit communication I have received from spirit entities in live ghost box sessions, this is a very big NO-NO!

First, let's address the issue of the lack of common courtesy and disrespect. Because we use a mechanical device to receive live spirit ghost box communication and to make a connection with spirit entities that have no physical form and are not tangible to us, cannot be seen, touched, or smelled, some often tend to associate the live spirit communication we are receiving with the inanimate object we are using to facilitate the communication, i.e., the ghost box. This often happens when we start to gain some time and experience in performing live spirit ghost box communication sessions. An operator can start to lose sight of the fact that the phenomenon we are experiencing is a very special gift to be treated with awe and reverence and not to be taken lightly. When we lose this awareness and become complacent in our practicing of live spirit ghost box communication, we forget that we are allegedly communicating with the disembodied spirits of once living human beings! When we lose sight of this, we start to lose respect and common courtesy for the human beings we are initiating live spirit communication with. This again stems from the unconscious notion that we are communicating with the ghost box itself, an inanimate object, as opposed to the spirits of human beings.

We must never lose sight of the fact that spirit entities were and still are human beings and deserve the same respect and courtesy that would be afforded any living human being here in the physical world. Look at it this way, if you were to telephone a friend, you would not call their phone and, when they answered, just set the phone down and go about some other business, leaving your friend and the telephone connection unattended. This would be an unthinkable act of disrespect and complete and utter disregard for your friend and their feelings. The only difference between the two situations is that after a while your friend could hang up the phone and sever the connection. This cannot be done with a live ghost box session. I will explain why. When you turn on a ghost box, there are not only the spirit entities that will be attempting live spirit communication, but also a spirit technician that must oversee the live ghost box session for however long the ghost box is in operation. When a ghost box is turned on and the connection is made with the spirit realm, the open connection creates a doorway or portal between our two worlds that is needed to facilitate the flow of combined physical and spiritual energy necessary to form and deliver the live spirit communication being sent between our physical world and the spirit world. This open portal or doorway is subject to infiltration by spirit entities that may wish to pass into our physical world. The portal can be used by benign spirits as well as negative ones. This being the case, the doorway needs to be guarded vigilantly, which falls under the responsibility of the spirit technician.

Along with the responsibility of guarding the open portal, the spirit technician must also help other spirit entities to send and receive live communication, and also relay communication if the communicating spirit entity is an earthbound spirit in a distant location. This responsibility of the spirit technician makes it necessary for him or her to stay in attendance of an open live ghost box session no matter how long the session stays in progress. If a ghost box operator keeps this fact in mind when turning on a ghost box, they will surely give the live ghost box session their undivided attention and not leave an individual spirit entity whose sole purpose it is to help in any and all ways "holding the box," as it were.

To sum it all up, the ghost box operator doing the ghost box session should always be diligent and attentive to the live ghost box session, making sure that there is continuous interaction between the ghost box operator and the spirit entities that he or she is communicating with. There is no reason why a ghost box operator cannot devote their utmost attention during the short time it takes to do a live spirit ghost box communication session. Remember, we are communicating with conscious, intelligent, feeling, and emotional entities who deserve our respect and attention, so DO NOT leave a ghost box running and unattended!

The next topic I would like to speak about is of great importance to the success of any and all attempts at live spirit ghost box communication. Let me state emphatically, "Never use a Faraday cage for a live spirit ghost box communication session." This will cover an explanation of the Faraday cage and its use in conjunction with live spirit ghost box communication.

First, a ghost box is a device designed to receive radio broadcasts. The foundation of a ghost box is the radio broadcast signal that it is receiving. Without it, there would be no ghost box sweep and subsequently no building material for an entity to use to form live spirit communication. If a Faraday cage were to be utilized in concert with a live ghost box, it would totally eliminate the reception of any radio broadcast or frequency, therefore rendering the ghost box useless. The object known as a Faraday cage is designed to block any and all outside energy signals and frequencies from reaching any device placed inside it. In essence, it accomplishes the very opposite of what we are trying to achieve, which is the reception of a strong and clear radio broadcast signal in order to operate our ghost boxes and allow them to facilitate live spirit communication.

The idea of using a Faraday cage was first initiated during the days before ghost box communication. It was used as an experiment with traditional EVP in order to determine if a spirit entity could leave a message in the form of an EVP on a recorder without the aid of an ambient energy source. I have not seen any evidence of the success of this experiment. Traditional EVP and live spirit ghost box communication are two totally different things and are achieved using two totally different methods; however, both theories on how the communication is derived are based on the reception of a form of energy, be it a radio broadcast signal for a ghost box or EMF energy for a traditional EVP.

Of course, if you do wish to do this experiment yourself using a ghost box in a Faraday cage, it is a simple thing to build a Faraday cage. As a matter of fact, we all have a ready-made Faraday cage in our homes, a microwave oven. A microwave oven is, in essence, a Faraday cage. If the ghost box operator is so inclined, they can just place a running ghost box into a microwave oven, close the door, and proceed to perform a live ghost box session. I promise you at the end of the live ghost box session performed via a makeshift Faraday cage, any and all live spirit communication or sweep sound for that matter will be nonexistent! Also and I do not know if any of you realize this, a Faraday cage is a completely enclosed box without an open front or any other open area. If any part of the Faraday cage were to be exposed, it would negate the purpose of the Faraday cage in that the open area of the cage would allow for the entry of energy and frequency, thus rendering it a moot endeavor.

This information is especially important for novice live spirit ghost box communication operators becoming familiar with live spirit ghost box communication. Suppose a novice individual interested in exploring live spirit ghost box communication read an article or post about using a Faraday cage during a live ghost box session and decided to implement a makeshift Faraday cage in the performance of a live spirit communication ghost box session because they believed it was the correct thing to do. They would receive virtually no signal and would soon become disappointed with live spirit ghost box communication and walk away from what could have been an enriching and rewarding experience. For all individuals who are in search of information, please do not take anything and everything you read to be accurate. With the free and easy exchange of information available today, anyone, even those who are not as knowledgeable as they could be, can and is posting information online that is misinformation. If you are a novice or have any questions at all, please seek out someone who has a reputation for experience in the area that you are inquiring about and explore more than one avenue of information. This will ensure that you will be receiving the best advice possible, and that will lead to success.

Chapter 16

Are We Communicating With Aliens or Extraterrestrials?

During the first days, weeks, and months of fumbling my way through trying to figure out what this new device that was called a ghost box actually was and what it was capable of, I knew that I was getting coherent communication through the use of the ghost box, and me being a paranormal investigator and researcher for a number of years, I immediately attributed the words and messages I was receiving to be from entities that were the disembodied spirits of human beings. In the beginning, it never dawned on me that the live communication I was receiving could be originating from a source that was not the realm where the spirits of deceased human beings dwelled.

As my live spirit ghost box communication research progressed and I began to formulate solid theories and accumulate information based on information gathered from my daily work with the ghost box, and the live communication received from those live ghost box sessions, the live communication I was receiving became clearer and more detailed. Once I started to understand more and more about how the ghost box worked and I developed a skill for deciphering the relevance and content of the live communication I was receiving, I began to think "outside the box" (no pun intended). At this point, I asked myself the question, "Was I only communicating with the spirits of deceased human beings?" I knew through the study and research of the live ghost box communication I received, and having become familiar with certain individual entities that communicated with me on a consistent basis, that I was in fact communicating with the spirits of deceased human beings, BUT! Were they the only entities I was communicating with?

Before I delve into my opinions and theories, let me say that it is a fact in live spirit ghost box communication that the entities communicating with us seem to carry the same characteristics as humans in the physical world. They will play practical jokes, mislead, embellish and downright lie to us, and I'm sure this is done for a myriad of reasons, the same as it is in the physical world. I have found that entities out of sheer boredom will spin tales and tell ghost box operators exactly what they believe the operator wants to hear, and can even become aware of a subconscious topic and/or question that is being thought of by the ghost box operator and will play upon that to deceive and frustrate the operator, or have it serve to keep the ghost box operator involved in the live ghost box session longer than the operator planned to be. I have personally experienced all of these situations and more in the practice of live spirit ghost box communication research over the years and have received countless reports of other ghost box operators having the same experiences.

The most common experience that will bring the identity of our communicating spirit counterparts into question is when we receive a message or answer to a question that will either directly or indirectly by a deliberate statement or by way of innuendo lead us to contemplate the source of the communication as possibly being alien or extraterrestrial in nature. As a matter of fact, the creator of the first ghost box, the late Frank Sumption, adamantly believed that he was communicating with aliens and believed he himself to be an alien living on this planet, awaiting retrieval or rescue by his alien species. I am not quite sure if Mr. Sumption had come to this conclusion solely through his experience with a ghost box and the communication he received, or if there are other mitigating factors at play, but he was nonetheless convinced that some of the live ghost box communication that is received through a ghost box is alien in nature.

I myself have received numerous live ghost box communications that have led to my questioning whether the source could be extraterrestrial. I have received communication in what could be considered the quintessential alien voice of little green men. I have heard sounds that have mimicked the sound of what I would associate with the sounds a UFO would produce. I have done complete live ghost box sessions on the subject of whether or not alien communication exists and what its origin and purpose would be, and have received live ghost box communication that strongly stated yes, it was from an alien source. On the other hand, I have received live ghost box communication in other ghost box sessions stating emphatically against the communication being extraterrestrial. This type of flip-flop live ghost box communication does, I am sad to say, exist in live spirit ghost box communication. It is common for a ghost box operator to receive completely conflicting answers and statements to a specific subject or questions within the same live ghost box session. This being the case, it is taxing on the part of the live spirit ghost box communication researcher or investigator to be capable of forming a solid arguable theory or opinion on the subject of the origins of live spirit ghost box communication, this subject included, of course. I don't believe that this can be resolved as long as we are restricted to the level of communication we are currently capable of.

Now on to my thoughts and theories as to the possibility of ghost box communication being derived from alien or extraterrestrial sources. I can say with a strong degree of certainty that we do communicate with spirits of deceased human beings. I base this on years of experience as well as countless live spirit communications that answer personal and private questions and adhere to criteria set forth by accepted protocols and guidelines, many of which I am responsible for formulating, as well as live spirit communication I have received from departed friends and family confirming their identities by rendering information only they would know. This has confirmed for me beyond a shadow of a doubt that we are absolutely receiving live communication from the spirits of deceased human beings via a ghost box. That being said, we must ask the questions, "Are spirit entities the only source of live communication that is received with the use of a ghost box?" "Are any of the live communications that lead us to believe they may come from physical beings that are not residents of this planet merely a trick by human spirit entities that have an ulterior motive?" Hmmmmm! Is pretty much the only definitive thing I can say!

Of course, like anything that is supernatural—UFOs, ghosts, vampires, Bigfoot, etc., etc.—there are those who staunchly believe and those who only believe that the believers are missing a few cards from the deck. Whether or not there is a basis for the possibility of alien or extraterrestrial communication through the ghost box is, in the end, a matter of the belief system of the individual live spirit ghost box researcher.

Now, let's delve into this idea. "Is live alien communication possible in any form, including that which comes through the ghost box?" Being a believer in the existence of spirit beings and our capability to interact with them, and given that those beliefs are not commonplace among the masses, I have to say that the possibility of there being alien existence and their ability to deliver live ghost box communication is a tangible possibility.

"Can aliens communicate with us, and are they

communicating with us through the ghost box?" Like I said, there are pros and cons to that question. I have had live ghost box communication that I would serve up if need be as an example of possible extraterrestrial communication, and I do believe that given a race of alien beings was capable of traveling countless light-years through space and possibly time to reach us, or to even send immediate live communication through the vastness of space and time from wherever their point of origin was in the cosmos, it would certainly stand to reason then that they should be capable of delivering that live communication through our crude form of receiver, i.e., a ghost box, and if so, why are they communicating with Bruce Halliday or Jane Doe? Why are they not communicating with the president of the United States or other heads of state. Surely if they were achieving live communication with us, they would want their efforts to be gleaned by our most brilliant and important human beings.

Now let's ask the question "How do they hear us?" In order for the live communication we receive to be relevant and validating, we must receive answers to direct questions or statements that adhere to the subject at hand. This entails the entity sending the live communication in real time as we hear it through the ghost box. Of course, we do not have any broadcasting or audio transmitting devices that are used in live spirit ghost box communication. This fact tells us we have to be heard without the aid of a microphone or other audio transmitting equipment. When we consider live communication that is spirit based, we "assume" that the spirit entity may be present and can hear us or that a spirit entity of astral origin has the energy-based connection with the ghost box operator that allows for the spirit entity to hear us as we speak aloud. This is a theory that can be considered in conjunction with live spirit communication, but how can a race of what we would think of as organic or physical beings be capable of hearing our voice without the aid of some sort of audio transmitting equipment? Do they have the ability to connect with us energetically or telepathically? Do they have the ability to "astral project" themselves to the location where the operator is conducting the live ghost box session? Do they have some sophisticated technology somewhat like our spy satellites that allows them to eavesdrop on us without our knowledge? These are all possibilities that can be considered, but again back to the root of the question: do they exist, can they communicate, are we being tricked, or is this simply our imagination running away with us?

Let's consider the circumstances, weird noises that are reminiscent of alien sounds, answers, statements, and messages that will on occasion directly pertain to the live communication as being alien in origin. These factors will take us on a path to considering the possibilities of live alien communication through the ghost box and most likely lead to frustration as we get no closer to the truth than when we started. Considering this outcome, did we fall victim to a spirit entity practical joker, was it the demented pleasure seeking of a less than benevolent spirit entity, or just a way to garner continual and future attention by a spirit entity through our continued live ghost box communication? Sorry to say that these questions not only pertain to the question of possible extraterrestrial communication but actually all our live spirit communication at this point in time. We can surmise, analyze, research, and theorize, but truthfully as it stands, the outcome to the question "Are we communicating with aliens?" is a frustrating, "Six of one, half dozen of the other."

I tried to touch briefly on the question of possible reception of live alien communication through live spirit ghost box communication. I have many other theories that I have formulated and documented through research and gathered spirit information that has explored the possibilities of sources for live spirit ghost box communication, like telekinesis, cerebral manifestation, contact with other physical dimensions, and contact from the future, just to mention a few. For now, I will just submit this explanation as to my ideas and opinions on an alien or extraterrestrial source of live communication through the ghost box.

There is another topic I would like to discuss that entails prophetic or prediction messages of live spirit ghost box communication. I often get this question: "Can we get live spirit communication about the future, and how much are spirit entities allowed to tell us?" This is a question that has taken me some time to receive the answer to. The answer was delivered to me through many live spirit ghost box communication sessions in quite a few parts. The incident itself can contain many variables, but the rule is steadfast and staunchly adhered to. Throughout the years I have attempted to get an answer to this question, "Are spirit entities allowed to give us information regarding future events?" The short answer to this question, which I have received straight from the spirit's mouth, is "NO!" I have performed countless live spirit ghost box communication sessions that were either dedicated to or contained questions of whether or not a communicating spirit entity was able to deliver live spirit communications that contained information on future events, or messages that pertained to important current events. I have come to understand through live spirit communication received during many live ghost box sessions that any and all spirit entities that are capable of communicating live with human beings that are still in the physical existence have very strict conditions and restrictions that need to be adhered to when delivering live spirit communication to physical human beings in the performance of a live ghost box session. During the many years of gathering information from my spirit counterparts as well as my trusted spirit technicians Mike and Lisa, I have not only been able to acquire definitive yes and no answers to specific questions, but I have been given the courtesy of an explanation as to why it is forbidden for them to administer any live spirit communication that would be of a prophetic nature.

The consensus I have reached is the culmination of many, many hours of live spirit communication and is as follows. The spiritual realm and existence as far as time, space, and consciousness are completely foreign to and separate from the physical world. Time in the spirit realm is not linear as we perceive time here in the physical. Time in the spirit world does not move continuously in a fluid forward motion; therefore it is not subject to the same constraints that we must adhere to in the physical world. As far as I could understand, if we were capable here in the physical world to see time from one point to another, it would look as if we were watching a moving train or automobile that left point A at 12:00 and reached point B at 12:15. If we could witness the whole journey from point A to B, we would be witness to the journey in a straight and uniform motion viewing it in a linear fashion; each increment of the journey would be in a straight forward moving motion. In the spirit realm, time is fluid and fluctuating; in essence, it is not time at all as we perceive it. As it was explained to me by my spirit communicators, the way a spiritual entity is aware of time is just that, a sense of awareness. In other words, we in the physical world can actually feel time; it is an integral part of everything we do. We are not only consciously aware of time here in the physical, such as time to go to sleep, time to wake up, time to go to work, and time to pick the kids up from soccer practice, etc. We are also unconsciously aware of time, our internal physical clocks react to the hours in a day, sunrise to sunset, the changing of the seasons, the unconscious ever-changing effects of aging, and the impending realization that time is running out on our physical existence.

When a spirit entity perceives what we would think of as time, it is in a sort of dream state, the interaction with other spirit beings, the awareness of eternal existence with no beginning and no end. Their perception of time is as if you were floating in outer space. You would be aware that you were in the midst of a vast infinite void with no parameters or borders to let you know where it began and where it ended, but you would still be aware of space itself. Time in the spirit realm, because it is not linear and in a constant state of forward motion, can be experienced by a spirit entity in the past, present, and future, sort of a crystal ball of existence. Because this is the reality in the spirit world, there are times when an entity can view past events and also be aware of events that will take place in the future while constantly existing in their own present. I know this is a bit deep and hard to follow, but this is basically how I have come to understand it through the live spirit communication I've received.

As far as the constraints imposed upon a spirit entity who attempts and succeeds at communicating with an individual here in the physical world, because they may have knowledge of some future event that will affect an individual or even mankind as a whole, the communicating entity is bound by strict regulations and restraints regarding the type of information that can be distributed to an individual in the physical world. It is akin to "the butterfly effect" when discussing time travel. For example, if a communicating entity was to tell the ghost box operator here in the physical world the time and/or date of that individual's death or that of a close friend or family member, most assuredly the individual here in the physical now possessing that knowledge would alter any circumstances that would bring about the foretold event, thereby altering its outcome and the outcome of countless events that would have led up to or followed the specific event. This, I have been told, would be catastrophic for mankind as a whole and could possibly alter the course of events for the future of the entire world.

During my many years of live spirit ghost box communication and after receiving countless messages from spirit entities in the spirit realm, I have had instances where I have received live spirit communications warning me of an impending disaster or ensuing health concern. I was even told at one time the exact date of my death. I am happy to report that none of the prophetic messages I received have come to fruition thus far. When I questioned my spirit technicians Mike and Lisa about this, I was told that those types of messages are communicated by spirit entities that are untruthful and negative in manner. I was assured that if the spirit entity sending those types of messages was a legitimate communicating spirit entity, it would be the last time I or anyone else would receive any live spirit communication from that specific spirit entity.

Throughout my whole career in live spirit ghost box communication, I have received only one message of an event that was at the time yet to be publicly known by anyone that actually came to pass. Quite a few years ago now, I received a random live spirit communication during a live spirit ghost box communication session while using an old Joe's Box, which, by the way, at the time was new. The live spirit message was as follows, "Patrick Swayze critical danger." When presented by me, the message was confirmed by other live spirit ghost box communication operators and researchers who concurred that the message did say what I claimed it said. Shortly after that, maybe two or three weeks later, there was a public announcement made in the media that Patrick Swayze had an advanced form of cancer, which consequently led to his death. This was the only instance where I had ever received a live spirit communication pertaining to a situation that was not at that time known to anyone but Mr. Swayze and people close to him. However, it can be argued that this was not a spirit communication predicting a future event but the case of a spirit entity that was aware of Patrick Swayze's existing condition and spilling the beans to me before the news broke to the public. This is the most likely scenario. This would explain why I was permitted to receive this information, due to the fact that Mr. Swayze's condition was already existing, and the information I received in a live spirit communication would and could not alter that fact or interfere with any future events.

In conclusion, any and all communication we receive from sources not of the physical world are subject to constraints, and any messages or answers we may receive as a live spirit communication that are to the contrary should be taken with a grain of salt and not considered a valid prediction or warning of things to come.

The final subject I would like to touch on in this chapter deals with the topic "Do communicating spirit entities know if we receive their communication?" I recently received a live spirit communication during the ghost box session where the communicating spirit entity asked, "Do you hear me?" This simple spirit question started me thinking about a question I myself and am sure other live spirit ghost box communication researchers and investigators have not thought to ask. When spirit entities are sending us live spirit communication during a live ghost box session, are they aware of our receiving their live communication if we do not acknowledge hearing it verbally, as in repeating what we have heard live?

Through my years in live spirit ghost box communication research and practice, I have been able to arrive at the conclusion that, given the current equipment and abilities of the operators in the live spirit communication field, we are only capable of hearing approximately 25% of the communication sent and received in any given ghost box session live as it is delivered. Of course, the percentage varies with conditions at the time of the live ghost box session, but on average it is around 25%. Therefore approximately 75% of the delivered and received live spirit communication is missed and not heard live during the performance of the live ghost box session. Of course, even a novice ghost box operator knows that you should never do a live spirit ghost box communication session without recording it, and that upon review of the ghost box session recording, if diligent enough, the ghost box operator will discover the majority of whatever live spirit communication was delivered through the device. So the question stands; are communicating spirit entities aware of our receiving a specific message and/or answer sent if we do not render a verbal confirmation by repeating aloud what we heard immediately upon hearing it during the live ghost box session?

Let's examine a couple of accepted theories that

research and experience by many valid ghost box researchers has led us to. We accept that the spirit entities we interact with during a live ghost box session can hear our verbal speech when we speak aloud. The fact that we receive live spirit communication in the form of answers and statements to specific questions and topics that we physically verbalize leads us to that belief, but what happens when we miss the majority of the delivered communication, and in doing so do not physically verbalize an acknowledgment of hearing said live spirit communication?

There are some researchers, investigators, and ghost box operators who believe the spirit entities we communicate with have the ability to receive our thoughts and feelings. Let me first say that it is a very, very common occurrence in a live spirit ghost box communication session where the ghost box operator will think that they heard a certain word or phrase of live spirit communication, but will only retain it as a momentary thought and not render a verbal confirmation due to the fact that the alleged live spirit communication was not clear or precise enough to make an on-the-spot decision as to what exactly was heard. Given these instances of split-second thought that very well may be retained subconsciously by the ghost box operator, is the communicating spirit entity aware of the ghost box operator's subliminal receipt of the live spirit communication, and therefore satisfied that their live spirit communication was received, or in the event that the communicating spirit entities are not capable of reading our thoughts, believe that their message and/or answer went unheard by the ghost box operator, resulting in frustration for the communicating spirit entity, which may lead to them stopping any further attempts at communicating.

In the live spirit communication I mentioned at the beginning of this subject, which was delivered to me by a spirit entity in a recent live ghost box session, "Do you hear me?" I was not able to hear live as it was delivered by the spirit entity; consequently I discovered it in the review of the ghost box session recording, which was a couple of days later. What was the conclusion made by the communicating spirit entity at the time? Did the spirit entity wonder if the message got through? Did the spirit entity ponder whether the ghost box operator in the physical heard the message? Did the ghost box operator choose to ignore the live spirit communication and not respond? All questions I would ask if I were the spirit entity and attempted to speak directly to someone and was completely ignored. It may be a good practice during the review of the recording from a live spirit ghost box communication session if we, as responsible researchers and operators, try to keep this in mind, and upon finding live spirit communication in the session recording we did not hear during the live ghost box session, we verbalize the live spirit communication found in the recording aloud as a post-session acknowledgment of hearing and receiving the communication that our spirit friends work so hard to send us.

Let's examine some of the other theories of whom we may be communicating with. There are other theories that have been discussed among live spirit ghost box researchers, investigators, and operators that pertain to the subject of who we are communicating with during a live spirit ghost box communication session. These theories entail the "alternate/parallel universe" theory and the "other dimensions" theory. These theories entertain the possibility of a live spirit ghost box operator making contact with and receiving live communication from beings that reside in another dimension or possibly another universe separate from our own.

This theory is intriguing in a number of ways. Firstly, let's examine the idea of communicating with beings from another dimension. It has been suggested that a part of the live communication that is received during a live ghost box session is not entirely comprised of messages delivered to us by the spirit entities of deceased human beings who once had physical lives here on Earth in our reality, but that there is some live communication that is being delivered during a live ghost box session that is being formed and sent through the ghost box beings that reside in a dimension that is separate from ours. There has been speculation by some that these other-dimensional beings are physical beings like ourselves; the only difference is that they reside in a different dimension. Of course, this is pure speculation due to the fact that at this point there is no way to prove the existence of any type of being other than a physical human being here on Earth, let alone the existence of other-dimensional beings. It is, however, proposed by some that there are beings in other dimensions that can pierce the barrier between their dimension and ours and use the live ghost box in session to form and deliver live communication to the ghost box operator.

I personally am not a subscriber to the other-dimensional theory; however, in the interest of research, I have posed questions pertaining to this topic in live ghost box sessions I have performed. To date, I have yet to receive any live communication, spirit or otherwise, that confirms this theory one way or the other. My personal opinion on the other-dimensional theory is that if live ghost box communicators were receiving communication, myself included of course, from beings in another dimension, a live ghost box operator at some point would have received some piece of live communication that would pertain to this theory either confirming or denying it. Any such live communication if received, of course, would have absolutely no means of verification by the ghost box operator, since live spirit ghost box communication as it stands now has not reached that level of sophistication. The live spirit ghost box communication researcher, investigator, and operator of today can barely validate the live communication that is delivered by spirit entities that must consist of specific answers to questions or details of a topic that can be verified by the operator here in the physical world.

Let's examine the alternate/parallel universe theory. Much like the other-dimension theory, this idea entails receiving live communication from entities that exist in an alternate/parallel universe from our own. Let's define both types of universes pertaining to this theory. The first is an alternate universe. This is a universe that is theorized to be situated in a different dimension of space and time than the real world experienced by human beings. The second is a parallel universe. This is a universe that is a separate universe that coexists with our known universe but is very different. There are individuals who practice live spirit ghost box communication who believe that part of the live communication that is received by the ghost box is delivered from an alternate or parallel universe, delivered by beings that are similar to human beings. If an individual were to subscribe to this theory, he or she would have to ask, are the beings inhabiting these alternate/parallel universes human beings like us? If they are human, do they have a spirit? Does their spirit entity go to an alternate/parallel spirit world? If they do have a spirit realm where their spirit entity goes after death, are we receiving communication from the beings in the alternate/parallel universe, or are we receiving live communication from the spirits of those beings in the alternate/parallel universe? All questions are to be carefully considered if you are to subscribe to the alternate/parallel universe theory. Knowing live spirit ghost box communication as well as I do and knowing how painstaking it can be to research a specific topic pertaining to live spirit communication and the, who, what, where, and how we obtain it, I am glad I do not subscribe personally to this particular theory. I would not look forward to trying to obtain information about the alternate/parallel universe theory based on live communication received via the ghost box.

There is one other theory that pertains to the origins of the live spirit communication we receive, the "cerebral theory." This theory considers the possibility that the live communication that a ghost box operator receives during the performance of a live ghost box session is emitted telepathically from the ghost box operator's mind and is, in fact, the thoughts of the individual performing the live ghost box session. These thoughts are received by the ghost box and transformed by way of telepathic and cerebral energy into coherent, audible, and intelligible words of live communication that are then delivered through the ghost box and heard live in real time by the ghost box operator who subliminally sent them. It is further offered by the theory that this action can account for the instances where a live ghost box operator will receive answers to specific questions before asking the question out loud. It is stated in the theory that because the ghost box operator is aware in their mind of the specific answer to the questions they intend to ask, the answers are sometimes cerebrally delivered through the ghost box before the ghost box operator has had a chance to verbalize them. The theory further states that because the ghost box operator already mentally retains the information, he or she will seek validation through live communication; the attempt to validate the live communication received in the live ghost box session is moot and therefore inadmissible. Because live spirit ghost box communication, like all other fields in paranormal research and investigation, cannot as yet produce "proof" of the evidence and data that is gathered, it gives rise to the formulation of all manner of theoretical thought and conjecture.

Until it is possible for paranormal research and

investigation to provide irrefutable proof of the evidence that is gathered, who can say who is right, or who is wrong. We in the paranormal research and investigative fields must strive to view with an open mind the theories that abound in our chosen endeavor to find the truth, and continue to work for the day when we can offer the world that irrefutable proof.

Chapter 17

Is It better To Use One Ghost Box, The Effect Imprinting Has on Communication

I have always noticed through my time in the field of live spirit ghost box communication that there are some live spirit ghost box communication researchers and ghost box operators who like to collect and use as many models of ghost boxes as they can, continually rotating different ghost boxes for each live spirit ghost box communication session they perform. I would like to address this subject and offer my opinion as to why it is more beneficial for the operator to choose a single ghost box to do the bulk of his or her live spirit ghost box communication sessions as opposed to using many different ghost boxes.

After many, many live spirit ghost box communication sessions, gathering information from other live spirit ghost box researchers and investigators over the years, and information delivered by spirit entities through the ghost box, I have come to believe that because of the act of supplying communication between our world and the spirit world, and the exchange of mutual energies between the physical ghost box operator and the communicating spirit entities that occurs when a ghost box is in session, the ghost box acts as sort of a sponge, for lack of a better term, soaking up the energy emitted by the physical and cerebral energy of the ghost box operator conducting the live ghost box session. Any given ghost box, the more it is used, will continue to absorb and retain this energy. I call this process "imprinting." It happens when a ghost box operator uses a particular ghost box often enough for their personal energy signature to become part of the ghost box's energy signature. In turn, a ghost box that has an operator's imprint on it is more easily recognizable by our spirit friends on the other side, especially our spirit technicians. This familiar energy will make the bond between the ghost box operator and the communicating entities stronger and will allow for better and stronger live spirit communication.

A ghost box that has been imprinted with the energy signature of the ghost box operator acts as a calling card that allows the operator to be recognized as someone familiar and trustworthy by the spirit entities attempting to communicate. I believe that using a particular ghost box frequently and allowing yourself to imprint on said ghost box will definitely help you in receiving higher quality, larger quantity, and more frequent communication, as well as helping to strengthen the bond between you and the spirit entities you're communicating with. A certain amount of live spirit communication will exist no matter what ghost box you decide to use; your spirit technician will be there to assist you in sending and receiving communication. That being said, I do believe that using a ghost box that has been imprinted and has a familiar energy signal can and does allow for a better exchange of the ghost box operator's energy and that of the communicating spirit entity's energy, which allows it to flow easier and stronger, thereby strengthening the live spirit communication and allowing it to be received more effectively. You can always use different ghost boxes, of course, but as far as having a stronger and better exchange of communication during a live ghost box session, I believe using a ghost box that you have imprinted on will definitely be more beneficial.

I have owned and used almost every type of ghost box that has ever been hacked or built. At the time of this writing, I only own four: two hack radio ghost boxes and two custom-built ghost boxes. I have one particular ghost box that I use almost exclusively, and I have come to rely on it to give me the best live spirit communication sessions I can achieve. I attribute this to two things. One, it is a quality built ghost box, and more importantly, I believe that because I have imprinted so deeply on this particular ghost box, it allows for a superior flow and exchange of energy and thus produces the best conditions for live spirit ghost box communication. Many people believe that the ghost box is simply a tool to be used in an effort to elicit spirit contact. My belief, which stems from many years of research and experience, is that the ghost box is not only a tool, but a conduit that has its own distinct energy that allows for the exchange and melding of our physical energy and that of the spirit entities we are communicating with. The imprinting process that is achieved over time between a particular ghost box and its operator is in my opinion crucial to the advancement and success of live spirit ghost box communication.

Whenever I discuss this subject, someone invariably asks the question "If I use many ghost boxes, won't they all become imprinted?" The short answer is yes, but think of it this way: if you were thirsty and wanted a glass of water, would you take ten glasses and fill them one-tenth full and drink from all ten glasses when you could fill one glass and quench your thirst in a much better and more productive way? I am not suggesting that all live spirit ghost box communication operators and researchers limit themselves to one single ghost box indefinitely. Of course there are times when the ghost box operator is faced with immediate existing conditions and must choose a ghost box that will allow for the best reception and operation in a particular area and situation. My suggestion is that, if circumstances allow, use a specific ghost box as often as possible to allow that given ghost box to imprint your energy signature and thereby afford you the best live spirit ghost box communication possible.

I would now like to discuss and explain a theory that I have formulated based on my observations on the progression of combined physical and spiritual energy during the performance of a live spirit ghost box session. I call this subject "energy phase transitions in a live ghost box session and how they affect live spirit ghost box communication."

After many years of performing live spirit ghost box

communication sessions, I became aware of an occurrence that took place during the performance of a live ghost box session that followed a certain transition. This transition directly affected the quantity and quality of the live spirit communication I received and my ability to hear it live in real time during the ghost box session. Of course, there are many factors that come into play during a live ghost box session, such as energy exchange, box imprinting, quality of radio broadcast signal, and the ability and willingness of our spirit friends on the other side to attempt and complete the delivery of live spirit communication. These are just a few of the factors that need to come together to perform a successful live ghost box session.

Taking all these variables into account, I still began to notice a pattern in how prevalent, clear, and valid the live spirit communication was at any given time during the session. I started to document this pattern and pay careful attention to the time evolution in a live ghost box session as it pertained to the abundance and quality of live spirit communication, and the ability for me to hear said live spirit communication live as it was delivered. After many live ghost box sessions and due diligence, I arrived at the conclusion that a live ghost box session will and does in essence follow an energy progression and decline during its duration. A live spirit ghost box session, whether it be a controlled session in a place such as a home, or conducted out in the field during a paranormal investigation or event, will follow a basic transition of progression and decline.

This transition will begin, of course, when the ghost

box is turned on and the session is initiated. At the onset of the live ghost box session, the energy level and its flow between ourselves and our astral counterparts will be at a minimum. As the ghost box session progresses and we start to ask questions or make statements and receive the beginnings of live spirit communication, usually in the form of one-or-two-syllable words, this will be an indication that the energy levels in the session are at a low stage due to the live ghost box session just beginning. As the ghost box session progresses, so does the amount and strength of the energy flow. You can now start to discern a noticeable change that occurs in the quantity and quality of the live spirit communication. You will begin to hear more spirit communication live as it is delivered, and it will come in closer proximity to your questions or statements. The ghost box session is now on the upswing of the transition. This will be noticeable if the ghost box operator is paying attention to the time progression of the live ghost box session. You will notice that this rise in energy usually occurs within the first five minutes of the ghost box session. Of course, these times are not by any means carved in stone, remembering all the other factors that come into play during a live ghost box session.

As the live ghost box session matures, you will reach a point of "optimum" communication. This is the point in the ghost box session where the energy synchronization and flow are usually at their peak. This is the time when it is possible for the ghost box operator to receive the best live spirit communication of the session. This peak transition usually occurs at around nine to eleven minutes into the session. After this peak, the session will begin its decline. By decline I mean it's a downward transition. As you continue, you will begin to notice a drop off in the quantity and quality of the live spirit communication. This may or may not be readily apparent during the session, as we do hear only a limited amount of communication live in real time, but it will become more noticeable in the review of the ghost box session recording, where you can follow the live spirit communication more accurately.

Actually, you will be more aware of these transitions in the ghost box recording review overall. As the session continues to follow this downward transition, the communication will become less and less, and it will eventually fade to almost being nonexistent. This usually occurs around the twenty-minute mark. This is not to say the live spirit communication will stop completely, but it will return to the one-or-two-syllable communications that we hear at the beginning of a session, which will come farther and farther apart as you let the live ghost box session continue. Think of it as your cellphone losing power. It will start to work slower, and its performance will be at a bare minimum as the battery power lessens. When it reaches a certain point, it will shut down completely, but if you let it rest a minute, you will still be able to turn it on for a few more seconds. The same premise applies here. The live spirit communication will not stop completely, but will get to the point where you will hear nothing but low-quality attempts. This is an indication that the energy of the session has been drained.

I have determined that the optimal time for a live

ghost box session to run should be ideally fifteen to twenty minutes, and at that point should be terminated. This time frame will allow for the best and most productive live ghost box session and also show a sign of caring and respect for the spirit entities that work so hard to deliver that live spirit communication to us. We need to remember as physical beings our communication being sent to our astral friends is in the form of physical speech relying mainly on our physical processes to create and deliver said speech. The amount of energy expended by us is very minimal. On the other hand, our spirit counterparts are relying upon their spiritual energy in combination with our physical energy to form and deliver their live spirit communication through a device that is not in their realm but in our physical world. If you think about it, the drain on the communicating entity's energy must be very strong. This has led me to the conclusion that, like batteries, our astral friends' energy is limited, and once exhausted, they lose the ability to form and deliver any form of quality live spirit communication.

I have decided to call this theory "energy phase transition." I believe it helps us to better understand how and why a live spirit ghost box communication session performs the way it does. It also allows us as ghost box operators to be aware of and considerate to our spirit friends on the other side when performing a live spirit ghost box communication session.

To end this chapter I would like to explain my belief on the subject of "What causes a drop-off or dry spell in live spirit ghost box communication?" which is a period of time that occurs when there is a lack of any substantial live spirit communication during the performance of live ghost box sessions. For those of you who are wondering why at times a live spirit communication ghost box operator will lose the quantity and quality of live spirit communication that has been achieved and enjoyed over time and suddenly have the live spirit communication that the operator is accustomed to, for lack of a better word, "DIE" (pun intended), here is my theory on dry spells in the overall reception of live spirit ghost box communication that I have experienced over the years.

All live spirit ghost box researchers, investigators, and operators at some point or another get a lull in live spirit ghost box communication. I have formed a theory as to why a live spirit ghost box communication operator will experience periods of time where there is a decline in the live spirit communication that occurs during a live ghost box session. I have based my theory on information I have received in live spirit communication from spirit entities when addressing this problem in live ghost box sessions. From what I have learned, the combined energy we build with our spirit counterparts in the spirit realm and the spirit technicians that oversee our ghost box sessions goes into a state of fluctuation for indeterminate periods of time. These fluctuations will tend to drain the mutual energy connection we establish during a live ghost box session and affect the communicating spirit entity's ability to form and deliver live spirit communication.

Live spirit communication is not solely dependent simply upon the ghost box and an adequate radio broadcast signal. Its success is also based upon the equal transference of mutual energy between the ghost box operator and the communicating spirit entities. When there is a disturbance in the harmony of this mutual energy exchange, my belief is said disturbance causes a decline in live spirit communication. This decline in live spirit communication is not because our spirit friends on the other side are bored with a certain ghost box operator, or are upset with an individual for whatever reason. I find that if there is a disgruntled spirit entity, said spirit entity will usually voice their concerns through live spirit communications until they are satisfied that we are aware of the problem and understand it.

These drop-offs are nothing to be overly concerned about. They usually last only a short time. The trick is to continue your live ghost box sessions in spite of the lack of communication, and to approach each session with the most positive attitude and emotions that you can muster. In live spirit ghost box communication, having a positive attitude and good karma is essential to successful communication as well as being a deterrent to any negative entities or energy that may wish to sabotage your live spirit communication. Like many things in life, positive begets positive, and negative will attract negative. I find that a positive attitude and minimal amount of frustration during a ghost box session will help to produce satisfactory results and aid in the fluidity of energy exchanged, thereby creating the most optimal conditions for good live spirit communication.

Believe me, I understand how frustrating it can be to have high expectations for a live ghost box session and devote time and effort to the session only to have it produce little or no communication. With a high level of frustration comes negative emotions, thoughts, and feelings that serve to make the existing problem worse. Think of negative energy as something you are not supposed to throw down a drain. At the beginning, the drain is clear, and the water flows easily down the drain. Now you scrape your dinner dishes into the sink and allow the leftover food scraps to go down the drain, inevitably clogging it and restricting the flow of water. The water will not flow easily down the drain again unrestricted until the clog is removed. The energy exchange during a live ghost box session is the drain and the water flowing easily through it; the negative energy is the scrapings that clog that drain, stopping the flow of energy and impeding the free flow of live spirit communication. I realize that everyday life can tend to frustrate and irritate even the calmest person, and that it is easier said than done to curtail that negative energy, but believe me, if you want to get your live spirit ghost box communication back on track, try not to scrape any negativity down the proverbial ghost box drain. Positive energy begets positive energy and positive results. Take it from someone who has experienced more than their fair share of dry spells.

Over the years I have performed more than one live spirit ghost box communication session in search of answers pertaining to imprinting and the benefits of using one or two chosen ghost boxes as opposed to using a plethora of different ghost boxes randomly for live spirit ghost box communication sessions. When I recall the various live ghost box sessions I have done regarding this subject, one in particular always stands out in my mind. I was not very long into my live spirit ghost box communication research when I began to become aware of the difference in live ghost box session success when I used a certain ghost box over others. As I considered this awareness, I decided to devote a whole live ghost box session to attempt to gather information and confirm my suspicions that devoting a majority of live ghost box sessions to one specific ghost box was beneficial. Of course, at the time I had not yet begun to realize just how important it was.

I gave the matter some serious thought over a couple of days and proceeded to construct a series of questions that I would ask my spirit technicians and any spirit entities willing to aid in the success of a live ghost box session dedicated to this subject. When I was satisfied with the questions I had and confident that I would be able to gather the information I needed, I sat down to perform the intended live spirit ghost box communication session. I, of course, grabbed my favorite ghost box, which I used more than any other for my daily live ghost box sessions, and proceeded to fire it up. With the list of questions in front of me, I called out to my trusted spirit technicians Mike and Lisa, asking for confirmation from them that they were in attendance and willing to help with the session. I received my response from both of them, which I heard live in real time, confirming that they were there and ready to go.

I spoke my first question. "Mike, Lisa, can you help me with information about using a certain ghost box?" Looking back, I realize the question was not very succinct. I was still feeling my way around this subject, so my initial questions lacked pinpoint accuracy. However, my spirit technicians got the gist of the question and answered it with a "Yes." My next question consisted of why it seemed that I had better success in a live ghost box session when I used one ghost box over another. I remember the response they delivered vividly: "Energy." Luckily, I was able to hear this response live and repeated it out loud. This response forced me to inject an additional question into my list of questions. Very often it is necessary for the ghost box operator who is performing the live ghost box session to adapt on the fly to circumstances and pieces of live spirit communication that arise during the course of the live ghost box session. My next question was now, "What do you mean by energy?" The answer to this question, delivered by Mike, my spirit technician, was "Together."

Before I go any further, let me take a moment to address a question you may have at this point. For those reading this who are not very familiar with or new to live spirit ghost box communication, I'm sure you can see here I was receiving short one-word answers to my direct questions. I am assuming that it is obvious that the majority of the live spirit communication we receive must be scrutinized by the ghost box operator, not only during the live ghost box session but also in the review of the session recording. More often than not, the live spirit communication received in a live ghost box session is, let's say, for lack of a better word, cryptic. This is not to say that our spirit entity friends are not capable of delivering more precise and lengthy live communication; on occasion they most certainly are. I have received answers to questions and statements of live spirit communication that have been in full sentences of more than ten words. However, we must remember that the formation and delivery of live spirit ghost box communication is not an easy task. A live spirit communication consisting of enough words to complete a sentence is rare and requires optimum and precise conditions to be accomplished by the delivering spirit entity. Therefore the majority of live spirit communication is sent in short bursts consisting, on average, of two, three, or four words. This is done intentionally by the delivering spirit entity.

Think of it like this: suppose someone was talking, and in mid sentence, if you were to place your hand over their mouth and muffle the words in the middle of the sentence they were speaking, and then removed your hand, allowing them to emit the last two words of the sentence, of course, to anyone hearing the spoken sentence, it would be incomplete and therefore not make very much sense. It is the same with live spirit ghost box communication. If the communicating spirit entity were to begin to deliver a full sentence of live spirit communication and the conditions and operation of the ghost box stifled the middle two or three words of that sentence, whether it was heard live during the ghost box session or discovered in the review of the session recording, it would probably make little sense and leave the ghost box operator scratching their head. I believe this is why the majority of the live spirit communication we receive is deliberately delivered in short bursts containing two or three pertinent words that will allude to a specific answer or response without losing any of the vital core meaning. Because of this, the ghost box operator must put on his or her Sherlock Holmes hat and attempt to decipher and make sense of the delivered live spirit communication as it pertained to a specific question or statement.

Now that I have rendered that explanation, allow me to get back to the original story. Ok, where was I? Oh yes, "Together." I was not able to hear this response live, but discovered it later in the review of the session recording, which, of course, prompted me during the live session to ask the question over again. This, by the way, I'm sure, becomes very tedious to our spirit entity friends, but is, unfortunately, an occupational hazard in live spirit ghost box communication. After repeating the previous question, I received a response that I was able to catch live in real time. It was, "Box has energy." I immediately repeated the three-word phrase upon hearing it live, and paused for a second to allow this response to sink in. I realized that because it was still relatively early in the live ghost box session, I had to maintain focus in order to be able to hear as much of the spirit communication as I could live. It was not the time to pause and reflect on the live spirit communication I had already heard, especially since the live ghost box session had only been running for about five or six minutes.

I glanced down at my list of remaining questions, realizing that the answers and responses I had already received and heard live made my next two questions redundant. I scanned down the question list and came to my next question, keeping in mind the live spirit communication already received caused me to restructure the next question. My next question was "Does the quality of live communication have to do with the operator, the ghost box, or both?" I waited quite a few seconds listening intently for a response from my spirit technicians and/or spirit entity communicators. I was just about to ask the same question for a second time when I heard a live spirit communication come through with the answer, "Yes, two, together." I was able to hear the first and last word of the live spirit communication and asked, "Did you say two together?" I immediately received the answer, "Yes." At this point the live ghost box session had reached around the seven-or-eight-minute mark. I was finding it increasingly difficult to concentrate, as I was fighting in my mind between keeping focused on the live ghost box session at hand and trying to piece together an explanation based on the live spirit communication I had already heard during the session. This is when I decided to end the live ghost box session, leaving a number of my intended questions unasked. I would save these questions for the next live ghost box session.

I addressed my spirit technicians and any spirit entities who had participated in the live ghost box session, thanked them for their help and cooperation, and said goodbye. As I always did, I let the ghost box run for a few seconds before cutting the power, and as I usually did, I received the live spirit communication response "Goodbye." I quickly said, "Bye," and turned the ghost box off.

As I uploaded the live ghost box session recording

from my digital voice recorder to my computer, I found myself very eager to review the live ghost box session recording and to discover any and all live spirit communication I had missed hearing live in real time during the live session. I proceeded to open the ghost box session recording in my audio editing program, which allowed me to review the recorded audio in increments. I would start at the very beginning and isolate the section of the recording that contained my first question and everything produced by the ghost box up to the beginning of my next question and/or statement. I would then proceed to copy that section of the recording and produce a separate single audio clip of the selected piece of audio recording. This would allow me to focus solely on the question that I asked or the statement I made and the ensuing ghost box sweep; every second of the recorded ghost box sweep was scrutinized whether it contained a live spirit communication that I was able to hear live during the live ghost box session or not. If the isolated audio clip did happen to contain live spirit communication that was heard during the session, it was heard in the audio example along with any verbal acknowledgment made by me in the confirmation of hearing the spirit communication live. If the audio clip did not contain an instance of my hearing and acknowledging live spirit communication, I would closely review the selected audio for any and all live spirit communication that had been delivered and missed by me during the live ghost box session. I have stated this a couple of times in previous chapters of this book, but I believe it is worth repeating here. As it stands, the average live spirit ghost box communication researcher, investigator, and operator is only capable of hearing around 25% of the total live spirit communication as it is delivered live in real time during the performance of a live ghost box session. The bulk of the live spirit communication will need to be discovered upon review of the live ghost box session recording.

After repeating this review process for the entire live ghost box session recording, I was left at the end with a number of single audio files containing my question or statement and any relevant live spirit communication that was delivered. Any and all remaining examples of live spirit communication that were discovered in the live ghost box session recording but were not associated with or relevant to any questions were kept as single audio files containing only the live spirit communication delivered by the spirit entity. Having completed the review of the live ghost box session recording, I was now able to listen to all the information rendered by my spirit technicians and communicating spirit entities in the form of live spirit communication sequentially as it had been delivered during the live ghost box session. I decided to write down all the words and phrases of live spirit communication that were received from the first to the last so that I could examine them without having to repeatedly access and listen to individual audio files, which was not very conducive to being able to associate one word to another fluidly.

As I went through the process of trying to make sense of the pieces of information from the often cryptic words and short phrases of the live spirit communication, all the different elements of the live spirit communication began to become cohesive. I began to slowly understand the explanation that the culmination of all the relevant live spirit communication arrived at. This was only the result of one live spirit ghost box session dedicated to obtaining information on the subject of why a higher quality and quantity of live spirit communication was received when a specific ghost box was used. I knew I had a bit of a way to go in arriving at a full understanding of what my spirit entity counterparts had begun to explain. I felt confident that with the results of this live ghost box session and the information I was able to glean from it, with further live ghost box sessions and the continued cooperation of my spirit entity friends and technicians, I would be able to arrive at a full understanding of this phenomenon. The subsequent live spirit ghost box communication sessions dedicated to this topic brought forth more helpful and enlightening information by way of live spirit communication. Based on the information derived and understood from those live spirit communication sessions, I was able to formulate the theory of imprinting and utilizing a specific ghost box and how it affects live spirit ghost box communication.

Since formulating, documenting, and publicizing this theory, I hope that any and all live spirit ghost box communication operators who have knowledge of it have utilized the information to achieve better success in their individual efforts with live spirit ghost box communication research and investigation. Imprinting on a specific ghost box is a very real aspect of live spirit ghost box communication and can be tested by any live spirit communication ghost box operator who is willing to put in the time and effort it takes to cultivate the information needed through live spirit communication gathered in dedicated ghost box sessions. Although this theory has been challenged by a couple of individuals, it has yet to be disproven by anyone and has been accepted by the live spirit ghost box community as a whole. There is an old saying, "Anything worth doing is worth doing well." In my experience, any question, idea, or recurring experience in live spirit ghost box communication can be answered, confirmed, or explained with the help of communicating spirit entities and the perseverance of dedicated live spirit ghost box researchers, investigators, and operators.

Chapter 18

Negative Communication Through the Ghost Box, What Are We Dealing With?

With ghost box communication, as with any other type of interaction with the paranormal, there is a certain amount of uncertainty in the unknown or unfamiliar that can come in many forms, including negative ones. I have had a number of ghost box operators mention to me that they recently experienced incidents that were unsettling although I would not call them necessarily "negative" but at the least unsettling. Although different in nature, these experiences were, I believe, frightening to them on the basis of being totally unexpected and out of the normal realm of what is usually experienced in live spirit ghost box communication. I am positive that every person in the world who is working or has worked with a ghost box can tell you that a decent part of the content of the live spirit communication we receive must be taken with a grain of salt.

In my experience, I have found that there are entities that will attempt to manipulate a ghost box operator into continuing a live ghost box session after the operator is ready to end the live ghost box session. A spirit entity will do this by delivering live spirit communication that is, let's say, not completely accurate, but serves to catch the attention of the ghost box operator by sending messages of a personal nature or having the communication contain content that is so intriguing that the operator will need to try to attain further information. Most of the time a simple request of "Wait" or "Don't go" by the spirit entity will suffice to make the operator continue with the live ghost box session longer than planned. I believe that this tactic on the part of the spirit entity is an attempt to retain the energy connection they have made with the physical world and/or to try to gain access to our physical world through a portal that has been opened by the live ghost box in session. There are also entities that, in my opinion, are bored and have nothing better to do than to tease and/or provoke the ghost box operator into believing that a situation is something other than what it actually is. Sometimes you will receive a prediction of some future event; sometimes you will get live spirit communication that will pertain to a publicized event such as a criminal investigation or the like. The topics and communications, of course, are always unique to the live ghost box session they are delivered in, but basically fall into the "being fooled" category.

Only experience will teach a ghost box operator how to recognize and decide what is immediate BS or what may need further investigation. My policy and what I try to convey to anyone who comes into live spirit ghost box communication is that we never take any live spirit communication at face value, and NEVER! approach any person who may be the subject of the live spirit communication message with any information that is received that may be important in content and most of all would serve to possibly impede a criminal or missing person investigation before being absolutely sure that the live spirit communication in question is valid. When we decide to delve into these unknown areas of existence, we also must take into account that there is the possibility of encounters with negative entities and/or negative situations.

"DARK HEADS" is a slang term that was originally coined by me back in the early days of live spirit ghost box communication to refer to any negative spirit entity or energy after discovering spirit entities that were trying to deter my attempts at live spirit communication. Dark heads in essence are any spirit entities that exude negative energy and carry a bad attitude and karma. You can usually detect a dark head easily by the foul language and negative messages and/or responses they offer. Dark heads will also attempt to deceive you and block any live spirit communication between the ghost box operator and their benevolent spirit contacts, such as spirit technicians and the spirits of friends or family. They are believed to be lower-level entities and can usually be stopped or blocked from interfering in a live ghost box session by our spirit technicians, with the help of the ghost box operator's positive attitude and energy. On the flip side, if you as the ghost box operator are in a bad mood, had an argument with the wife, or a bad day at the office, and are steeped in negative tension and energy, this will serve to reinforce the negative energy of a dark head and give them fuel for their fire. This is where our communication with friendly spirit entities becomes affected. We are usually told by our spirit technicians that dark heads are blocking our interaction with any positive spirit entities attempting to deliver live spirit communication. When this takes place, the live spirit communication will suffer until the problem is alleviated. This occurrence during a live ghost box session tends to frustrate the researcher, which only serves to compound the problem and reinforce the negative energy.

The best course of action when you suspect or are confronted by dark head activity that is disrupting your attempts at live spirit communication is to stop the live ghost box session and attempt another ghost box session when you are in a better frame of mind and the problem has been eliminated. I have stated again and again that the more positive the energy from the ghost box operator is, the stronger the bridge of communication becomes, and therefore we receive better, clearer, and more lengthy live spirit communication. I and other live spirit ghost box researchers who have been around long enough to have some experience with dark heads all have stories to tell. I have actually had one of my Joe's Box circuit boards fried during a live ghost box session by an attacking dark head.

The best way to combat these negative entities is to approach a live ghost box session only when you have a good attitude and are in a positive frame of mind in order to supply the energy connection created by the live ghost box session with an optimal amount of positive energy. This negativity and/or negative entity is capable of traveling from its own realm into our physical world via an open doorway or portal, if you will, that is created when the ghost box is in session. This portal is the result of the live ghost box having to develop a sort of umbilical cord between our world and the spirit world in order for the live spirit communication to travel back and forth between the physical world and the spirit realm. I help combat this infiltration by doing a short protection ritual before performing a live ghost box session, and asking my spirit technicians on the other side to protect against any negative entities that may want to create a problem or travel through the portal that the running ghost box creates.

Remember also that when doing a live ghost box session at a field location or investigation, there is a threat of having a dark head becoming attracted to the energy of the open ghost box session at the location you are investigating, and possibly having that dark head follow you when you leave. A protection ritual is also a good idea in this situation. Pretty much every time you turn a ghost box on, do your protection ritual first. "It is better to have it and not need it than need it and not have it."

A good practice for the operator to use at the close of a live ghost box session is to ask the spirit technician to return any wayward spirits that may have traveled through the open portal back through to the spirit realm, or they will be stuck here in the physical world after the ghost box is turned off. Not doing so could result in poltergeist activity, which more often than not, is an attempt by the stranded spirit entity to gain the attention of the ghost box operator so that he or she may initiate a new live ghost box session, which would allow the wayward spirit entity to return to the spirit world. I speak of this through experience. It has happened to me personally, which was what helped me develop this theory.

After asking the spirit technician to retrieve the wayward spirit entity, the ghost box operator must wait to hear a verbal confirmation from the spirit technician live that it is clear to shut down the ghost box.

This is a must; the ghost box operator has to hear the confirmation from the spirit technician live in real time to be assured that it is safe to shut down the ghost box with no fear of stranding a spirit entity on our side.

As for negative entities and their effect on us and our attempts at live spirit communication with a ghost box, negative entities do exist; they do try to infiltrate our live ghost box sessions as well as our emotions, thoughts, and actions, and even invade our physical world by way of the open ghost box session. Negative entities can be dangerous. Stay vigilant, follow good practices and protocols, and stay focused during any and all live spirit ghost box communication sessions. The following story will help to illustrate the capabilities of a negative force and what it can accomplish if left unchecked.

Back in the early days of live spirit ghost box communication research, there were only two types of ghost boxes available, the Frank's Box and the Joe's Box. Both models of ghost boxes were very hard to acquire. I was lucky enough to own both models. I had a personal preference for the Joe's Box, not because it was a better ghost box but simply because the area where I lived at the time had touchy radio broadcast reception, and the Joe's Box was able to give me a better-quality live ghost box session, as it was able to receive a better radio broadcast signal in my location. At this time I worked closely with a fellow live spirit communication researcher. We exchanged information, data, and evidence derived from our individual research efforts. My colleague and I had also developed the habit of speaking nightly over Skype and doing live ghost box sessions. Some days I would run the ghost box session as he participated live through Skype. Some days he would run the live ghost box session, and I would be the remote participant.

One evening I answered his Skype call per usual to find him distraught and upset. I asked what was wrong and why he was in such a state. My colleague proceeded to explain that earlier in the day he had decided to do a live spirit ghost box session using his Joe's Box. He informed me that he started the live ghost box session as he usually did; however, approximately five minutes into the live ghost box session, he began to hear strange sounds coming from the speaker of the ghost box. Immediately following the reception of these strange sounds, his Joe's Box made a loud popping sound and went dead. He attempted to restart the now silent Joe's Box with no success. I asked if he was able to determine what had happened, and he went on to tell me that he removed the back of the Joe's Box to expose the circuit board and discovered that it had been fried. We discussed the possible causes of this incident. We speculated that it may have been a faulty battery that caused a power surge, possibly a faulty connection or solder point on the ghost box's circuit board, or maybe the ghost box just overheated. Honestly, we were both at a loss for an explanation of how this ghost box could be working perfectly fine one moment and destroyed the next, never entertaining the idea that this incident may have been related to negative entity activity.

As I said earlier, ghost boxes at the time were scarcer than hens' teeth and not easy to obtain, so this incident that rendered my colleagues Joe's Box unusable was a blow not only to him but to live spirit ghost box communication research, which at the time consisted of only myself and my colleague. Between the two of us, we owned a total of four ghost boxes, each having one Frank's Box and one Joe's Box. Following this disaster, combined, we were down to three working ghost boxes that would have to serve as the tools to facilitate pretty much all the live spirit ghost box communication research being performed at that time.

The evening following my colleague's misfortune, we initiated our daily Skype call. We decided to do a live ghost box session, which I would perform using my working Joe's Box. I retrieved my Joe's Box and digital voice recorder, checked the batteries in both, and asked my colleague if he was ready to begin. We had decided that the topic of this live ghost box session would be to obtain information pertaining to the incident that befell my colleague's Joe's Box. I started my digital voice recorder, stated my name, the date, the ghost box that would be used, and the topic of the live ghost box session. I then hit the power switch that brought my Joe's Box to life. After a second or two to warm up, the ghost box began to emit a relatively strong ghost box sweep.

The way we conducted these remote live ghost box sessions was that because I was the live ghost box session operator, I would pose the questions, and my colleague and I would listen and respond to any live spirit communication that was heard. I would, of course, afford my colleague the opportunity to pose any questions he may have at the appropriate times. Because this live ghost box session was to be based on the specific topic of what had happened to my colleague's Joe's Box the previous evening, it was decided that I would ask all the questions during the live ghost box session, and he would offer input as to any live spirit communication he was able to hear and understand on his end.

The Joe's Box was running like a well-oiled machine with no indication of a problem when I began the live ghost box session. My first act was to acknowledge, greet, and receive confirmation of attendance by my spirit technicians. I asked, "Mike, Lisa, are you there and available to help us today?" I immediately received a clear response of "Yes, here." I heard this response live and acknowledged it, as did my colleague listening live over Skype.

My second question was "Are you guys aware of what happened to the Joe's Box last evening?" A few seconds went by, and I received a resounding "Yes." I heard this live and went on to ask if my spirit technicians knew what had happened to the Joe's Box and why. Although my and my colleague's experience was somewhat limited at this point in time, I was able to recognize that my spirit technicians attempted a response. Unfortunately I was not able to understand the communication live. I later discovered it in review of the live ghost box session recording. Not hearing my spirit technicians' response live, I went on to the next question. "Can you tell me if it was a mechanical fault that caused the incident?" To this question I received a very loud and clear "No," which was so deliberate that it made my colleague comment, "Wow, that was clear," and remember, he was listening to the live ghost box session and hearing any live spirit communication remotely over Skype and did not have the luxury of hearing the audio directly leaving the ghost box speaker.

As I mentioned earlier, we did not attribute this incident to anything paranormal. We assumed, which in hindsight was a mistake, that it had to have been a problem with the Joe's Box power supply or circuitry, knowing now that a good researcher never assumes, he or she investigates. After hearing the resounding answer of no from my spirit technicians, I posed the question, "If it was not a mechanical problem, what caused it?" Listening for an answer of live spirit communication, I was able to once again discern an attempt by my spirit friends to deliver an answer, but I was not able to understand what they had said live as they delivered it. At this point I began to notice some weird guttural sounds mixed into the live ghost box sweep, but they were not distinct enough to be really noticeable. I asked my colleague on Skype if he was able to hear those weird sounds, and he replied that he was not, which I attributed to his hearing the live ghost box session secondhand over Skype.

I continued to ask questions pertaining to the previous responses received and heard live and the topic at hand. We were receiving adequate live spirit communication that we agreed was relevant to the questions and topic, some of which we were able to hear live. One response we were both able to hear live as it was delivered contained the words "negative" and "evil." My colleague and I were beginning to get a picture of what might have actually occurred that resulted in the destruction of his Joe's Box. Approximately ten minutes had gone by, not that we were really keeping track of the live ghost box session progression time wise. At this point the weird sounds I had heard began to become more pronounced and stand out more above the live ghost box sweep. They became more abundant and were accompanied by attempts at live communication delivered in a sort of growling voice. Due to the increased level of these sounds, my colleague, even listening through Skype, became aware of them. His reaction to me was, "Wow, that does not sound good." I agreed.

After a minute or so more of asking questions, I realized that I was not only not hearing any answers or responses from my spirit technicians, but I was not hearing anything that indicated live spirit communication at all, just the increasing sounds of negativity that had taken over the live ghost box session from the spirit side. I called to my spirit technicians Mike and Lisa in an attempt to reestablish contact with them. As I was in mid-sentence, a very loud growl came through my Joe's Box speaker. As I held it in my hand, my Joe's Box crackled a bit and then made a loud popping sound. The ghost box went dead, and a wisp of smoke rose from the air vents located on the back cover. I could detect the smell of burning plastic, and at that instant I realized that whatever negative and/or evil entity overpowered the live ghost box session had now fried my Joe's Box! Of course, my colleague was privy to this whole incident from beginning to end and told me that if he had not been witness to the live ghost box session and the events that took place, he would have found it hard to believe.

After my initial rage at now losing my Joe's Box, my colleague and I discussed the events that took place and tried to come to an explanation of what had occurred, who or what caused it, and what we would need to do to prevent this type of incident in the future. After giving the incident much thought and going over the entire scenario from the time my colleague informed me of his encounter and the frying of my own Joe's Box, I arrived at the only logical conclusion. I surmised that the dark sounds that I had heard during the live ghost box session and the invariable destruction of both my and my colleague's Joe's Boxes were due to the deliberate attack of a negative entity. I also concluded that this negative entity had not perpetrated this act from a position in the spirit realm, but had to have been in the physical realm, in direct proximity to both ghost boxes at the time of their destruction. The negative entity would had to have manipulated the energy in and around the two Joe's

Boxes in such a way as to have the energy intensify enough to actually cook the ghost boxes' circuit boards.

I use this story as an example of the real and present risk that can be posed by a negative entity. Whether a dark head is present at the location of the live ghost box session or interjecting themselves into a live ghost box session from the spirit realm, the ghost box operator must be constantly vigilant and aware of any signs or activity that would indicate the presence of a negative entity, and do everything in their power to guard against any dark head infiltration or activity. Our spirit technicians are very capable and can be relied upon to do their best to protect the live ghost box session, its operator, and the portal the live ghost box creates. However, the ghost box operator cannot rely solely on the spirit technician for this protection. He or she must be an active part of the protection. Together the ghost box operator and his spirit technician can put up an effective defense against the attempts of a malicious dark head entity to wreak havoc. Always remember, "An ounce of prevention is worth a pound of cure."

Chapter 19

Crossing Over a Spirit Entity in a Live Ghost Box Session Explanation and Procedure

The "cross over session" is basically a live ghost box session that is done specifically to help an earthbound or lost and confused spirit entity to cross over or make the transition to the spirit realm. The term is used to describe the act of a spirit entity that is still here in the physical world and needs to make the transition to the spirit world or plane of existence where the disembodied spirits of human beings go after they have left their physical body and life. A crossing over session is usually initiated when a live spirit communication is received during a live ghost box session that renders a plea for help from a spirit entity communicating through the ghost box. We can pursue information about this live spirit communication with questions that will help the ghost box session operator understand the situation that the communicating spirit entity is in, and what they want from the operator, or how he or she can help the requesting spirit entity. The spirit entity has obviously

.

sought out the ghost box operator and made a plea for help.

I have found the help we can offer comes in a few different forms and is not restricted to just offering the wayward spirit entity the help it needs to cross over. Many times when a live spirit communication is received from a spirit entity asking for help, the ghost box operator invariably discovers that the spirit entity is that of a recently deceased individual. Often a newly transitioned spirit entity will be confused, disoriented, and in denial of their having died and are now in spirit form. When and if this is the case, the ghost box operator can help the confused spirit entity to understand what has happened to them and why they are where they are. The ghost box operator can help resolve issues between the spirit world and the physical. However, investigators generally should not automatically contact someone with a message from their dead relative that was received using a ghost box. It does not usually go over too well.

Before any contact with individuals the operator may believe the live spirit communication is meant for, the ghost box operator should assess the live spirit communication. Is it relevant to the situation in which it was received, does it contain a specific name and/or piece of information that would be recognized by the physical person you are presenting it to, and is the live spirit communication important enough to attempt delivering it to someone who most likely has never heard of live spirit ghost box communication and will not have any idea what you are talking about? For example, if the ghost box operator received a message from a spirit entity he or she was trying to help, and the communicating spirit entity wished a message forwarded to someone in the physical world, would the operator attempt to deliver a message that simply said hi or something similar? Not a great idea, so make sure before making any live spirit communication pertaining to a specific individual public, or privately bringing it to the individual's attention, that the live spirit communication is relevant and viable.

There is a process that should lead up to the actual act of rendering assistance in crossing the wayward spirit entity into the proverbial "light." My theory on why astral entities seek help from us to cross over is that the ghost box in session opens a portal or doorway to the other side and in doing so creates a strong flow of energy between our physical world and the spirit world. This, in turn, will attract a wayward spirit entity in search of a way to get where he or she is supposed to be, i.e., the spirit realm. Because the operator is the facilitator of the live ghost box session, the earthbound spirit entity will seek his or her help in understanding the opportunity created by the live ghost box in opening a passage between the physical and spiritual worlds. The wayward spirit entity will solicit the ghost box operator's help in directing them to the point where they can "cross over." The crossing over session may be done immediately upon receiving the plea for help from the spirit entity, or may have to be done after some questioning in the same live ghost box session. The situation can call for the ghost box operator to help the spirit entity to understand its situation, where it belongs, and why. The main thing is to help the spirit entity to get where they need to be. Most of the time in doing so, the spirit entity will need more than just a basic crossing over session. The ghost box operator will have to deal with each unique situation individually, but the basic protocol remains the same. Crossing over a lost and helpless spirit entity is one of the noblest tasks we as live spirit ghost box communication researchers, investigators, and operators can accomplish in the field of live spirit ghost box communication.

Helping others, whether it be helping a grieving person to contact a loved one or friend who has passed, or helping a spirit entity to realize its destiny and to cross into the light of spirit energy and find the way home to the loving arms of the spirits of family and friends and take its place back among the whole spiritual consciousness, is a calling we as live spirit ghost box communication practitioners should strive to accomplish. A basic crossing over session is a specific live ghost box session designed to aid a spirit entity that is earthbound and asking for help to make its transition from the physical world to the spirit world. Remember when going into a crossing over session that your spirit technician is always there and will help you to accomplish this honorable task.

A crossing over session can be accomplished either during the live ghost box session when the spirit entity's plea for help is heard, or can be a specific live ghost box session initiated by the ghost box operator for the express purpose of attempting to help an entity cross over to the spirit realm. Remember, and this is very important, the live ghost box operator must be prepared to conduct a crossing over live ghost box session where the operator can hear and act on the responses given by the communicating spirit entity live in real time. The ghost box operator must continue to strive to hear the spirit entity's live communication as it is delivered and be able to respond to that spirit entity based on the live spirit communication being received. If the ghost box operator were to miss even a small portion of the delivered communication, it would create confusion and misunderstanding on the part of both the operator and the communicating spirit entity, thus diminishing the chances of the success in the crossing over session. If necessary, the operator must be prepared to ask specific questions multiple times in an effort to hear any and all responses live in real time. This is crucial to the success of the crossing over ghost box session and, more importantly, the fate of the wayward spirit relying on the ghost box operator for help. It is essential for the ghost box operator to follow through with the steps a crossing over session entails, and to be secure at the end of the live ghost box session that the goal of the crossing over session was accomplished.

Whatever the situation may be, there are simple protocols to follow that will help to attain the goal of a successful crossing over session. First, ask that the spirit entity requesting help identify him or herself with a name. When and if you receive this name, from that point on refer to the spirit entity using their name. This will allow you to distinguish that particular spirit entity from any others that may be present during the live ghost box session.

Ask for a confirmation that the spirit entity is, in fact, seeking help. If you receive this confirmation, proceed to ask if the spirit entity is aware of its situation and its surroundings. Based on the answers you receive, you can either move on to the next step in the crossing over session, or try to explain the situation to the spirit entity that is asking for help. Use compassion and good judgment when and if you need to explain that the spirit entity is, in fact, dead and is here in the physical world, and that they need to cross over to the spiritual realm, which is where they need to be.

If the operator can be comfortable in knowing that the spirit entity basically understands the circumstances, the operator can ask what their immediate surroundings are and what they are able to see around them. Ask purposely if they can see a bright light. If the spirit entity acknowledges that they can see a light, you will need to walk them through entering that light with explanations and reassurance. Remember, this spirit entity is lost, scared, and confused. Right now the operator is the only conscious energy that it has to hold on to. The wayward spirit entity will need to have trust in the ghost box operator and be confident that the information and instructions he or she is receiving are the right things to do. Do not rush, and do not demand that the spirit entity go towards or into the light. Simply be a friend who is there to hold their hand through a difficult time. Verbally lead the spirit entity to the light, tell them that everything is OK and that there will be people there who love them and are waiting for them. Ask them to look into the light and ask them what they see. If they can see the light, you will usually get a response of them seeing something or someone familiar to them. This is when you help them to take the last steps into that light and to help them cross over and essentially "go home."

After you are confident that all went well, ask for the spirit entity by name and ask the attending spirit technician for confirmation that he or she has crossed to the other side. Ask your spirit technician to reassure and help the newly arrived spirit entity to become comfortable on the spirit side.

You may ask, "Why doesn't the spirit technician simply come to the physical side and bring the lost spirit entity over to the spirit world?" Good question! I believe, after many crossing sessions and many answers from spirit technicians and communicators, that we, as live spirit ghost box communication operators, have a certain energy bond between our world and the spirit world. I have always likened this connection to an umbilical cord that facilitates the flow of that energy back and forth from our world to theirs. This energy flow opens a doorway that allows for the exchange of energy. I feel that the ghost box operator is vital to guiding the lost spirit entity to the proverbial "light" while it is on the physical side, and with the help we get from our spirit technicians on the other side, together we can accomplish the crossing over session. Always bear in mind that the spirit entity you are helping is putting their trust in you, and you need to repay that trust with kindness and the best effort you can make to help them.

I would now like to render my explanation on "how to follow up on an important live spirit communication missed during a live ghost box session." If you have ever used a ghost box for live spirit communication and hopefully recorded your live ghost box sessions and reviewed them, you will know that the bulk of the live spirit communication we hear in real time as it is delivered through the ghost box during a live ghost session only makes up a small amount of the actual live spirit communication that is delivered. Through my time in live spirit ghost box communication practice and research, I have concluded that as it stands now, even the most seasoned and experienced live spirit ghost box communication operator is only capable of hearing approximately 25% of the total live spirit communication that is delivered in any given ghost box session. It is very frustrating and concerning to be reviewing your live spirit ghost box communication session recording and discover a pertinent and important message to a question that was not heard live during the performance of the live ghost box session.

I consider myself to be a diligent live spirit ghost box communication researcher. I try to perform a live ghost box session daily, which has been my practice for almost two decades now, and anyone who practices live spirit ghost box communication will tell you it is no speedy task to review a live ghost box session recording. It can be quite daunting and take a good amount of time. This being the case, when an important live spirit communication is found in the recording, it can be days after the communication was actually received, therefore denying us the opportunity to address the communication at the time of its reception. For example, the operator may ask the question during a live ghost box session "Are there any spirits that wish to communicate?" and the response of "Please help me!" may be communicated from the spirit entity. Unfortunately, the ghost box operator did not hear the communication live during the ghost box session; it was discovered days later in a review of the ghost box session recording. At this point it is too late to immediately address the live spirit communication or receive any further information pertaining to it.

This is a circumstance that is faced all too often by an operator in live spirit ghost box communication. Of course, any opportunity for immediate assistance or advice on the part of the operator has passed, although this is the case when we as live spirit ghost box communication operators can do what is called a "follow-up session" or " follow-up questions" that address the specific live spirit communication that was discovered in the previous ghost box session recording. With the assistance of spirit technicians who are present during every live spirit ghost box communication session, the operator can attempt a new live ghost box session to communicate with the spirit entity that delivered the original communication in question. It is possible that the same spirit entity can be reached by the spirit technicians and brought forward to reestablish live communication, and it is also possible that the target spirit entity may be on hand already. Simply apprise the attending spirit technician of the situation and politely ask for their help.

If everything comes together, which there is no

guarantee that it will, the ghost box operator will have the opportunity to communicate with the original spirit entity, address the original live spirit communication, and attempt to gather further information and/or answers regarding the original communication and also offer any assistance that may be needed. During the follow-up session, the ghost box operator should keep the questions and/or statements basic, ask questions, and make statements that are uncomplicated and that will require short basic responses by the communicating spirit entity. This will afford the operator a better chance of hearing any communication sent live as it is delivered. This will also give the communicating spirit entity a better chance at forming and sending live spirit communication due to the basic nature of the answers and/or statements required. Do not ask for a lengthy explanation of the original message or any answers that require a complicated response on the part of the communicating spirit entity.

If adequate and useful communication regarding the original message is heard live by the ghost box operator, he or she should attempt to evaluate the live spirit communication heard and adjust his or her questions and statements accordingly. Simply treat this specific part of the live ghost box session as if you were speaking with a person here in the physical world, try not to be forceful or demanding in your questioning, and allow ample time and patience for the communicating spirit entity to send the communication. Also if you are conducting a follow-up live ghost box session pertaining to a message or request for help or if the message you discovered was sent by what you believe to be a spirit entity in distress, you should approach the live ghost box session accordingly. Try to keep in mind how you would interact with an individual here in the physical who was scared, confused, or emotionally distressed. There are spirit entities that we come into contact with that are actually confused, scared, and even unaware that they have died and are in spirit form. So examine the original live spirit communication and structure your approach to the follow-up live ghost box session accordingly.

Try to resolve the situation live during the ghost box session. This is not a simple task and may take time and the repetition of questions or statements in an attempt to hear the communication being sent live, but believe me, the end result will be well worth the effort. Remember that as live spirit ghost box communication researchers and operators, we have a duty to the spirit entities we initiate contact with, and serve as liaisons between our physical world and the spirit world. As such, we have an obligation to do whatever is in our power to render comfort and assistance when we are able.

Here now is my explanation of a "contact confirmation question ghost box session." The contact confirmation question ghost box session is a live spirit ghost box communication session that is done for the express purpose of making contact with a specific spirit entity and attempting to confirm the identity of said spirit entity. This is accomplished by asking a question or series of questions to validate that the spirit entity that is communicating is in fact the individual they claim to be. This procedure is usually done during a private contact live ghost box session in which a request has been made to the ghost box operator by an individual to attempt to contact a specific spirit entity. The questions that are to be asked during the contact confirmation ghost box session are received from the party that the live ghost box session is being performed for. The questions are asked by the ghost box operator performing the live ghost box session, without the ghost box operator having any knowledge of the answers to the questions submitted by the person for whom the live ghost box session is being performed. The questions are asked, and assuming there is a response, the answers communicated by the spirit entity are either heard live in real time and/or recorded for discovery in the review of the ghost box session.

The ghost box session recording is then reviewed by the ghost box operator, and the questions it contains are individually reviewed with any following live spirit communication that may have occurred. The specific section of audio is then isolated and saved as an individual audio file. This audio file will be sent to the person who requested the personal ghost box session for review and validation that the communicated answers are either correct or incorrect. If the answers to the specific questions received in the live ghost box session are correct, the ghost box operator can be relatively sure that the correct spirit contact was made, and the questions that were answered consisted of live spirit communication from the spirit entity that was the focus of the personal live ghost box session.

This contact confirmation question live ghost box

session protocol should be followed whenever this particular type of live ghost box session is done to attempt to receive positive live spirit communication in the form of responses from specific spirit entities that the ghost box operator is attempting to contact. The contact confirmation ghost box session will help to confirm the identity of a spirit or spirits that the ghost box operator is attempting to contact on behalf of the person requesting the live contact ghost box session. It is very important that the ghost box operator performing the contact session does not have any prior knowledge of the correct answers to the specific questions submitted by the individual requesting the session. Any knowledge of answers to the session questions by the ghost box operator would negate the validity and integrity of the contact confirmation question session. This not only allows the requesting party to have confidence that the live spirit communication received was in actuality from the spirit entity they wished to contact, but also serves to reassure them that the ghost box operator was not capable of influencing the outcome of the live ghost box session.

The contact confirmation question ghost box session can be performed as part of a larger live ghost box session that entails specific topics or random questions. It should always be the preliminary section of any more complex live ghost box session. Always perform and complete the contact confirmation question portion of the live ghost box session before proceeding with the remainder of the planned live ghost box session. Needless to say, live spirit ghost box communication audio lends itself to personal interpretation by the individual listener. This includes the ghost box operator who performed the live ghost box session. As the ghost box operator and reviewer of the live ghost box session recording, make absolutely sure of what you believe the live spirit communication consisted of that was received in the live ghost box session. The ghost box operator should be confident in what the live spirit communication says and that it is clear enough for the requesting individual to hear before labeling the audio file with a description and submitting it to the requesting party. Most individuals who request a contact confirmation question session will not be as adept at listening to live spirit ghost box communication as the ghost box operator who conducted the session, and therefore should be subject to live spirit communication audio files that are as clear and easy to understand as possible.

Chapter 20

Are There Animals in The Spirit World?

I have performed numerous live spirit ghost box communication sessions with the express purpose of finding out if our beloved pets when they die make the transition to the spirit world as we do, and if they are waiting there for us when our time comes to make our transition. I have done specific ghost box sessions to try to gather information and receive answers to this question. I have come to the conclusion from live spirit communication received in those ghost box sessions that, yes, our pets do make the crossing and do wait to be reunited with us when we arrive in the spirit realm. With the belief in this occurrence, some may ask, "If animals can cross and become spirits, why is the spirit world not filled with billions of animal souls, lions, tigers, elephants, etc.?" This is a valid question and one I have pondered since my decision to accept the messages from our spirit friends and adopt the belief that animal spirits do transition and cross to the spirit world. I did not receive any specific explanation as to why not every creature that exists carries a soul and the ability to cross to the spirit world when their physical existence ends; however, through continued research and a culmination of the information I have received from spirit entities during live ghost box sessions, I have been able to formulate a theory that pertains to this subject.

We, as human beings in the physical world, build a strong emotional and spiritual bond with some of the creatures that share our lives. There is a common bond that all living creatures share, the fact that no matter what form we take physically, be it human or animal or even insect and fish, all life on earth is made up of the same essential building blocks. Of course, our connection to every single living thing on this planet is limited to unconscious primal energy that goes relatively unnoticed, except possibly in the rarest of instances like when a dolphin will save a drowning person or the case of a fully grown silverback gorilla cradling an injured child that had fallen into its zoo enclosure until help could arrive. These instances are extremely rare, but they are examples of our primal bond and sharing of energy and a form of subconscious connection with all living creatures.

I will try to give my answer as to why I believe the spirit realm is not completely overrun with animal spirits. I believe that the basic bond of energy we all share with the other creatures of the earth, as I explained earlier, is all encompassing. However, this energy bond transcends the basic in the relationships that are shared between certain animals and human beings. I speak of the animals that have chosen by one means or another to become close and trusted everyday companions, coworkers, and lifelong friends of man. The energy bond I speak of can play many parts between human beings and our fellow creatures. Among the animals that have chosen, whether willingly or unconsciously, to be our companions in many different ways, these are our beloved pets, dogs, cats, and birds, among many others. I believe that the reason these creatures are capable of existing in spirit form and are able to interact with human spirits in the spirit realm is due in large part to the bond that exists, not only of basic living energy but also the bond of unconditional love, trust, and respect that is shared by most of us with the creatures we so openly share our home, our beds, and our lives with, the creatures that depend on us for their sustenance, their protection, and their well-being, and that we depend on for our comfort of thought, unending flow of affection received, unconditional love and loyalty, and our very sanity at times.

These bonds are a form of energy that transcends the basic building blocks of merely the affiliation of all living creatures. These close relationships and the energy traded between them are akin to the energy shared between a parent and a child. Have you ever witnessed an elderly person walking a pet dog in the park? Next time you have the opportunity to, pay attention to the unspoken attachment that is shared by them and the reliance that you will witness between them for each other's very existence. They are more than master and pet but "soul mates" in a sense of the idea, that is to say, their souls have connected and bonded; the love and life that they have shared so closely has cemented their reunion in the next existence. That is what I believe makes it possible for our pets to make the special transition and become spirit entities that will continue to comfort us and share our love in the life we will share with them when reunited in the next experience.

You may ask, "Why isn't the pet frog I had when I was twelve going to be waiting for me when I get to the spirit world?" What I have come to learn through information granted me from spirit entities through many years of live spirit ghost box communication has culminated in this answer to that question. Given that we as physical human beings share a special energy connection with all the world's living creatures, I have come to believe that certain animals have been endowed with a special energy, one that allows for a special and unique connection with human beings. These, of course, are the animals that human beings have chosen to share the intricacies of our lives with, the creatures we live with, work with, play with, and give our unconditional love to, the animals that help us see when we are blind, the animals that find us when we are lost, the animals that protect us when we are in danger, our beloved friends and companions. The energy connection exists between all animals and human beings, but only those certain animals that we develop that special bond with have been given the gift of an enduring spirit that will continue to share our existence when we transition to the next experience.

At the time of this writing, I had recently lost my trusted and loved friend and companion of sixteen years, my dog Rocky. From the first time I picked him up as a tiny six-week-old puppy to the time he closed his eyes here in the physical world and started his journey to his spiritual life, I don't think in all the sixteen years that we shared our lives together we ever spent a day apart. Rocky was a constant friend, partner, companion, and confidant; he was there by my side through good times and bad, never judging, never angry, never selfish, and never dismissive. The bond that existed between Rocky and me was very strong; it was like we almost knew what the other was thinking at times. Rocky was always there; one of the hardest things I have ever had to do was when I had to bid my friend and companion goodbye. As Rocky took his final breaths in this world, I whispered to him that we would be together again and for him to wait for me when he arrived in his new home. I assured him that there would be people there who would love and watch over him until we were reunited. Rocky may not have understood my words in those last moments, but from the look in his eyes, I knew that he heard what I said. Rocky peacefully took his last breath, and I could just picture him galloping into the light that would lead him to the place where he would be waiting for me.

Shortly after Rocky's transition, I performed a live spirit ghost box communication session to ask my longtime spirit technicians and friends Mike and Lisa if they could locate Rocky and let me know that he made his crossing safely and was happy and ok. My first question to my spirit technicians was, "Is Rocky there, and is he ok?" I immediately received the answer, "Yes, he's here." I heard this live spirit communication live in real time and breathed a sigh of relief. Before I could ask a second question, I received the live spirit communication message, "Rocky is with Elvis." I also heard this spirit communication live. I knew my spirit technicians were referring to a dog that was my companion before Rocky, an English bulldog named Elvis whom I loved just as much as I did Rocky, and had spent eleven years of my life with. With that live spirit message, my spirit technicians had actually answered one of my intended questions before I even asked it.

I proceeded with the live ghost box session and asked a few more questions about Rocky and received numerous live spirit communications in the form of answers and statements. By the end of the live ghost box session, I felt a great sense of relief and comfort knowing that Rocky had made his transition to the spirit realm successfully and was in good hands. It has been almost eight months since Rocky has passed, and I still continue to receive updates from my spirit friends during my live spirit communication ghost box sessions about Rocky and how he is getting along while he waits for me to arrive so that we can continue our eternal life together. It is live spirit communications like these and many more that have preceded them that allow me to state without compunction that, yes, our animal friends do transition to the spirit realm just as we do after the physical experience is completed.

The next topic I would like to address is merely a

short explanation of my opinion on "the scientific theory of neuron firing separation and my opinion of it." I have heard this scientific theory quoted many, many times throughout my paranormal research and investigative career by proponents of science, and nonbelievers in anything spiritual or paranormal. It is called "the neuron firing separation theory." This theory is used by science to dismiss the possibility of a human spirit and the existence of a spiritual afterlife that follows a human physical life. It is also used by scientists to negate any and all claims made by individuals who have experienced an NDE, or near-death experience. It is reported by those who have experienced NDEs that the individual experiences a sensation of leaving the physical human body and traveling to a place of total love, peace, and happiness. Most report that upon arrival in this paradise, they are greeted by friends and family who have previously departed the physical life. Some even report meeting and speaking with angels, God, and Jesus. There have even been reports by individuals of visiting a place they recognized to be what they would describe as Hell.

There have been many hundreds of documented cases of NDEs, and the vast majority of the individual details in the descriptions are strikingly similar. Science felt a need to investigate these near-death experiences and formulate a scientific theory that would negate the possibility of their being based in reality. The explanation that science came up with for the experience of an NDE was that the human body's natural process of dying entails that at the very moment before brain death occurs, there is a state of euphoria, a feeling of warmth and peace is experienced at the moment of death, which is created by the physical act of all neurons in the brain firing simultaneously. This physical act occurs immediately preceding the moment of actual death, where the brain ceases all function and gives the individual the last cerebral experience of being in, let's say, a state of grace, the sighting of a bright white light, feeling what is perceived to be total peace and love and safety, and the fleeting vision of deceased loved ones and friends.

Let's consider, and this is just a theory that I have developed, let's consider that the simultaneous firing of every remaining neuron in the brain acts as a sort of cannon shot. Let's look at it this way, suppose the brain is the cannon and the neurological energy is our soul. Scientists will tell you that the simultaneous firing of the neurons emits energy in the form of electromagnetic energy. Suppose the purpose of this instantaneous and complete firing of all the remaining neurons in the brain serves to separate the soul from the physical body. Let's think of it as firing a cannon that separates the cannonball from the cannon itself. Suppose this final physical blast of neurological energy serves to release and separate the soul from the physical body so that it can move on to the next plane of existence.

There is another fact that has been established by science that states that all the energy that exists in the universe has always existed and will continue to exist for as long as the universe exists, no matter what form it takes. To accept this scientific truth would mean that the energy created by the final firing of neurons in the physical brain at the moment of death could not and does not dissipate but continues to exist in an altered form, "the soul." This is a theory that I have formulated just as scientists have formulated the scientific theory of the firing neurons creating an artificial state of grace. Why does one theory hold more credibility than the other? Is it because the scientific theory comes from the "trusted" field of established science, and my soul separation theory comes from someone who researches and investigates a less accepted form of research, investigation, and discovery, such as the paranormal? Strip the outer stigma of legitimate and illegitimate and you are left with only two equal opposing theories, both of which cannot be proven, only speculated on. The only thing that science can prove as far as this their theory on this phenomenon is that there is a simultaneous firing of all neurons in the brain at the time of death; beyond that, there is no way for them to "prove" that this firing of neurons causes the effects that they state in their theory. Anyone who could substantiate their claims is obviously deceased at the point where they could be questioned about it.

I find science to be like an overly strict parent; it's all "Do as I say not as I do." Because science says it is so does not always make it so. It's way past time for science to step out of the role of the dictator and step into the role of the open-minded researcher. It's time for science to embrace new ideas, new theories, new possibilities, and stop trying to bully mankind into believing whatever they are told without question simply because the data and information have been tested by standards science itself set. It is very easy to dismiss something you refuse to investigate with an open mind. Hey, science, come and do a live spirit ghost box communication session with me, and I guarantee you that you will walk away from it scratching your head and saying hmmmm!

Chapter 21

Contacting and Communicating With a Specific Spirit Entity, Is It Possible?

Can a specific spirit entity be called upon during a live spirit ghost box session to come forward and communicate with the live ghost box session operator and/or any individuals who may be present? The short answer is yes. Now to elaborate a bit on that short answer.

Many live spirit ghost box communication researchers, investigators, and operators oftentimes find themselves in a position during a live ghost box session having to attempt contact with a specific spirit entity. This could be due to a myriad of reasons: the ghost box operator is performing a private live ghost box session for an individual who wishes to receive messages and/or answers to specific questions from a loved one or friend who has made the transition to the spirit realm, the ghost box operator is attempting to contact one of their own loved ones or friends, there is an individual present at the live ghost box session who wishes to communicate with a specific entity, or the ghost box operator is attempting to contact and communicate with a famous individual who has crossed to the spirit realm. There can be many variations in these instances depending on the wants and needs of the individual requesting contact with the spirit entity.

Let's first examine the reasons that the actual live spirit ghost box communication researcher, operator, or investigator may find it necessary to contact a specific entity during a live ghost box session. There are two circumstances in which the live ghost box operator will attempt contact and communication with a specific spirit entity. One is in the performance of a planned and controlled live ghost box session where the operator has prepared a topic and list of questions pertaining to a specific spirit entity and is dedicating the entire live ghost box session to contacting and communicating with that spirit entity, or the ghost box operator finds himself in a position during the performance of a live spirit ghost box communication session where he must attempt to contact a specific spirit entity due to circumstances that have arisen during the course of the live ghost box session.

There is one instance that can apply to both circumstances, which is if the ghost box operator is conducting a live ghost box session during a field investigation and the ghost box operator is attempting to contact and communicate with a specific spirit entity that is reported to be in that location, or if the ghost box operator may have had a specific live ghost box session intended for that investigation, which is most likely, and had prepared a list of questions to be asked of a specific spirit entity at that location, or the ghost box operator during the course of an impromptu live ghost box session at the investigation location received live spirit communication from a spirit entity claiming to be a specific individual known to be associated with that location.

In most cases, the reason for a ghost box operator to attempt contact and communication with a specific spirit entity is in performing a private live spirit ghost box communication session that has been requested by an individual seeking to contact a deceased loved one or friend who has made their transition to the spirit world. In the event of one of these private sessions, the ghost box operator will gather basic information from the requesting person, name of the deceased, date of birth of the deceased, location where the deceased lived, date and location of death, circumstances of death, and relationship to the individual requesting the contact session. The ghost box operator will also request that the person asking for the private session render any questions that they would specifically like the ghost box operator to ask, assuming that contact with the specific entity is made. It is very important that the person giving the questions to the operator not divulge any answers to the questions submitted; to do so would negate the validity and integrity of any live spirit communication received that was a specific answer to the questions supplied by the requesting person. When the ghost box operator has the information he or she needs to perform the live ghost box session, he or she can then initiate the live ghost box session.

The first procedure in this type of live ghost box session would be to establish contact with the spirit technician who is overseeing the particular ghost box session. Once the operator has determined the presence of the spirit technician and has received the name of the spirit technician, he can now solicit the spirit technician's help in locating and retrieving the specific spirit entity who is the subject of the live ghost box session. The ghost box operator should now give the spirit technician the identifying information about the target spirit entity that was acquired from the person requesting the session, name, date and place of death, etc., and ask the spirit technician to locate the specific spirit entity and bring them forward to communicate. The operator should ask the spirit technician to acknowledge if and when the target spirit entity is located and available to communicate. Based on the spirit technician's confirmation that the specific spirit entity has been located and is available to communicate, the ghost box operator can ask directly for the specific spirit entity. The ghost box operator should address the spirit entity by name and be polite and respectful, ask if the spirit entity can confirm their identity by saying their name. Based on the response from the communicating spirit entity, the ghost box operator will now know how to proceed with the private ghost box session. The operator can either continue with the assigned questions, or if the operator is not convinced he or she is communicating with the correct spirit entity, they can request further information and assistance from the spirit technician.

The next instance where a ghost box operator may

find him or herself in a position to have to attempt contact with a specific spirit entity is during the performance of a live spirit ghost box communication session that is being conducted at a field location during a paranormal investigation. Many times these days paranormal investigations are carried out on location at celebrated alleged haunted locations such as hotels or inns, abandoned mental asylums or hospitals, and private homes that have been publicized in the media as being haunted. These publicized locations will usually have a backstory involving specific individuals who were known to have stayed at, resided in, or been incarcerated at one of these locations, many times with reports of paranormal activity perpetrated by the spirits of the former inhabitants.

Today it is standard issue for a paranormal investigating team or individual to have a ghost box in their arsenal of evidence-gathering equipment. It is very rare today to find a paranormal investigation equipment case without one; actually, there are probably several. Most paranormal investigating teams will have a designated ghost box operator, someone who is assigned to perform the live ghost box session during a field investigation. This individual will usually have prior knowledge of the location and any reported details of paranormal activity and any suspected entities that are believed to be responsible for said paranormal activity.

When the ghost box operator performs a live ghost box session at a field location, although they can receive live spirit communication from the spirit realm, it is more than likely the majority of any live spirit communication will be delivered by a spirit entity or entities that are earthbound at the location of the live ghost box session and in direct proximity to the operator and the live ghost box. There are two possible scenarios here; one, the investigating ghost box operator has prior knowledge of an alleged haunting by a specific spirit entity or entities, and two, the cause of their departing the physical life.

When the ghost box operator begins the live ghost box session, they should ask for the confirmation of a spirit technician that will be overseeing the specific live ghost box session. No matter what the circumstances of the live ghost box session, there will always be a spirit technician that is assigned to every live ghost box session that is initiated no matter when or where. Once the ghost box operator receives confirmation that the spirit technician is in place and ready to go, the operator can proceed with the live ghost box session as planned. When the investigating ghost box operator has prior knowledge of the location and any spirit entities that may be present there, he or she will usually prepare a list of questions and statements pertaining to the location and the specific spirit entity that is to be contacted and communicated with. The ghost box operator will then proceed to deliver questions and statements in an attempt to garner live spirit communication from the specific spirit entity and also any other spirit entities that may wish to communicate. In a live ghost box session at a field location when the ghost box operator has prior knowledge of the location and specific spirit entities allegedly in residence there, he or she will focus the live ghost box session on making contact and communicating with the specific spirit entity associated with the location. This will be done in an effort to gather live spirit communication that will verify and validate facts about the specific location, and specific details about the specific spirit entity located there, including details about the spirit entity's ties to the location and activity there during his or her physical life, including the circumstances leading to their death.

When investigating a field location that is reportedly haunted, the investigating team or individual does not always have specific details about the location or any inhabiting spirit entities that may be present there. In this case, the purpose of the investigation is to determine whether or not the designated location is being haunted or has a spirit entity that may be grounded there or simply in visitation. This type of field investigation is usually prompted by a report of some type of paranormal activity at the location; the only details known are usually what the residents, occupants, or workers submit to the investigators. Things like poltergeist activity, lights flickering, items falling from shelves, basically things that go bump in the night. When the ghost box operator performs a live ghost box session on an investigation of this type, the main goal of the live ghost box session is to attempt to contact and initiate live spirit communication from any and all spirit entities that may be present.

As always, the ghost box operator will establish that there is a spirit technician overseeing the live ghost box session and receive confirmation from the spirit technician that they are there and ready to work. The live ghost box session operator should start with a few basic questions that warrant short direct and specific answers, such as, "Are there any spirit entities here in this location with us now that would like to communicate?" This type of question by the ghost box operator, if heard by a spirit entity that is at the location, in proximity to the ghost box, and is willing to communicate, will usually garner a short one-word response like yes, yeah, or here. When and if the ghost box operator receives the live spirit communication, and assuming he or she hears it live in real time, the operator can now start to ask questions that will entail slightly more detailed answers from the communicating spirit entity. The ghost box operator will usually proceed with, "My name is Bill. Can you tell me your name?" If and when an answer is received and heard by the ghost box operator, he or she can continue the line of questioning that will hopefully lead to determining who the spirit entity is, why they are there, and if they have been perpetrating the experienced paranormal activity.

This type of live spirit ghost box communication session to contact a specific entity and gather information and can also sometimes help a wayward earthbound spirit entity that is lost and/or confused to find their way to cross into the spirit realm. In situations like that, as in all aspects of live spirit ghost box communication, the spirit technician plays a vital and integral part not only in the success of the live ghost box session but in helping the wayward spirit entity to find their way home.

There are other instances that would warrant a

specific contact live ghost box session where a live spirit ghost box researcher, investigator, or operator would attempt to contact and communicate with a specific entity. One of these, in particular, seems to be all the craze as of late, the attempt to contact a specific celebrity or historical figure that has transitioned to the spirit world, for example, Michael Jackson or Elvis Presley. The trend seems to be ghost box operators attempting to contact and communicate with the spirit entities of most recently transitioned celebrities like James Gandolfini or Ray Liotta. It seems like we no sooner hear that a celebrity has died, and almost immediately there are videos posted to social media with examples from live ghost box sessions claiming live spirit communication with the deceased individual. I am not saying that this type of specific spirit contact and communication is not possible; God knows I have experienced more than my share of things that were, let's just say, less than possible. All I'm saying is, come on, people, let a spirit entity settle in for a minute before calling them to a live spirit ghost box press conference.

Another instance that calls for a specific contact live ghost box session is when a live spirit ghost box operator is called upon by either a requesting party or the operator takes it upon themselves to attempt to contact a specific spirit entity to gather information on a missing person or cold case. I have performed quite a few missing person and cold case live spirit communication sessions in the course of my career. Cold case live ghost box sessions almost always entail a victim who has been murdered or abducted and is presumed dead. A cold case session is done for the express purpose of contacting the spirit of the deceased victim in an attempt to gather facts and information about the actual crime and/or murder; who better to ask about it than the victim themselves? All cold cases are not necessarily murder cases. Sometimes they can be a case of an individual who had been abducted and the individual or their remains have never been located. A cold case live ghost box session can be requested by either the family of the victim, an investigator, law enforcement, or any combination of the three. In my experience, most of the cold cases I have performed live ghost box sessions for were requested by a family member of the victim; however, I have done live ghost box sessions requested by investigators working with law enforcement.

Whoever the requesting party is, the cold case live ghost box session is basically the same, with minor variations according to the circumstances of either the case or requesting party. It is still a contact ghost box session for a specific spirit entity. The cold case live ghost box session is performed using the same basic protocols used for every specific contact ghost box session. The ghost box operator is given information pertaining to the victim and the alleged crime that was committed. The information is usually made up of the victim's name, birth date, and place of residence; however, information forwarded to the ghost box operator performing a cold case ghost box session will also include facts about the case that have been verified: where the victim's body was found, cause of death, etc. It is the goal of the ghost box operator to attempt to contact the specific spirit entity, which in most cases will be the victim in the case, and render the questions that will glean any information from the spirit entity that will help in solving the cold case or supply further clues that will aid in the investigation of the case.

Of course, a cold case can also involve a victim who had been abducted. In this case, it is not certain whether the victim is deceased or still living and being held against their will since no physical remains have been discovered. This is where the job of the live ghost box operator performing the specific spirit entity contact session becomes a bit more complicated. The ghost box operator will have information that pertains to the individual who has been abducted and to the crime itself; however, the ghost box operator will have to rely mainly on the spirit technician to try to discover whether the abduction victim is deceased and residing in the spirit realm and, if so, to locate the specific spirit entity and bring them forward to communicate. The ghost box operator must now determine if the spirit technician has discovered the spirit entity of the deceased victim and receive a confirmation of that. If this is the case, the operator can proceed with a line of questioning that is similar to the questioning in the aforementioned cold case session. If it cannot be confirmed by the live ghost box operator that he or she has made contact with the specific spirit entity of the abduction victim, the operator must continue to rely on the spirit technician for assistance in gathering information about the case. When a live spirit ghost box communication operator agrees to perform a live ghost box session to try to obtain information about a criminal case and/or murder victim, the ghost box operator must take all steps necessary to ensure that the information received through the live spirit communication received in the live ghost box session is of high quality and cannot be mistaken when listened to. The operator must use very good judgment when deciding what live spirit communication they will present to the party who requested the specific contact ghost box session.

I have performed many specific contact live spirit ghost box communication sessions over the years, cold case sessions, missing person sessions, private contact sessions, and sessions to contact specific prominent individuals to obtain information. Let me explain the specific contact ghost box session to contact and communicate with a prominent individual. What I mean by a prominent individual is a specific individual who had been a prominent figure when in their physical life, for example, Thomas Edison. Mr. Edison was a prominent and well-celebrated individual in his physical life.

I chose Thomas Edison as an example for two reasons. Thomas Edison, in the course of his inventing career, actually worked on a device that he believed would allow him to communicate with the spirits of deceased human beings. He called this device "the telephone to the dead." Unfortunately Mr. Edison never completed his work on this device. The creator of the first ghost box, Frank Sumption, actually derived the idea for the ghost box after reading an article in a *Popular Science* magazine dedicated to Thomas Edison's attempt at a spirit communication device. I have attempted and successfully contacted and received live spirit communication from the spirit of Thomas Edison in numerous live ghost box sessions. There are audio and video examples of the actual live spirit communications that I have posted to the internet on my Facebook page and YouTube channels respectively. Mr. Edison on occasion has even rendered live spirit communication with details and advice on how to improve the ghost box. In addition to Thomas Edison, I have also specifically requested contact with his rival Nikola Tesla in a number of live ghost box sessions, and have received great live spirit communication from him also. These are just a couple of examples of a specific contact ghost box session to attempt contact and communication with a prominent individual.

A prominent individual does not necessarily mean a celebrity figure. As I said earlier, there are some live spirit ghost box communication operators who will attempt a specific contact ghost box session to try to receive live spirit communication from a spirit entity who was a publicized celebrity in their physical life, and most examples of this are attempts made to contact and communicate with celebrity spirit entities that have just passed and made their transition to the spiritual life. For example, you can have a celebrity like Betty White, world renowned and recently deceased. Not twenty-four hours after Ms. White's passing, there were YouTube videos of live ghost box sessions made by individuals claiming to have made contact with and received live spirit communication from the spirit of Betty White. This occurs like clockwork every time a celebrity figure passes away.

Please do not misunderstand me. I am not denouncing the performance of a live ghost box session to attempt contact and communication with a celebrity figure. I am simply attempting to convey the personal uneasy feeling I get when I see these instances of alleged live spirit ghost box communication with a celebrity who has not been dead for more than a day. When I see this occurrence, it just seems to me that the individual posting the video or audio under these circumstances is doing so to publicize themselves and not to gather evidence that will help to advance live spirit ghost box communication research. I cannot say that I have never attempted to contact or communicate with the spirit entity of a famous celebrity, but I can say over the last seventeen years I can count the times on one hand, and I have never attempted contact with a celebrity spirit entity that had been deceased less than ten years. The specific celebrity contact ghost box sessions I have performed were in pursuit of information and to increase the validity of live spirit ghost box communication and not to claim, hey, look, I am the first individual to have so-and-so celebrity speak to me through a ghost box. For whatever reason a ghost box operator decides to perform a specific contact live ghost box session, it should be performed carefully and with the utmost attention to protocol and any repercussions that may arise from the outcome of the live specific ghost box session.

I feel it is necessary and relevant to this subject for me to reiterate my earlier statements about deceitful and manipulating live spirit communication that we can and do receive during a live spirit ghost box communication session. There are unfortunately some spirit entities that for various reasons will deliver less than honest and sometimes downright deceitful live spirit communication. These spirit entities I have found are not malicious or carry negative energy; they simply tell the ghost box operator what they believe he or she wants to hear in order to keep the operator engaged in a direct connection and continued back-and-forth communication. These trickster spirit entities do not have any malicious intentions; they simply tell the operator what they need to keep him addressing them. I have come to believe that the physical energy that the ghost box operator emits during a live ghost box session that is combined with the energy of the communicating spirit entity is like a sort of drug to them; a spirit entity seems to crave this physical energy connection. Also, I believe that once they have established live communication with the operator here in the physical world, it may seem to them that for a moment they have recaptured being a part of the physical world again.

I have performed many live ghost box sessions in which I have inquired about the reasons behind untruthful live spirit communication. Although never being able to pin down one specific answer to the question of why a spirit entity would lie, I have been able to piece together from information gathered the scenarios I just mentioned as to why this occurs. We must also remember that there are negative and evil spirit entities that will jump at any opportunity to infiltrate a live ghost box session and spew lies and negativity. Even with the protection afforded by our spirit technicians, negative entities can and do manage to crawl into a live ghost box session and disguise themselves as benevolent spirit entities and even lead the operator to believe they are the specific spirit entity that is the target of the live specific contact ghost box session.

No matter how vigilant the ghost box operator is, his or her job is not an easy one. The operator must conduct the ghost box session, ask the questions, state the topics, focus on trying to hear the spirit entity's communication live as it is delivered, and then scrutinize the delivered communication that was heard live and determine its relevance to any question or statement that was presented, and doing all this while listening to the constant sound of rapid gibberish emitted by the ghost box in session. Not an easy task. With all of this happening simultaneously, the ghost box operator is sometimes apt to miss a deliberate deception; however, most of it makes much more sense to the operator upon reviewing the ghost box session recording. The seasoned ghost box operator can usually recognize untruthful live spirit communication and/or negative manipulation.

Conclusion

The driving motivation for me to put pen to paper and produce this work was first and foremost the passion that I have for live spirit ghost box communication and research of the paranormal, and a desire to share this passion and the knowledge it has supplied with everyone. In this writing, my goal is to share the accumulated knowledge and experience I have gleaned from over twenty years of paranormal research and investigation with the past sixteen plus years dedicated solely to the practice and study of live spirit communication through the use of a ghost box. My journey began at the very dawn of this miraculous method when there was virtually no knowledge of its existence and very few individuals who even knew what a ghost box was let alone had the opportunity to work with one. From its creation, live spirit ghost box communication has allowed physical human beings like myself to communicate and interact live in real time with entities that are no longer a part of this physical realm. It has spanned two decades now and has afforded me the chance to accumulate the knowledge I have been so blessed to acquire from my daily research and from continuous communication with otherworldly entities that have been dedicated and selfless in their efforts to accommodate the ongoing barrage of questions and requests that have come from me and other researchers in the field over these many years, it has allowed me to formulate and document many theories and practicing protocols adhered to in the field today.

The vast amount of knowledge and understanding of the spirit realm and its inhabitants that I have gathered over these many years has culminated in my burning desire to share what I have learned with the world. Over the course of my career in this field of research, I have always tried to be forthcoming with the data and knowledge I acquired, I have tried to disseminate this knowledge and experience by way of written articles, live broadcast appearances, social media platforms, and personal interactions. The interest in the field of live spirit ghost box communication has grown exponentially over the years and has integrated itself into every aspect of paranormal research and investigation, this being the case I felt it was time to compile the knowledge and experience that I have to share into one comprehensive work. This book is the culmination of all that I have learned over the course of my career in live spirit ghost box communication practice and research. In this book, I have covered the many aspects of live spirit ghost box communication as well as stories of my true life experiences with spirit entities through their communication and interaction. This book will address the creation of the first ghost box and its history and evolution, noteworthy individuals in the field, the different aspects and protocols of performing live spirit ghost box communication sessions, and how to discern, evaluate, and understand live spirit communication, who we may be communicating with and how they communicate with us. I have tried with this writing to create a completely comprehensive guide to live spirit communication with the use of a ghost box. This work is meant to be invaluable as a book that can be referred to indefinitely not only by the novice but by the experienced researcher as well. It is my profound wish that this book will help any and all interested in or practicing in live spirit ghost box communication to employ the tried and true methods outlined in this work to achieve a high level of success in their efforts to connect and communicate with beings that are not of this physical world.

In writing this book it was also my hope that it would reach and intrigue individuals that may not be involved in live spirit ghost box communication or even know what it is, the person who has that nagging itch to learn about what they have always been told is impossible. This work is meant as much for them as it is for the paranormal researchers and investigators already active in the field. It is also my hope that this book will help to dissuade the myths and negative inferences that are unfortunately associated with the field of live spirit ghost box communication, and that it will afford a new open mindedness. This book is meant not only to explain and teach but to give individuals with no prior knowledge of live spirit communication or the paranormal the opportunity for them to open their minds and thoughts to the possibility of the existence of things that can not be readily explained by logic or science. Nothing would give me greater joy than to have every practicing live spirit ghost box communication researcher and investigator, and paranormal field investigator who reads this book to attempt to put the techniques and theories outlined here into practice, and for anyone who reads this book that has never been involved in any aspect of the paranormal to take their first steps into gaining a greater and richer knowledge of things paranormal and possibly attempting to try live spirit ghost box communication for themselves. All are welcome to contact me through my Facebook page or my Youtube Channel "Halliday Paranormal" I will be happy to help in any way I can.

About the Author

Bruce Halliday is a renowned paranormal researcher with over twenty years in paranormal research and investigation, and is known as one of the first two people who originated and developed live spirit ghost box communication research over sixteen years ago, and is responsible for most, if not all, of the working theories and protocols in the field. His debut book, *When Spirits Speak: Live Spirit Ghost Box Communication,* details his long and expansive journey in GBC and is the premiere reference guide to the subject.

He has appeared on numerous radio shows and

podcasts discussing his expertise in live spirit ghost box communication and ITC.

www.ingramcontent.com/pod-product-compliance
Lightning Source LLC
Chambersburg PA
CBHW032342280326
41935CB00008B/419